KNOWING FEMINISMS

KNOWING FEMINISMS

On Academic Borders, Territories and Tribes

Edited by Liz Stanley

SAGE Publications
London • Thousand Oaks • New Delhi

First published 1997

SAGE Publications Ltd
6 Bonhill Street
London EC2A 4PU

SAGE Publications Inc
2455 Teller Road
Thousand Oaks, California 91320

SAGE Publications India Pvt Ltd
32, M-Block Market
Greater Kailash – I
New Delhi 110 048

British Library Cataloguing in Publication data

A catalogue record for this book is
available from the British Library

ISBN 0 8039 7540 6
ISBN 0 8039 7541 4 (pbk)

Library of Congress catalog record available

Typeset by M Rules
Printed in Great Britain by Redwood Books,
Trowbridge, Wiltshire

Contents

1

Introduction: On Academic Borders, Territories, Tribes and Knowledges

Liz Stanley

Knowing feminisms and the in-between

What this book is about, what this book is for: two proposals for readers. *Knowing* feminisms: feminism as the source of new knowledge, that which runs counter; as the source of action which is based upon such knowledge; as a means of turning analytic attention upon the objects of knowledge-production; as a source which redefines who and what is subject, who it is that can know, as well as what it is that is known. Feminism as the analysis of old knowledge and the source of new knowledge: it makes you think. Knowing *feminisms*: counterveiling that which is not feminist, analysing injustice, insisting upon change; but also encountering difference, dissent and disagreement within; struggling to accept the epistemological ramifications of difference; difference in knowing as well as difference in being: situated knowledges. Feminism as itself a focus of analytic attention and inquiry: it makes you think about this too.

In recent feminist explorations of the sites and problematics of difference, the notion of 'borderlands', analysed by Gloria Anzaldúa (*Borderlands/La Frontera*, 1987) as '*la frontera*', has become of critical importance. Here in the borderlands difference is often experienced neither as separation nor as silence, but rather as an interface expressed through a babel of voices speaking together, speaking past each other, in which some voices sound, resound, more than others, and in which echo connotes power. This interface is a frontier that sees the coming and going of peoples, the speaking and silencing of voices, the casting of gazes which look but do not necessarily see. Around this frontier are gathered the differences of 'race', ethnicity, sexuality, gender, class, age, dis/ability, and more; and it is this frontier which constitutes the cultural space in which 'difference' becomes the point at which fundamental epistemological disputes surface around seismic linguistic and ideational shifts. The frontier thereby provides 'the space between' for debate, contention, disagreement.

Anzaldúa's '*la frontera*' is a powerful idea, invoking a borderland in which a second and subordinate cultural group 'grates against the first and bleeds', an area 'set up to define the places that are safe and unsafe, to distinguish *us* from *them* . . . a vague and undetermined place created by the emotional

residue of an unnatural boundary. It is in a constant state of transition. The
prohibited and forbidden are its inhabitants . . . Do not enter, trespassers will
be raped, maimed, strangled, gassed, shot' (1987: 3). Of course Anzaldúa is
writing here about a literal *frontera* along the border between Mexico and the
USA which then creates a symbolic as well as cultural borderland, for it is the
constitution of states which produces the possibility of statelessness as a
condition of mind as well as of living. The rapings and maimings, stran-
glings, gassings and shootings that Anzaldúa writes of are very real ones
produced out of massive shifts and migrations of peoples and the formation,
from out of what was once simply land, of distinct and separate, but certainly
not equal, nation-states. In Anzaldúa's words, '*Los atravesados* live here . . .
those who cross over, pass over, or go through the confines of the "normal"'
(1987: 3), and the borderlands create people whose everyday ontological
condition is one of constant liminality, of constant 'crossing over' between
two states of being.

The notion of borderlands signifies that there is also a territory *between*,
on the borders of – precisely a state and a space of liminality, the in-between.
Borderlands are a kind of space, social as much as physical or geographical,
which are co-inhabited by people of different cultures, classes, ethnicities,
religions, languages, as well as sexualities and genders and politics. A borderland is a contested zone, if not always politically, or in terms of national
identities as in, for example, Northern Ireland or Ruanda or the former
Yugoslavia, then certainly socially in terms of the re/construction and
re/negotiation of identities and biographies and thus also of knowledges.
Thus the US Christopher Street riot in which 'fags and dykes' fought back
against contemptuously harassing police, thereby helping to bring 'lesbians
and gay men' into existence: the ghetto became a corridor into political life.

The academic frontiers and borderlands that are the subject of this book
are also epistemological borderlands, as sites of interface between different
knowledges, different knowledge-claims, in which difference is spoken
through the conjunction *knowledge*/power. These borderlands are differently
constituted, where the prior production of symbolic frontiers – those who
have knowledge and those who merely experience – has given rise to material
organisations and institutions and governing bodies and 'states'. These spatial complexities of knowledge/power give rise to ontological problematics:
just who are the people who 'cross over, pass over, go through the confines of
the normal', who inhabit the academic borderlands and live in 'constant liminality'? Or rather, who and what do they become, what 'are' they in an
existential sense?

As the tourist guide-book says, 'The institutions and organisations of
Academia are masculinist in two closely related senses. The first is that historically the knowledge-makers, guardians and teachers of this tribe have
been male. For many centuries this was a profession and status barred to
women, and only within the last century have women been admitted. The
second is that 'knowledge' is by definition rational, scientific and universal.
These seminal characteristics are counterposed against those of emotionality,

the natural and particular, and these and related characteristics – termed 'binaries' – are associated with the known characteristics of the sexes. Women are 'other' to the citizenry here. They are the labour that makes it work – the secretaries, kitchen staff, cleaners, minor administrators, support staff and librarians – but they are largely invisible as 'people' therein. The status of citizen is reserved for those who are male/academic. Sex outweighs the otherness of 'race', at least in the formal institutions of Academia; but class is of the essence, for 'education', the chief product of this place, is considerably more than just book-learning – it is an ineffable grace of mind that only the lineage of centuries can bestow. Moreover, gender among the Academic tribe has both the power to magnificently increase size and attractiveness (in the male) and can produce near invisibility (in the female).'

Example 1: A door to a classroom on 'Feminist Thought' opens; in come a porter and two architects chatting and measuring; I remonstrate; oh sorry they say, we didn't realise there was a lecturer here. Example 2: I walk down through the building to another meeting of this class; a student clutches my sleeve preventing me from moving; give this note to my lecturer, they say; I answer, I am not a servant, take your hand off my arm and say please when you want things done for you. Example 3: In the same class I am half-way through explaining a particularly abstruse point in feminist deconstructionist ideas to a perturbed student; another member of the class talks over me with an instruction to go and have it explained by a male colleague in the department 'because he lectures on this in the theory course'. Example 4: Bearing examination papers, I enter an examination room; a suited man bustles up to me: stop, you can't come in, go outside until I say; fine by me if you don't want a co-examiner for the next three hours I respond, and go away. These examples concern the fixing of women in particular positions within the academy. Unless you status-mark others, dress in obviously smart ways or are by other means clearly distinguishable from students and secretaries (smart, but not smart skirts), or teach in mystificatory and so 'clever' ways, then changing combinations of 'they' assume you are a student (female, stupid), or they take you for 'women' (those nose and bum wipers of the academy known as 'the secretaries'), or they treat you as by (sexual) definition inferior or invisible members of your profession. And this 'they' is not a unitary group confronting a unitary 'us'.

We are, however, all passing women in the academy, not just those of us who manage sexuality or 'race' or disability or class in this way. Franz Fanon remarked upon the masks that black people under colonialism wear, never being 'out' to their oppressors, while Simone de Beauvoir noted the similar way in which women constrain themselves as Other to men. How comforting: 'women' do this. But for those of us who are not men, passing is a necessary condition of entry into the academy as a member: behaving as though we are safe, tamed, reasonable, colleagial. How is it possible to be so subservient as to 'be reasonable' in the face of inequality, exploitation, oppression? Yet we do it all the time, we apparently pass as one of that 'they' that we are other to.

What – and who – am I as a woman and a feminist within the academy?

For many, I am positioned and fixed according to assumptions concerning position and thus function and status because of my sex and age. My four examples are of course not 'feminist' in any *a priori* sense; they concern responses to women in a putatively male space, and the feminism here lies in the way that such events are experienced as well as analysed, as being about status and power of gendered kinds. However, once understood within such a frame, this then transmutes like a new kind of philosopher's stone. There is nothing either inferior or diminishing about being or being seen as a student or a secretary; what *is* diminishing are the twin assumptions that women in the academy can be nothing but these and that to be them is to be at the beck and call and governance of males, for no matter what position men may be in the academic hierarchy in relation to each other, their common assumption is that women are indeed a priori lower. What feminism provides is a comprehension of the blinkered stupidity of such a way of thinking about the world, as well as the resultant injustices that arise from it.

These gendered ontological problematics thus have feminist epistemological consequentiality – or rather feminism analytically creates such epistemological consequentiality around them. Feminism sees new knowledge, sees 'coming to know' in a different way, as having its origin within such ontological problematics and the practical inquiries that arise from them. It has articulated ontological difference as the site of epistemological distinction: a feminist theory of knowledge linked to a feminist way of knowing, and this in turn linked back to a feminist way of theorising being. Moreover, ontology (a theory of being and living) and epistemology (a theory of knowing) become two symbiotically-linked 'moments' within a feminist praxis. What results is a truly radical approach to theorising knowledge, one which refuses the scientistic distinction between mind/knowledge and body/experience, instead situating knowledge as in and of grounded experiences viewed in a particular and feminist analytic way.

It has become conventional to speak and to write about such ideas and attendant issues in connection with the presence of 'women's studies' within the academy. This term both is and is not appropriate to describe the intellectual and academic activities discussed in this book. Insofar as 'women's studies' is constituted by separate or semi-separate organisational existence within educational institutions, then for most of the contributors it either does not exist or exists in relation to ideas and research and publications rather than separate classrooms, degrees or jobs or departments. Moreover, to make the complex more complex, it may exist in relation to such organisational facts of academic life, but not in relation to any convincing inter-disciplinarity, and instead take the form of the consanguinity of slices of disciplines which pertain to the topic women/gender: women and health, women and science, women and this and that. And, to make it even more complex, exclusion paradoxically may permit the easier or greater expression of feminist ideas and feminist practice within the zones of exclusion. Contributors write of the possibilities of exclusion and the limitations of inclusion, as well as conversely. They also write in relation to women's studies and/or feminism and/or gender; some contributors situate themselves firmly in relation to one of these as constituting a particular kind of gaze upon the academy as well as presence within it, but some utilise elements of all three to indicate shifts over time which may be organisational, personal or relate to the wider parameters of intellectual life in which the configurations 'gender', 'feminism', and even 'women', have changed markedly.

'Higher education' is less a figurative and symbolic space than it is a concrete and very grounded organisational place in which, within any one institution, there are the overlapping territories of intellectual allegiances and the discrete territories of departments, faculties and schools, all in complex interaction with each other. Within this organisational edifice the intellectual space of ideas and knowledges sits uneasily, often hardly remembered let alone invoked in the ordinary round of the activities that constitute 'doing the business' required by government policy and funding council injunction. Moreover, both the intellectual space of 'education' – for it does still exist, in the interstices and squeezed until the pips squeak though it is – and the organisational place of 'universities' are marked by the separations and hierarchies of status and reward: Foucault's notion of knowledge/power is as appositely applied within and on 'us', as it is without and on 'them'. At its simplest, this can be seen in the fact that the greater the status and monetary reward, then the less likely there are to be women in organisational positions; and the greater the intellectual approbation, the less likely it is that what women do will be included within it. Indeed, there are clear signs that higher education is becoming one of the last bastions against the recognition of 'women's worth': it is salutary to note that business, manufacturing and government organisations are all more likely to value and to promote women than educational ones. 'Academic man' is a living reality, however Neanderthal he often seems in the flesh. And at another level, the gendered nature of knowledge/power is witnessed by the apparatus of science, objectivity, detachment, rationality and the use of these in simultaneously creating hierarchies in which one form of knowing – scientistic, apparently detached and presumed to be objective – stands over and against others.

However, feminisms in the academy do not simply face, confront, receive, these dominant ways of knowing. In a very real sense feminism has been itself a creator and maintainer of intellectual and political borderlands in its own right, which have been brought inside by students, staff, research, writing, publication, teaching, and to which 'the academy' has necessarily had to respond. This has occurred through rejection, negotiation, admission, acceptance, assimilation, silencing, ignoring, or indeed all at more or less the same 'moment'. But whichever, this response has occurred around some kind of *acknowledgement*, whether of the looming presence or the looming absence, of feminist ideas if not of feminist persons or practices. Inside, some of us have become 'them', while the rest of us pass to one degree or another.

The contributors to this book explore a wide variety of the ontological and epistemological borderlands and border disputes thus created. They do so in their own ways, some stressing organisational problematics, others bio-graphical resonances, others ideas and powers, most some combination of them. They explore the intertwining ontological problematics and epistemo-logical consequentialities sketched out above. The pages of this book offer another kind of space, in which its contributors can explore these intellectual concerns in relation to 'what is happening' in academic life as experienced from their particular vantage-points. They reflect upon different aspects of academic and intellectual life, including at those other borders and bound-aries that exist, for example between academic organisations and those of 'outside' groups, organisations, audiences, institutions. This constitutes the broad shared framework within which the differences of the contributors are located. Such differences are occasioned both by different feminisms and by the different disciplines within which these feminisms are located, as well as the differences of age and status, class, 'race' and sexuality, and type and status of institution. Moreover, mapping and theorising such sameness/dif-ference must also take note of that 'meta-difference' which is created out of the fact that both feminism and the academy are experiencing independent change, as well as also changing because of the growing relationship of inter-dependency between them. 'Everything is changing at once' has been heard more than once recently in the bulging classrooms of contemporary academic life. The resultant chapters are consequently points of departure, and not clo-sures, for readers wanting to reflect upon their own vantage-points, experiences and interpretations.

Organisations, lives and careers

Feminists are ontologically outsiders, 'Other' to the academy. This 'otherness' exists in the sense that 'the stranger' in Georg Simmel's analysis is other: the stranger is someone inside but marked off, different and, although within, not within in the same way that 'real' insiders are. The stranger *travels between*, and in doing so brings their ontological borderland with them, indeed who wears it like an almost visible marker which sets them apart in their difference. This difference is not merely experienced; it is *lived*, it becomes the stuff of which 'a life' is thus composed, and it is central to identity and feeling, and thinking.

But feminist academics are not just 'women, full stop'. Those categorically important features of life as it is lived, such as 'race', sexuality, class, age, all make a difference, as does how people understand and act upon such matters. People do not inhabit conveniently separated pure identities: 'black? over there please', 'Romanies, in that one please', 'lesbians over there, heterosexu-als in here', 'old people, no not there, in *there*'. Goodness knows 'biological [sic] sex' is a myriad enough, so what chance anything else being singular? And the political analysis of the ontological problematics that underpin and help give rise to feminism are not of merely arcane interest, for they have direct and very powerful ramifications for how people understand their lives and the possibilities they perceive those lives as not/having.

Some of the contributors have chosen to examine wider changes through the lens of their particular biographical trajectories, while for others this has remained implicit, a part of the backcloth to the themes and issues they foreground in their writing. But whichever, it is important to remember that such changes *always* have auto/biographical implications, *always* impact on collectivities of individual lives and careers. Embedded within these overlapping textual accounts of disciplines, feminist ideas, institutional re/arrangements, then, lie the interconnected biographies of thousands of people, as academics, students, researchers, administrators, secretaries, and a vast array of 'support staff'.

The term 'career' is often used to indicate general developments and patterns in a life, as well as in occupations. Ironically, various of the changes attendant upon shifts in educational funding policies in Britain have made one kind of academic biography/career, that of the social science or humanities researcher, become nearly extinct. Much more typical now is the successive arrival of cohorts of new researchers who then, lemming-like in their later 20s or early 30s, leave for other careers, mostly outside of academic life altogether. Nonetheless, and perhaps because of its very precariousness, research in these areas continues to attract well-qualified, energetic and productive women researchers: here organisational entry can be affected, for barriers are as few as the long-term career rewards. It is of course no accident that there is a relationship between low-status academic occupations and roles and the relatively high presence of feminists and other women. The invisible colleges of high-position, high-status, networks and associated processes of gatekeeping – the boy's club, the 'good ol' boys' – remain as important in academic life as they ever were, albeit cross-cut by an ethos of greater openness and the existence of procedures and practices apparently designed to regulate entry around formal qualifications and measurable attributes. The re/definitions of 'competence', 'skill' and 'importance' in gender terms is as important here as it has been in the workshops and factories of industrial capitalism. To the (marked) extent that higher education remains if not the preserve then still the shelter and support of 'the good ol' boys', then the existence of educational 'interstices' remains an important way-station for women in general, feminists in particular, to establish themselves and legitimate their credentials, including promoting the competing knowledges that have arisen from the flames of feminism itself.

Of course 'feminism' has never been as unitary as the use of the singular presupposes; it has always been marked by difference, tension, division; and it has always encompassed competing knowledges, competing feminist worldviews. There has never been the lining up of a single and undivided feminist epistemology confronting an equally single and undivided masculinist one, no matter what rhetorics of such binary oppositions have existed (and on both 'sides'). And, over the last twenty-five years or so, there have been considerable (in both main senses of this word) changes in the constitution, structure, concerns, activities and preoccupations of 'feminism', as it has been perceived from 'outside' as well as from 'inside'. However, understanding the

links and tensions between individual and collective biographies, and the
intellectual and political changes that have occurred to the organisational as
well as ideational face of feminism, is clearly no simple matter. Understanding
the process of the formation of ideas necessitates 'biographising' social structure and 'structuralising' biography. Conscious deliberation on these matters
by those in the heart of the storm of change, as are the contributors to this
book, speaks both to the immediacy of the moment and also traces the actually longer-term shifts that have occasioned 'now', the moment, and will
eventuate 'then', the future. It is important not to see 'now' as uniquely without origin, but rather to trace its ancestry, its links with other social
movements, other re/formations of identities, other accompanying economic
and social structural changes. We are not alone.

Gaining entry into high status professional and other occupations via low
status sectors is a strategy that many of those ontologically 'Other' have
adopted, and sometimes, as with feminists, with marked success within the
academy. At the same time, within some disciplines and institutions there
have been successful organisational and intellectual closures against feminist
ideas. However, perhaps paradoxically, this has sometimes not only permitted
but actively facilitated the development of feminist work, albeit in the margins
and on the borders, in the organisational and intellectual 'interstices'. What
this raises is the conundrum that 'success', in the form of the incorporation of
some versions of feminism, also brings with it costs, the intellectual and epistemological costs of assimilation and the consequent overlaying of an
erstwhile oppositional epistemological frame by one which looks from the
inside out, seeing out there sedition, dissension, irrationality, chaos. Descartes'
nightmare peopled by wild women, 'Other' feminisms, other feminists.

As the mention of Descartes' troubled nightmares indicates, what should
not be forgotten is the intensely *emotional* character of much of the reaction
and resistance to dissenting feminist ideas, including such reactions by incorporated feminisms to those *other* Others, the feminists who are not like 'us',
who are too extreme, too different, neither rigorous nor rational nor acceptable. *We* are not like *that*! Casting political, theoretical, analytical and
methodological conflicts and debates in emotional terms is to see the passions
at work here, ostensibly beneath the surface of intellectual life but actually
running sharply through every idea, every theory, every analysis. Prick them
and they bleed, the hotness and urgency spilling out into reviews, essays,
papers and articles. To read 'dispassionate' responses to feminist work, feminist ideas, feminist women, with a finger over the vein is to feel the pulse of
anger, denial and sometimes the stirrings of hatred. It all matters a good
deal, you see.

There is no *necessary* synonymity of constructions of knowledge, appropriate investigative methodologies, desired outcomes and praxes, between the
varieties of feminisms beyond that which gives rise to common use of 'feminism' as a marker of political and ethical stance (and, let us not forget, this is
a great deal of synonymity). The common insistence there is something
rotten in the state of the relationship between the sexes/genders may be what

binds us, with this 'something' the bone of fierce contestation. What results from such contestations are competing varieties of feminism intertwined with competing strands of conceptual and theoretical analysis within the various academic disciplines. At one time in Britain, for an actually very short period, it was possible to propose that the centre of academic feminism was constituted by Marxism, and all else degrees of peripherality. But soon (all too soon for some) such certainties were disturbed by the arrival of those 'other' feminisms, so that invocations of 'feminism' became marked by the naming of varieties, like naming the genuses of flowers: *Marxist* feminism, *socialist* feminism, *radical* feminism, *liberal* feminism, oh, and *revolutionary* feminism: and we should not forget that academic careers have been built upon the naming of these varieties and the maintenance of divisions between them. Now there are no longer even these certainties (not that there really ever were, for few of us understood our ideas and praxes for long within such confined and static terms).

Both feminisms and the academic disciplines are boundaried systems, but with (increasingly) complex borders. Consequently great interactional complexities arise in the interfaces between, both within any 'one' discipline and between it and other disciplines, and also regarding other organisations that these disciplines have dealings with. All of the academic disciplines are non-unitary and what is centre and what constitutes the peripheries is a contested matter. And it is not just the applied disciplines which have applications outside of the academy: the abstractions of philosophy and theology, for example, can drive corporate training programmes and the ethical committees of medics every bit as much as the ideas of accounting or engineering resound in the so-called 'real world'. Everywhere we look, the abstract and the academic meld into the concrete, become endemic in all fields of social life.

This is not to imply that fierce boundary-marking does not mark the borders, for it most certainly does; the ideological practices of organisational entities are intimately involved here, for their very existence is at stake. Difference is the name of the professional organisational game, marking off separations and distinctions, insisting upon the unique scope of particular professional knowledges and the inevitability and certainty of the translation of these knowledges into spheres of autonomous activity unamenable to the specificities of given rules. Professional autonomy is the central concept here, the jealously preserved and practically often unrealised grail that is nightly and daily defended against any attempted incursion into professional decision-making space.

Identity crises are at the centre of the disciplines as much as the professions; these are contested domains. Substantive work – concerned with what is 'out there' but also what is 'in here' – can illuminate the boundaries, the contested areas, the shifting centres of power and control, and thus become the motor force of changes over time. 'Biographies', it is worth noting, are not confined merely to persons, whether factual or fictional or heroic; complex organisations too have 'a life', a birth and a death, a character, experience epiphanies and dis/junctures and phases and trajectories, and engage with other organisational entities. These particular identity crises are fashionably associated with postmodernist and deconstructionist ideas but actually long precede the existence of these, lying at least in part in the long-term organisational features of disciplines as, inwardly, changing alliances of shifting and disputing networks and groupings, and, outwardly, settled and programmatic essences founded on unchanging truths about the natural/social world. The crisis that is the existence of shifting identity/ies is the name of the academic organisational game. No wonder feminism is often experienced as a threat rather than a promise, for, by making the game open, it gives the game away. 'Nothing is settled' shifts the known ground – good grief, things might *really* change!

The boundaries between feminisms and a discipline are no longer clear, not least because of the impact of some feminist ideas and the progress of some feminist women. 'Within' and 'without' consequently have become difficult to tell apart, and especially so when those who may remain in some sense ontologically 'Other' nonetheless come to call the departmental, theoretical or methodological shots and so gain the means to operate epistemological closure. This can be intellectually creative because the borderlands thus opened permit unaccustomed exchanges: hierarchy meets inversion. But, of course, the re/making of knowledges need not necessarily follow from a very few gaining organisational clout. However, at the least this leads to shifts in organisational composition: and whether this will lead to wider-reaching change remains to be seen. The re/writing of knowledge certainly encompasses the re/making of organisations and institutions; however, it is the converse move that is politically and ethically more ambiguous: a changing institution can change in ways that have little or no epistemological or political consequentiality.

There can be, indeed there often are, un/intended consequences of a feminist rewriting of knowledges, especially so with regard to 'other' audiences and perhaps particularly the mass media. Feminist work, on rape and advertising, Victorian novels and child abuse, portraiture and pornography, child abuse and the structure of households, has come to the tender attentions and peculiar practices of the mass media, grist to the ever-rumbling mills that churn out Greenham woman, absailing dykes, political correctness, Camille Paglia, and goodness knows what else next. Feminism, the wicked witch of the north, of the first world, the wicked witch in your (whose?) own home, *sells*. But paradoxically there is a good deal more realised in feminist terms about the seventeenth-century persecution of witches than there is about the construction and use of 'witch-like' imagery in the here and now, and in particular regarding the relationship of this to the stereotyping and corralling of 'feminism' itself. Note that 'post-feminism' conveniently sterotypes and lethally disempowers.

It seems that academic feminisms are by and large less than fully concerned about their own construction and reproduction, in organisational or epistemological terms. There is no 'feminist woman' at the heart of this multi-discipline of women's studies, feminism, gender studies: only the shivering, suppressed, oppressed, subjugated 'woman' that is the focus of collective theoretical and analytical attention. All the light is upon these poor categorical creatures, their plight, why it has occurred, what can be done about it, and little of the spotlight is turned upon those strapping resourceful women who provide this allegorical analytic gaze. And in taking such a stance to its 'research subjects', academic feminisms too much resemble the disciplines within which they are situated. At the centre is still a 'missing person': methods, their epistemology as much as methodology, serve to slice off aspects of the people who are the objects of academic attentions. The person missing is one who is complex and rounded, who is 'raced' and classed and gendered, who has a body and emotions and engages in sensible thought, and who inhabits space and place and time, and a person who may be a man but can be pathetic and weak, or who may be a woman but can be confidently powerful. The disciplines are concerned with 'bits' of social life, but even in their own terms what they choose to omit is considerably more than it need be: sociology, for example, still fails to assign bodies and places to 'social life', and economics still fails to encompass people at all. And as for the physical sciences, people are neither their objects nor their subjects: all subjectivities are banished by Method, so they say. So they say.

Difference: women, feminisms, gender

The very successes of feminism within the academy have occluded the provisionality of basic terms and concepts: 'women', and/or 'feminisms', and/or 'gender'. For some, the use of such terms may result from strategic choice, for others these may be almost accidental usages, and for still others their choice is an indication of clear political and analytical intention. Whichever, it should be recognised that a variety of terminological usages co-exist, sometimes indicating deep conceptual and political difference and disagreement, sometimes indicating nothing so much as casual choice. Nonetheless, these conceptual choices, howsoever made, are still analytically and epistemologically consequential, shaping as they do topics of interest, the epistemological parameters of inquiry, and the basis and claims of the knowledge that results. More simply, they also draw a line, create a frontier, between who is in and who is out, and so they help bring different styles of feminism into contest with each other. Gender? oh, I know your sort; wimmin? Yes, well.

'Contested feminisms' indicate not only the disagreements and sometimes conflicts that exist but also the preoccupation of different 'schools' or styles of feminism with each other, with their internal definitional, knowledge-producing and claims-making activities. Paradoxically, in the very 'moment' at which feminisms appear most to disagree they are also the most intimately involved, with their gaze settled firmly upon each other. In the same way that Foucault remarked on the vast preoccupying armoury of the Victorian injunction not to speak sex that spoke sex all the time, let us remark on the feminist gaze which inspects and scrutinises and criticises with all the brutal familiarity of sisters who have fallen out. This is a mutually preoccupying gaze – and why not? Why not a closer gaze, one more analytically predisposed? Why not one that takes both itself and 'other feminisms' as a crucial topic of analytic discourse, a prism through which the world is seen? Go for it!

'Seeing the world' here analytically draws in the relationship of women to theory, feminisms to theory, women to feminisms, and women to men; that is, it invokes the outwardness of the feminist gaze as well as its inwardness. Within these relationships lies both the epistemological grounding of any kind of feminist enterprise within the academy (for feminism is predicated upon the importance and possibility of an analysis of the grounds and bases of 'women's oppression') and uncomfortable and awkward feminist problematics concerning knowledge/power. Feminism is predicated upon the fact that its knowledge-base stems from its practitioners being members of the category 'women'. Herein lie the grounds to rebut feminist knowledge-claims from the 'side' of the (masculinist) academy protesting at emotion and subjectivity, and the grounds to reject such privilege from the 'side' of the 'women' that such knowledge-claims aim to colonise in a new form of intellectual imperialism. The terms and concepts of academic feminisms have political and ethical as well as epistemological outcomes, for speaking 'as a' woman gives rise both to different kinds of knowledge-claim and also to a very different relationship to the disciplines. Speaking 'for the' women can more easily become incorporated because speaking 'for the . . .' is the voice of the malestream, while speaking 'as a' woman is to speak sedition, involvement.

A further set of definitional and thus procedural issues surround how 'it' (women's studies, gender studies, feminist research) relates to the disciplines and thus how 'it' constitutes itself. Whether 'it' takes a cross-disciplinary, multi-disciplinary or inter-disciplinary form makes a difference, as does whether 'it' eschews all of these, instead settling determinedly *within* particular disciplines, occupying sometimes peripheral and sometimes what looks increasingly like central space. This is not to deny that the position of women, and the position of feminist ideas, can be markedly at variance. It is difficult not to read publishers' catalogues with the feeling that these seemingly witness a revolution in the form and substance of knowledge – but at the same time, to turn from these to contemplate the structures of departments and institutions is to contemplate a different world, one seemingly not marked by this revolution in thinking and writing at all. *Cherchez les hommes*? everywhere in departments and institutions! *cherchez les femmes*? everywhere in ideas and books! Seen from the view of feminism, 'knowledge' and 'academia' are drifting apart, a version of continental drift; so then, tidal waves and volcanic eruptions are called for!

Some commentators lay these intellectual and academic fragmentations at the door of deconstructionism, although they are more accurately associated with broader fragmentations of 'knowing', intellectually but also politically, which have always existed, sometimes subterranean and hidden or suppressed, at other times on the surface, fermenting or erupting, in intellectual life. Their present incarnation should be analytically coupled with massive changes in other 'known quantities' in contemporary social life, like 'Eastern Europe', 'the USSR' and 'the Third World', not to mention attendant changes to beliefs about women's 'proper place' within these (former) entities. Clearly there are massive shifts occurring around the nature of identities and knowledges, and equally clearly academia should be concerned with investigating whether and in what ways these apparently short-run changes might be linked to longer-run and more fundamental change in social, economic and political life. So too should women's studies, gender studies, academic feminisms, for their own unsettled character is caught up in these changes also.

Is the proliferation of nationalisms to be summed as the growth of ethnic fundamentalisms, the boys carving up territory on ethnic grounds this time, and little more? An earnest colleague shakes his head and tells me that this is a diasporic search for ontological certainty in the midst of the political and epistemological fragmentations that are postmodernity. Freshly horrified by television coverage of massacres and 'cleansings', I ask a friend, a former-Yugoslavian, to 'explain what is going on'. She shakes her head; 'I don't know', she tells me; 'he says, but there again she says, while another claims . . .'. She stares vacantly, deep in thought: 'You see during the war, and then again during the first world war, while during the 1880s, and before that, well in the twelfth century . . .'. There are, however, things that she herself knows with complete certainty: 'Well, I don't know, I really don't know, I don't really understand because people say such different things. But it's changed everything, you see; there's no going back. When I go there, there's no home anymore; it's all different, and back here it's different too . . .'.

This is a race war, one which perceives 'the Other' as constitutionally, biologically, essentially, different and threatening; they even say those Others look different from them, the shape of their faces, lips, eyes. And of course 'race' was the Irish in Britain for a long time – colonialism and imperialism come in different shapes and are not dependent upon skin colour, although this certainly helps in the 'othering' process, nor are they purely 'Third World' phenomena. Post-colonial studies are concerned with interstitial cultures centring notions of ambivalence and hybridity through colonial displacements, as well as with decentering 'western modernity' from a post-colonial perspective. But if there is no 'race' in a biological or essentialist sense, then 'racial purity' becomes a matter of politics, power; and if hybridity is an ontological state for those who are 'in-between', then perhaps there are *only* interstitial cultures but made seemingly unitary and whole through politics, power.

The university is a minor transit-camp for many displaced people. Diaspora: 'Where do you come from?' 'Oh just a little town out in the Diaspora.' I contemplate women's role in the diaspora if women already have no country anyway. The women diasporic travellers I meet generally express a sense of belonging to somewhere else, often what has passed or has never been. But although I'm supposed to be 'at home', I feel little of this; is this because lesbian women are among the other Others? Because feminist women are among the Other others? And when I feel an alien among lesbians and a stranger among feminists, is that just my personal oddity? Why is it that I don't want to feel 'at home' anywhere, indeed feel repelled by the idea of belonging, but don't experience its diasporic binary either? Should I pull myself together?

Within academic feminism, such ontological fragmentations have been read as signalling epistemological uncertainty, a loss of intellectual nerve and purpose. Read in one way, such fragmentations have brought with them a greater sophistication about the representational character of 'texts', but seemingly little else. But read in another, the former certainties can be seen as intellectual and political blinkeredness to intellectual complexities and differences, with their removal heralding a more open intellectual climate. Whichever (or both), what is certainly noticeable is the now considerably greater tolerance of difference within feminism's own gates, of differences writ in terms of theories, explanations, methodologies and epistemologies, as well as in the more customary sense of 'race' and ethnicity, class, sexuality, dis/ability, and so forth. Is it then a choice between closed certainties and action, and fragmented complexities and paralysis?

This loss of certainty and purpose has been experienced particularly in feminism's *academic* borderlands, and there are few who would cast the intellectual runes to speak with any degree of confidence about where academic feminism is moving either intellectually or politically. It might be comforting to see this as a product of the *malaise* of ageing and so to be experienced by every age-cohort: the collective academic form of a 'mid-life crisis'. Certainly 'ask the younger women' was one response to a recent public formulation of this issue, 'look at what they're doing', but this turned out to be fairly much the same as their elders. There are actually no simple answers 'possessed' by any group of people, nor are any expressed by the contributors to this book. However, if not 'the answer', the contributors do provide a set of intellectual steps for exploring 'the problem', and it is surely through thoughtful engagements that 'steps in the right direction' will come.

The politics of location

At least part of the difficulty in addressing the problematic of fragmentation and change is that all aspects of academic/intellectual life are apparently on the move at once. How then is it possible to review, to overview, anything or to know where things are going? The conventional social science answer here is found in the formulation *ceteris paribus*: hold all other elements constant and see what just one difference makes. However, life is not a model in the way *ceteris paribus* requires; its complexities cannot readily or successfully be reduced to these terms without the omission of exception, variation, indeed the omission of everything that is complex and interesting. The feminist response to this procedural problem has been to formulate a vantage-point, a place to look from; and this vantage-point has been one which seals together epistemology and ontology by situating the feminist knower within, at the heart, at the hub, of the things that happen and which, analytically because experientially, matter. The hub, after all, is the only bit of a moving wheel in some kind of stasis.

Situating the feminist knower has gone hand in hand with the insistence that actually *all* knowledge is located and thus specific, that it is grounded and consequently it has limits. It is arguable that this is the most revolutionary idea associated with feminism, of far more immediate danger to existing configurations of power than attempted re/orderings of the gender system. What it *does* is to require a shift in perspective, turning the academic gaze a little away from those 'others' that are its subject-matter, a little towards this 'gaze' itself, to the processes of knowledge-production and the claims-making attendant upon this product, and the related bartering and exchanging that occurs in the academic/intellectual market-place. These are political processes through and through, and one important illustration of this is that the apparently 'irrational' – like subjectivity – can be seen to be eminently 'rational' when viewed in a different context because viewed by locating the knower differently, precisely as feminism has done. The politics of location is essential to the epistemological position that feminism has advanced, and it is one which insists upon not only the specificity of knowing and thus of knowledges, but also on the ontological basis of *all* knowledge because grounded in specific and contextualised acts of knowing. This has reverberations for the totality of feminist thought as well as for feminist praxis within the academy, because it situates 'knowing' as a methodological matter, as an analytical problematic, *and* as an ethical requirement. This trinity – methodic, analytic, ethic – is actually one and indivisible.

Another important factor in coming to terms with the fragmentation of knowledges and identities is formed by that other 'fragmentation' constituted by *time*, by the passing of time and the changes this brings. Recognising the otherness of the past means recognising that no resurrectionalism of 'times past' is possible and the epistemological problematics thus engendered are actually emblematic of all social investigations, including those dealing with 'now', for evidence is always partial and incomplete and always dependent upon that central intellectual act of knowing. Time and time passing are, then, part of the problem, but also and for the same reasons part of the 'problematic' that sets out the procedures and methods for investigation and the terms and conditions of what is seen as a satisfactory explanation. This approach centres 'history', not in the conventional sense of providing a grounding for current knowledge, but rather through demonstrating the epistemological consequentiality of situating the knower and acts of knowing *in time* as well as in *place*.

Is prioritising gender necessary to a feminism concerned with such an ontological and epistemological project? This is to reformulate, in relation to what some perceive as an over-emphasis on the issue of gender to the exclusion of other and sometimes wider concerns, the question of 'what should feminism

be about?'; that is, what its intellectual and political task should be. This does
not mean that gender, nor any of the related concerns of gender studies and
women's studies, do not feature in this intellectual landscape. It does, however,
mean that they may no longer be seen as synonymous with the whole. To
treat them as the whole leaves largely intact the 'speaking for the . . .' intellectual position, whereas the call here is for a vision of knowledge which
acknowledges 'speaking as a . . .', and which recognises that all generalisations
originate as particularities, and all universalisms as specificities.

The borderlands in-between 'without' and 'within' thereby shift from this
pressure and from that, among them the processes of academic and intellectual incorporation and assimilation. One aspect of this has been the
making of a feminist theoretican canon within academia, together with the
creation of knowledge hierarchies and the superordinate place of 'grand'
social theory and those who produce it. Indeed, in some areas of intellectual
life feminist travelling theory is no longer a variant but has become 'it' itself;
and some feminist intellectuals have moved across this division, leaving what
the rest of us do as something different in kind from 'Theory', leaving intact
the evaluation of academic roles implied.

Cross-cutting this development is that other, in which 'abstract knowledge' is seen as a contradiction in terms for a 'borderlands' feminist
epistemology and ontology. In the in-between, all knowledge, howsoever
termed so as apparently to divorce it from the grounded and contextual and
specific, derives from the lives, ideas and acts of particular persons. And not
of supposedly 'great minds' either, but instead of shared minds, socially constituted, materially-based and collectively engaged in the processes of
knowledge-production. Ideas are common property, indeed ideas are no
property at all here in the in-between. 'Ideas' are social and material produc-
tions, and feminist ideas are neither individual inventions nor individual
possessions. The views and analyses which appear within this book result
from collective labours involving the sharing of ideas, and the chapters by its
contributors represent concerns expressed by many others within their particular disciplines and areas of work, as well as inscribing their own particular
'gazes' upon these. These chapters should thus be read as works in progress
investigating the fragmentations of contemporary intellectual life, as well as
exploring and analysing aspects of the particular vantage-point on these
matters constituted by feminism generally, more specifically by the ontological and epistemological borderlands constituted by its position within, but
not yet entirely of, the academy.

This book originated in a seminar series organised at the University of
Manchester in the UK, on the theme of 'Women's studies and the academic
disciplines'. During one seminar, the Manchester police helicopter hovered
continually backwards and forwards over the university, the noise all but
drowning out the speaker. In another, a large contingent from a particular
discipline became increasingly discomfited at what 'their' feminist was saying,
while another was notable for the complete absence of anyone from the particular discipline under discussion. One seminar was preceded by weeks in

which the public posters which advertised it all over the university were ripped down, replaced, then defaced, ripped down, shredded. In another seminar, most of the feminists present disapproved of the displacement of non-canonical themes and concepts. Another was one of those wonderfully charged intellectual occasions when minds meet and huge energy and excitement are produced, while in all of them some sparks of this were a current running through.

Like the seminar series, this book is concerned with the incursions of the regulatory and constraining state, the discomfort of those who perceive of the disciplines as 'theirs' and the withdrawal or absence of any recognition by others, the threat of violence and the actuality of exclusions and anger, the growth of canonical versions of feminism and incitements to rebellion, and, in the midst of this, thoughtful and challenging reflections on academic institutions, borders, territories, tribes and knowledges, as well as the diversity of the feminist engagement with these, and the impact of them on those of us within the academy but not entirely of it.

Read on!

2

Whose Women's Studies? Whose Philosophy? Whose Borderland?

Anne Seller

The philosophical establishment in this country, as represented by university departments and academic journals, has remained remarkably immune to women's studies. True, there is the odd course on some variant of feminist philosophy, but it is generally considered marginal, not the sort of thing that you concentrate on if you want to go on to graduate work or, harder yet, an academic career in philosophy. Indeed, such courses are more likely to be found within women's studies. The mainstream curriculum remains largely untouched: a question on Plato on women or Mill's *On the Subjection of Women* may be included, but they are marginal to such central issues as the theory of forms or utilitarianism. Papers are always welcome at philosophical societies, but I often suspect that this is to give the opportunity to dismiss the issue of gender as philosophically irrelevant. (A common form of argument is to show that whatever has been said was previously argued by some male philosopher in the past, or alternatively to show that nothing *philosophical* has been said.) The only thing that has changed is the interest of students: there is always a good turnout for these papers, always a high take-up of those odd questions on women. It is as if the increasing numbers of women on our courses were standing up and saying 'This bit is for me, and I am going to seize it'.

Feminist philosophers in Britain organised themselves into a Society for Women in Philosophy in the early 1980s. Then, as now, we were unsure of our identity, hence the absence of any reference to feminism in our title. We continue to meet on Saturdays to share notes, develop analyses. We write books, give papers at conferences, teach courses in feminist philosophy, and even get chairs. But there is an edginess there: is what we are doing 'real' philosophy? Few of us are actually in philosophy departments, but 'do' philosophy in Education, Languages, Schools of Continuing Education, etc. So most lack the confidence of an institutional identity, while at the same time that very marginality has been what made our challenges possible. You can't say very much when every sentence has to be defended against the charge of either nonsense or irrelevance. You need a certain critical mass of people, of *presence*, to force a suspension of disbelief before you can get the argument off the ground. That was the original argument for women's studies. We had a hunch that there was more to male bias in philosophy than the explicit bits of misogyny in the classics. We felt excluded in ways that we could not articulate, and created a space in which we could experiment freely as philosophers *and* women, away from the bullying voices of our discipline which is a tendency to define philosophy as the untrammelled exercise of reason. This is liberating in certain periods (anyone with reason can do it so, as Plato argued, even women can), exclusive in others. In a reformulation of an old Cartesian joke: 'Good morning, I've left my body outside so you can let me in even though I'm a woman.' Some examples, to show the problem: every woman who came to those meetings 'confessed' at some point that she did not think of herself as a philosopher, that she was not doing 'proper' philosophy. But each of us thought that the others were: 'proper' philosophers were always someone else.

It was only with the provision of a community which validated us that we began to discover what we had to say. The problem was we couldn't get our critical mass from women's studies at that time either, for just as we needed to defend our thought from the premature destructiveness of philosophers' critiques, we also had to defend it on the one hand from feminists claiming that philosophy was little more than male ideology, and on the other from the overwhelming embrace of approaches based on what seemed to be theories of psychology or literary criticism. Compared to philosophy, feminist critiques appeared to be having a genuine impact in both of these areas, and they were developing theories about ways of reading and interrogating texts, including philosophical ones. Philosophy is not so much defined by its subject matter as by its way of asking and discussing questions on the one hand, and a canon of texts on the other. If the former is displaced by deconstruction, for example, and the latter dismissed as a collection of books by dead white males, we seem to be left without a subject. In those early days, we hid ourselves away, trying to reinterpret psychological analyses of Cartesianism into philosophical arguments and to rethink such concepts as autonomy and rationality, protecting ourselves from the destructive criticism of male colleagues who deemed gender irrelevant, on the one hand, and the enveloping embrace of feminists who seemed to think that we should stop doing philosophy, in favour of critical theory or direct action, on the other. To be on the borders is always to be betrayed by whatever identity you adopt. We wanted to go on doing philosophy, and had our own tradition to grapple with.

It is scarcely surprising that so many of us found the continental/phenomenological tradition a more secure base to work from, for it both provided an identity within philosophy while giving an alternative to the dominating analytic tradition. It is generally assumed that phenomenological and analytical philosophers cannot talk to each other. We could because we wanted to, because we knew how to listen to each other and knew that 'I don't understand' did *not* mean, 'It's your fault, you are talking nonsense.' We are also a small enough group to know that we need each other. Camps can only develop when they have enough people, as has occurred within the US Society for Women in Philosophy. In this country, the Society for Women in

Philosophy remains an eclectic group, with an ever growing number of young women graduate students, and a continuing minority of women actually employed in academic philosophy departments. But within those institutions, we have been taken over by events. Government-led changes within universities have meant masculinisation in terms of a single-minded commitment to visible success in competitive situations, the language of toughness and leanness, and the hours demanded by aggressively managed institutions, and have made universities, regardless of equal opportunities policies, unfriendly places for women. Philosophy departments, entrenched in the view that it is a privilege accorded only the brightest and the best to study in them, have been slow to adapt to this new business ethic, and so have diminished in size. At the same time, as the competition heats up for limited jobs, those most likely to succeed will be those identifying with the profession as it identifies itself – that is, as it is identified by dominant males. For example, if you wish to contribute to your department's research rating, then publish in recognised, not marginal (women's studies), journals. Alternatively, women may successfully identify with an emergent feminist philosophy, a specialist subject dealing with questions raised by feminist theory which leaves the core curriculum courses untouched, and is more likely to find its home in women's studies. I will have more to say about this later. It means that as feminist philosophy succeeds, then the feminisation of philosophy, as an attempt to make the subject answerable to the questions and experience of women, recedes. My argument will be that our best hopes lie in continuing to roam around margins, rather than being packaged into accredited and successfully marketed subjects, but my main aim is to show what life is like in those borderlands between philosophy and women's studies.

The charms of philosophy

Philosophy has enormous charms for those on the margins. You don't need background to do it. It's a solitary activity, an invitation to step outside all our everyday assumptions and meanings, and to think about them with the mind of an outsider. 'You might all be merely inhabitants of my dream' is the fantasy of one disengaged from society. You can even leave your body behind: 'I am a thinking substance.' It's an adolescent reverie: limitless power to define and redefine reality, iconoclastic, answerable to nobody but my own personally defined canon of rationality. I am invulnerable when I do philosophy, I leave the limits of myself and define those of everybody else. No wonder that Plato thought it an unsuitable subject for the young: such games can be played safely only by those who in their heart of hearts know what reality is, and so know that these are games. To let the marginalised in can lead to cynicism or revolution and possibly both, to madness and death. Philosophy is only a consolation to old patriarchs: to the rest it is a banner and sometimes a delusion.

I discovered it with a sort of wild joy: as an adolescent in the 1950s I had

vowed never to become a woman, rejecting a destiny of high heels and tup-
perware parties. I was always asking the wrong questions, seeing disturbing
implications. My dreams were vivid, and I had difficulty knowing what was
real. I loved science because of its suggestion of buzzing motion behind the
seemingly solid world, its undermining of a common sense that I could not
share. My cultural background was of the BBC Home Service and Scott
reproductions: ducks over estuaries. When people discussed literature and art
it sounded like gossip in an upper-class accent, but philosophy required no
such acquaintance with the world. Like many adolescents, I was awkward,
isolated and rebellious, and I discovered philosophy not only as a place that
would end that isolation, reassure me that the questions I asked were not
mad, but also reflect my adolescent iconoclasm and lack of grace back to me
as critical intelligence and philosophical acumen. It gave me status as well as
shelter.

This isn't an unusual story. After all, the founding legend of the tradition
is of Socrates, who was executed because he refused to desist from asking
awkward questions, and he still captures the imagination of the young,
despite revelations of his anti-democratic political activity and charges that he
had it coming to him. Philosophy claims to require no credentials, is open to
all honest enquirers. It is sceptical, critical, an eternally mischievous child
asking improper questions. At the same time, those questions seem to be
about our deepest concerns: identity, meaning, what can be known, how we
can break through appearances to the real world. At its best, it empowers the
culturally dispossessed. It develops critical sceptical skill, teaches that it is
precisely the troublesome questions which are the important ones, canonises
those who are distanced from society.

This account shows the dilemma for the feminist philosopher, for this
description of the initial attractions of philosophy reveals some of those features which would seem to exclude women. My account could equally have
been of the isolated, disembodied self-absorbed adolescent male. Perhaps I
became a philosopher because I did not want to become a woman. One of the
main feminist critiques of our intellectual inheritance has been of how it has
disguised a particular perspective (white, middle-class male) as universal.
Philosophy's claims to universal reason (or failing that, universal scepticism)
make it a prime suspect in that, and we need to ask whether the philosopher's
questioning is exclusively masculine. The language, the questions, the conception of reason at work have all been developed within a tradition which has
excluded women, so we should suspect a male perspective which only becomes
visible to an outsider. Some examples will show this: philosophy has defined
the problem of abortion as the issue of whether or not the foetus is a person,
and hence has rights. If you can get the definition of personhood right, then
you can deduce the correct answer to the question of the woman's right to
choose. And there the issue is stuck. But the crucial question for most women
is not the issue of rights, but how to come to the decision of whether or not
to have an abortion (legally or illegally). And that, as Gilligan (1982) has
shown, often turns upon a consideration of a whole raft of responsibilities and

dependencies in order to find the 'right' answer. The question then becomes that of how to take a responsible decision so that a network of relationships is not irreparably torn. Looking at the question from the perspective of the women involved changes the issue, not to mention the way that you will explore and develop moral philosophy with a seminar of students discussing the problem. If medical ethics were written to include that perspective (rather than simply to seek criteria for taking hard decisions, which will be as close as possible to dominant moral sensibilities), it would be a different subject.

Before turning to my disillusion with philosophy, I want to say that if I have described a disembodied adolescent male, perhaps we should own up to how much of that creature there continues to be in all of us. I see him in my female students as well as myself. The question is not to deny him, but what to do with him. What I have done, and continue to do, is part of my identity. Like everyone else, I speak different languages, engage in different kinds of conversations, which do not all cohere. The differing parts of a person cannot be incorporated into one 'authentic' self. Which one I identify with at any moment may depend on who is trying to exclude me from what, but I am not willing to give any of them up. I am a feminist philosopher, not a feminist who gave up philosophy: and that is *always* the challenge that I face.

The disillusion with philosophy

For the feminist reader, this is perhaps obvious. Many such readers may look forward to the dissolution of philosophy as practised in the UK, into an abandonment of 'big ideas', or into a variant of the phenomenological tradition as practised in France and Germany, or into deconstruction and/or post-structuralism. For it is here that they recognise rich possibilities for women to write as embodied gendered thinkers, and to find ways of countering the masculine perspective which dominates our cultural institutions, and possibly to extirpate the adolescent boy mentioned above.

These are the areas that have been successfully developed into feminist philosophy, and I return to them later. Whatever their merits (and they are a rich resource for us all), they do not solve the problem I am concerned with here for two reasons. Firstly, all those alternative traditions are as male-dominated as the one I fell into with such delight (indeed, I recall Michele Le Doeff commenting at a SWIP conference in Britain on how liberating British philosophy was, precisely because it was dominated by an analytical tradition which facilitated critique and questioning of authorities). And secondly, I am one of several who want to engage with the British or analytical philosophical tradition: not abandon it, but change the terms of the engagement.

What went wrong? I can best describe it as the loss of subject to technique. I engaged with philosophy because it discussed questions I really cared about: questions of justice, identity, how I could be sure I was engaged with the real world, how language attached to the world, or whether language *was* the world . . . and I found myself in the coils of a logic which denied the possibility of answering such questions, and therefore questioned the sense of asking them. It was rather like joining a Marxist party because of a passionate concern to do something about social injustice, and finding yourself in a never-ending debate over interpretations of the Marxist canon. Doubts about identity, language, moral knowledge became a technical game in which my thoughts were seen as dissolvable puzzles. Meanwhile, to paraphrase Adrienne Rich, the disease went raging on, and I *still* want to discuss those questions, but as real questions. This makes me feel marginal to philosophy, for I believe that the big questions are probably only avoidable by very clever academics, and this avoidance is achieved by a faith in logic as the only technique for sorting them out.

If these questions are important to all of us, as I believe they are, then the discussion of them should be available to all. This means using different means of resolving them, not because we are not all clever enough to operate with that extremely narrow conception of reason that currently dominates philosophy, but because that is what it is: narrow and partial, and because in that form it has been used to dominate and exclude.

Let me back-track a little. Apart from the obvious empirical claims about who holds what positions and publishes what where, and which philosophers said what sexist things (all now well-charted), there are three reasons, or moments, for the claim that philosophy is male dominated, and each of those moments disempowers women in the university at the same moment as it empowers them.

A combative culture

In teaching critical, sceptical skills, the ability to question anything, we silence as often as we make critical. It is that logic mentioned above which facilitates this. If you can operate with it you acquire power. But if you are not prepared to put your back to the wall and defend to the death what you have said, you had better keep quiet, and if you want to explore an idea that you are uncertain of, do it secretly, with a friend. Public spaces are for public combat. Self-contradiction and hesitancy, which often accompany genuine thought, are confined to the private sphere. A feature of this is the way that a trained philosopher will take your question and turn it into his, redefine your problem out of existence. Doing philosophy requires a self-confidence which is still lacking in young women, an assertiveness which often is still alien to us, and, more importantly, might not be the most desirable way of pursuing the subject.

At the same time, once we have learnt to do this, once we are trained to pick out a thesis and probe its weakest spots, we are empowered, we can hold our own with anyone, and in particular answer back to those élites who make us feel inferior. At least one of my aims at the university is to provide my students with a safe place in which to learn how to use a dangerous weapon, because they need it to defend themselves. But in doing that, I prepare them to take their place in a man's world, rather than to create their own, and my lessons are riddled with ambivalence. There is a further ambiguity in these lessons, for what makes this logical facility so destructive is as much the presumption that it is the *only* form of reason as the competitive culture within which it is practised. Often seminars can feel more like a competition to silence others than a common search for truth or understanding. This brings me to the second moment:

Method

Philosophy seems to be dominated by the idea of a genderless, disembodied reason which, if employed properly, will lead to a body of certain and universal truth. This turns into a quite peculiar agenda, which could probably only have flourished in a culture where women, bodies and emotion are identified with each other, and reason is conceptualised as distinct from these. The story is a familiar one: the opposition of minds and bodies, reason and emotion, truth and opinion, reality and appearance. A body of universal truth becomes more and more of a chimera as this disembodied critical intelligence gets to work on it, and the project of finding methods for determining what to believe turns into what to many outsiders must look like a breathtakingly trivial concern with the existence of tables, other persons, or indeed the self. Such a project excludes not only women, but members of those cultures with more embedded concepts of personal identity. I remember trying to teach Descartes to Dakota Indians, and simply being unable to get over their amazed contempt for a man who did not know who he was and in those days, before the emergence of feminist and post-colonial theories, I had no vocabulary for understanding or developing other ways of talking about Descartes.

So women are apparently excluded and disempowered by such a project. But at the same time it develops a critical scepticism which can be empowering: it teaches that no 'truths' are final, no appearances certain. Thus, for example, women are now challenging conceptions of reason which exclude any reference to emotions. This becomes subversive of the privileging of a particular viewpoint, and we might expect resistance. But that resistance itself is constrained by the requirement to use *only* the weapon of rationality (at least officially). I find myself using both intelligence and experience to argue about reason with men restrained by a particular canon of rationality. I cannot simply walk away from that canon, as some feminists recommend on the grounds that rationality is a masculine construct, not only because to do so would be to leave institutionalised philosophy untouched, but also because to do so would be to deny myself and my students a subversive place within the university and a way of seeing through illusion and authority. I have to change the canon, but in doing this I find myself on the margins of feminism.

In attempting to feminise and democratise philosophy, am I using the master's tools to enlarge his house when I should be rejecting them in order to dismantle it altogether? The short answer to that is to remember that philosophy departments themselves are both threatened by and subversive of an increasingly authoritarian management and mindless acceptance of a market model for education within the universities. My argument with my department is at the same time an alliance with it against the silencing of all voices except those of a market economy. Which is the master's house and what his tools are depends on where you stand and what you are trying to defend at any given moment.

Substance

The third main way in which philosophy excludes women is in its subject matter: in what topics it takes to be problematic, what it considers worthy of discussion. Many of these appear to be defined from a masculine point of view. For example, the issue of what belongs to the public sphere, what to the private, has largely been discussed in terms of whether or which sexual practice should be legislated over, usually with the assumption that one is free in the private sphere. For many women, the private sphere remains an area of deprivation and violence until legislation intervenes, and this leads to a rethinking of the whole distinction between public and private. Or take theories of obligation: for most of the history of the subject, it has not been seen to be a problem that these simply fail to account for the obligation we have to care for our children. The commonest obligations for women are not voluntarily undertaken but simply given by the relationships and dependencies they stand in. But the dominant philosophical theories still treat the freely given promise as the most illuminating model for understanding obligation. Because of our historically marginal position to the subject, we now have an agenda of both redefining some of the central problems in philosophy and rethinking such central concepts as identity and obligation. As in the case of reason, I find that this exclusion leads me back into an engagement with the subject.

So the culture, the method and the substance of philosophy, while appearing to provide a place within the academy where all are welcome, require outsiders to behave as if they were one of the chaps. Perhaps they require us to behave like the privileged adolescent mentioned earlier, or, more accurately, they require him to grow up into one of the men that they have become. But is it just a game? If it is, and if playing the game is what gives access to power and independence and prestige, should we women do it too (and become fighter pilots and futures brokers and . . .)? Women's studies provide a base from which to discuss these questions, but, as I have indicated, I cannot give philosophy up. What it enabled me to see were the problems I wanted philosophy to address, the way I wanted its method and culture to change. This involvement makes women's studies at times an oddly insecure place for me.

Women's studies: feminist philosophy or feminising philosophy?

The ambivalence of doing philosophy within women's studies was brought out for me by an MA course, open to both philosophy and women's studies students. We began with a collection of papers written by philosophers who were feminists, reflecting on questions of knowledge and subjectivity. They were clearly written and argued pieces, looking at such issues as how to develop a concept of the self which is consistent with a shifting, changing subjectivity, or how to develop accounts of knowledge which overcome relativism without becoming yet another instrument of domination. The philosophy students loved it – it clearly satisfied a deeply felt need to focus on these issues. The women's studies students found the book hard to read, had difficulty articulating the problems, and felt something was going on which they couldn't really do and weren't sure of the point of. We turned to a collection of readings in post-modernism and feminism, many of them extremely difficult, written in arcane terminology and relying upon a knowledge of what was going on in such other disciplines as psychoanalysis and literary theory. The women's studies students, already familiar with some of the theories and terminology from other courses, engaged with the material enthusiastically and treated it as providing an account of the way that they wanted to read texts, an explanation of how they felt about their subjectivity, or an articulation of their political positions about not privileging voices, classes or cultures. The philosophy students were irritated by the lack of clarity in the papers and the amount of time they had to spend effectively translating them into a language they could understand. For them, it was as if the discussion only really began at the point that it seemed to end for the other group. They did not look to the papers for a theoretical base to their politics but, having struggled to clarify what was being said, held it at arm's length to subject it to a critical scrutiny which, at least in aspiration, was independent of their politics.

There isn't space to develop a full account of these differences, and the divisions were not as deep as I have described them: both groups left with the sense that there were different approaches to problems which made you see them in a new light, and at times a genuine dialect developed between political commitment and critical scrutiny, which is in my view characteristic of both women's studies and philosophy at their best. But I tell the story to demonstrate the way in which outsiders within the academy (and probably everywhere) form new clubs, with their own language, method and culture which inevitably become exclusive. You have to think in the correct way to get in. I had two groups of students who, although they shared a common politics and commitment to feminism, belonged to different clubs and so had difficulty engaging in a conversation with each other.

This raises questions about the nature of women's studies. For me it used to be a place from which we could interrogate institutionalised knowledges and make them answerable not just to women, but to all those excluded constituencies which men as well as women belong to. It took a commitment to feminism to create that place, because most of us had successfully entered the academic club and its language was also ours. It was our commitment to the democratisation of knowledge and culture which made us pay attention to our ill-defined discomforts with our subjects, and develop them into critiques. Implicit in these critiques is a notion of emancipatory education which provides the criteria for assessing our successes and compromises in the academy. I want to give two examples to show what I mean by emancipatory education:

Recently I have been involved in an experiment of doing philosophy with nine-year-olds in a special school for children with learning difficulties. I did it because the children's education consists of a series of skills to be acquired, broken down into manageable tasks: how to trace a letter, play for five minutes without violence, add blocks to blocks, all essential for them to function in society. But I wanted them to have a space in which they could think about anything they wanted, to confirm to them that their ideas matter and are worth expressing. They raised whatever questions they wanted about picture story books we read, and then discussed them. These children, on the very edge of society and failed by most of its institutions, raised and discussed with each other profoundly philosophical issues: what is the difference between a person and a pet? What is evil and what stops it winning? Are dreams real? Philosophy thrives at the margins. The children showed me that an empowering education would be one that not only enabled people to move freely and comfortably about their society, but one which enabled them to own and pursue their own questions, so that they jointly create those cultures which give their lives meaning.

I have tried to show my first year students at the university an agenda, a series of problems that their generation face: they live in a multicultural society and are pleasingly tolerant and non-judgemental, but because they have to solve problems together they also cannot avoid judging unless they seek an isolated, a-political non-responsible future. These are exciting times for philosophy, because changes in our world demand so much rethinking, and this is the space in the curriculum devoted to that. Women have emerged into the academy, into philosophy. We have burst open the assumptions of the enlightenment and liberalism. The translucency of language, the rational autonomous subject, the voluntary nature of obligations . . . all are questioned. My generation opened up that questioning. I try to give these students a sense of how much there is to take forward, how necessary they are to this task.

An emancipatory education is one which begins with the student's perspective and, behind that, a particular community which poses its own problems, background, beliefs, etc. Part of our aim must be to enable the student to help solve her community's problems, or to help solve our own community's problems, and that means developing a critical understanding of our culture and the way our particular positions are constituted by it. It means recognising that explanations are social achievements, realised in people's abilities to use them. It means cultivating habits of scrutiny, of listening, of understanding, and of respect. And it means a model of education which is based on communication and dialogue. My examples demonstrate how that *could* happen in philosophy. How do they relate back to the question of women's studies?

Women's studies developed a critique of knowledge as serving the interests of a particular dominant group – roughly speaking, white, male, property

owning and western. Our knowledge not only solves their problems and celebrates the meaning and significance of their lives, rather than other people's,
but has been used to either dominate or exclude others. The inclusion of
'others' (such as women) is to educate them in ways of furthering that dominant interest. Hence the charges by some feminists that female academics
were women taken over by male ideologies. Many of us continue to inhabit an
uncomfortable borderland between feminism as a political constituency and
our intellectual commitments, and this is brought home most clearly in
women's studies, where those students who take the subject because of their
political commitments will challenge almost any provision, from teaching
methods to social spaces, as 'unfeminist'. Thus they will be reluctant to pay
serious attention to thinkers they deem either irrelevant or inimicable to the
interests of women, and where they have an interest in philosophy it is very
different from that of those students who want to do something about the
absence of women's voices in philosophy. Thus, for example, women's studies
students tend to dismiss philosopher Hannah Arendt on the grounds that she
maintains a strong distinction between public and private, while philosophy
students turn to her eagerly as one of the very few women they can study. In
the literature, this difference is reflected in the dismissal of her as a 'female
male-supremacist' (O'Brien, 1981: 9) or 'a female mind nourished on male
ideologies' (Rich, 1980: 212), while in contrast, Andrea Nye produces a sensitive account of how, from her perspective as an outsider, Arendt is able to
demand that political theory be adequate to the major political events of her
time, rather than to abstruse academic arguments (Nye, 1994).

Feminist philosophy is in large part a response to that feminist critique of
philosophy as male reason enunciating masculinist ideology. It stands in contrast to, and often in argument with, what I shall call feminising philosophy,
the project I have earlier described of putting women's voices into philosophy.
The political impetus of feminism lies behind both, and no one of the three
areas of feminism, feminist philosophy and feminising philosophy is as distinct as these labels suggest. But they constitute the borderlands I inhabit, so
that I am always open to the charge of thinking like a man on the one hand,
or failing to do real philosophy on the other.

Feminist philosophy has become an institutionalised body of knowledge in
its own right, with its own canon, set of theories and agenda for discussion.
It cannot be summarised in two sentences, but some crucial elements in it are
the claim that the gender of those creating knowledge is relevant to the
knowledge that is created, and hence that neither abstract reason nor universal 'truths' can be valid or true. This leads to a method of examining the
situation or perspective of the text and the writer (and the silences or absences
in the text) rather than focusing on the questions the text puts. Gone are the
days when we could exclaim 'Never mind the speaker, the thought is all.'

This not only looks like a rejection of philosophy, and a silencing of the
adolescent voice in philosophy which I prize so highly, but it constitutes a new
club, developing its own career structure and gatekeepers. Just as at one
time (male) philosophers sought to exclude women on the grounds that they

were incapable of thinking like men, some branches of feminism seem to exclude (female) philosophers on the grounds that they think too much like men. But these strictures, although they may have induced self-censorship and discomfort in the early 1980s, are not the real problem. We can argue about what constitutes male ideology, take issue where we disagree with clearly stated views. It is much more difficult to challenge a recondite theory which claims that the very thought processes we use and language we speak is masculine, particularly when we try to express that theory in familiar terms. Yet this seems to be precisely what is being claimed by some contemporary feminist philosophers (Irigaray, 1985; Kristeva, 1985). This is not the place to examine such theories in detail: long may our discussion continue of precisely how our knowledge and thought are gendered, and how the institutionalisation of knowledge has silenced certain constituencies. But I do have three major worries about the way that feminist philosophy is developing.

Firstly, there is a tendency to turn philosophical texts into literary texts, and to treat them as a play of words and metaphors which are more or less pleasing within the discourse, but have no reference, meaning or truth outside it. This seems to remove, or at least diminish, our capacity to hold the text up to critical scrutiny, to ask awkward questions of it, to challenge its version of significance or truth. It undermines that critical edge which is the basis and point of feminism (Soper, 1990; Lovibond, 1989). As philosophical approaches are progressively displaced and explained away by psychoanalytic or linguistic theories, we are denied the very skills which we might have used to assess and criticise these theories, to render them answerable. So feminist philosophy can seem disempowering, denying us tools that we might use for emancipation. Clearly, we need to be able to move between the knowledge that our thought processes are gendered and our ability to use those processes to reveal structures of gender inequality. We need the borderland between feminist philosophy and philosophy.

Secondly, every time that I have introduced students to feminist post-modern texts, no matter how bright or mature or motivated the students are, their initial response has been one of total incomprehension, not just of what the writer is saying, but even of what the writer is trying to do, in the most general terms. Often, particularly amongst mature students, the response is one of anger, and I think this may have something to do with their having finally gained access to higher education, and suddenly feeling themselves excluded again, because they cannot make sense of the words in front of them. In a word, much of this material is inaccessible, and it casts out the uninitiated. There is a terrible irony in Spivak meeting such complaints with 'Do your homework,'[1] and yet elsewhere arguing that she would like to talk so that the subaltern can understand her (Spivak, 1988), and this is simply a reflection of the general paradox that the theory which draws attention to the silenced and excluded is at the same time one of the most exclusive conversation clubs in the world.

Thirdly, these theories and the terminology they are couched in are themselves based on linguistic and psychoanalytic theories which are not beyond challenge. The arguments between aficionados easily match the practice of Byzantine theologians in complexity, subtlety and relevance to the daily struggle to survive, understand the conditions of one's life, and have some faith in the future. That is part of their attraction: an ability to use the language marks one out as at an intellectual cutting edge. I suspect that we are developing new conceptions of human identity and knowledge, but the feminist commitment to emancipatory education must include a commitment to putting their theories into the language of their constituencies, or at the very least, their students. Ultimately, the difficulty of new ideas must be overcome as they become part of the currency of familiar languages. That is part of the challenge of teaching feminist philosophy.

But I still worry whether this is genuinely empowering education or simply facilitating the movement of our students into the élite. A friend of mine wants her extramural students to be able to answer back to those élites who so enforce a sense of inferiority with 'But Quine says . . .'. And that is certainly liberation of a sort – her students are no longer victims to clever chaps. Another argues that post-modernism is a back-hander for the oppressed: her students discover the liberation of reading novels from their own perspective, finding *their* agendas in them, only, a few months later, to discover that their voice is just one in a babble, making no more sense than anyone else's, as if at long last one gets an appointment with the consultant only to discover that diagnosis is done by dice throwing. And, she adds, you can deconstruct the courts all that you like, they will still send you to prison. I might add: you can deconstruct the university all you like; it is still a boys' club. Which is why, at the end of the day, post-modernism might serve to exclude as much as to empower.

I glory in the success of women's studies and feminist philosophy: we subversives have got ourselves established. But there are high risks attached: if you are ambitious, you want to be grounded in the canon to get to the position that you are aiming for. For students, that means a sort of efficient and competent conservatism: knowing what is required and delivering it. For academics, whose ratings and funding increasingly depend upon the presentation of their intellectual wares as attractively packaged and thoroughly labelled items in a supermarket of modular opportunities, it means watching customer trends rather than intellectual or political demands. I'm reminded of a women's university in India, committed to raising the status of women and therefore apparently founded as a university of women's studies, which is increasingly offering courses in tourism or counselling of the sort that can be found in any university, because to attract students they need to offer job qualifications. Their survival depends upon fitting into state economic programmes (which now happen to be acutely conscious of women). I worry that this is simply a more honest and visible way of achieving what we may be forced into surreptitiously: the university as the successfully integrated instrument of government economic policy, which includes women's studies as an imprimatur of being part of the élite. It may no longer *look* sexist, but the old dominations and exclusions remain.

That produces another borderland between the new managers, concerned with image, ratings and sales, and old-style academics, trying to hang on to intellectual commitment and the idea of education as developmental and critical rather than an accretion of discrete skills and information. It would take another chapter to discuss this, as Mary Evans does elsewhere in this collection, but within the efficiency-driven university we subversives look increasingly like old conservatives, setting our faces against change in order to preserve spaces where risks can be taken. The adolescent rebel rises in me again and recognises the other adolescent rebels, who are my allies even if they are wedded to abstract reason and universal truth.

Conclusion

I have been asked whether my bottom-line is political – the transformation of our universities into resource centres for *all* parts of our society – or intellectual – the preservation and development of rational investigation. My reply is both. The aspiration to emancipatory education demands a dialectic between political commitment and critical scrutiny which requires us to celebrate our borderlands, for all their heartache.

Notes

Passages from this paper also appear in Seller (1997) .

1. Spoken in a discussion with John Searle on Channel 4: *Voices: The Trouble with Truth*, transmitted 17 May 1988.

References

Barnett, Ronald and Griffin, Anne (eds) (1997) *The End of Knowledge in Higher Education*. London: Cassell.

Gilligan, Carol (1982) *In a Different Voice*. Cambridge, MA: Harvard University Press.

Griffiths, Morwenna (1995) *The Web of Identity: Feminisms and the Self*. London: Routledge.

Irigaray, Luce (1985) *This Sex Which is Not One*. Ithaca, NY: Cornell University Press.

Kristeva, Julia (1985) 'The revolution in poetic language', in Toril Moi (ed.), *The Kristeva Reader*. Oxford: Basil Blackwell. pp.90–136.

Lennon, Kathleen and Whitford, Margaret (eds) (1994) *Knowing the Difference*. London: Routledge.

Lovibond, Sabina (1989) 'Feminism and postmodernism', *New Left Review*, 178: 5–28.

Nicholson, Linda (ed.) (1990) *Feminism/Postmodernism*. London: Routledge.

Nye, Andrea (1994) *Philosophia*. London: Routledge.

O'Brien, Mary (1981) *The Politics of Reproduction*. London: Routledge and Kegan Paul.

Rich, Adrienne (1980) *On Lies, Secrets and Silences*. London: Virago.

Seller, Anne (1996) 'Whose knowledge? Whose postmodernism?' in R. Barnett and A. Griffin (eds) *Higher Education: The Knowledge Crisis*. London: Cassell.

Soper, Kate (1990) 'Feminism, humanism and postmodernism', *Radical Philosophy*, 55 (Summer): 11–17.

Spivak, Gayatri Chakravorty (1988) 'Can the subaltern speak?' in Cary Nelson and Lawrence Grossberg (eds), *Marxism and the Interpretation of Culture*. Urbana: University of Illinois Press.

3

Feminist Pedagogy to the Letter: A Musing on Contradictions

Gina Mercer

Postcard from Townsville, tropical Australia – 1

Dear Liz,

   Sitting on the verandah looking at the round breast-shapes of green paw-paws and languidly pondering which bunch of bananas I should pick next. It's really green and steamy . . . a bit like living underwater. And I'm wondering what you'll think of these letters when I find them for you. Will they have the power to cross the borders between this physical space and the cold brisk city you inhabit? Or will my words appear, to you and other northern hemisphere readers, to be lush and straggly like this permaculture garden?

   I like Virginia Woolf's notion of women inhabiting a separate women's country, but perhaps that concept is too false and cosy, draping and disguising our important differences. Since you rang and asked for these letters and gave me the title of your collection, I've thought that maybe, as women, all we share are multiple borderlands where snow and big city meet tropical rain and rapid garden with ambiguous results.

   Still – in the letters, as you'll discover, I write about becoming accustomed to straddling, whether it be the straddling of borders, fences or different subjectivities. Oh, now I need another postcard.

* * *

Postcard from Townsville, tropical Australia – 2

Dear Liz,

   I try to imagine your garden . . . terracotta pots of herbs and geraniums on a balcony? Luscious roses, gracious oaks and crisp clean lawns? A few well-loved indoor plants, cyclamens perhaps? Or no plants in your life at all, just a minimalist white monastic space which needs no nurturing?

   Maybe that's all we can do, try to envisage each other's spaces and enjoy their differences whenever we get the chance to glimpse them through the gates of writing. I'm really looking forward to developing my straddling stride when I come to read the rest of your collection . . . .I anticipate revelling in the other women's jungle patches, formal plots, productive allotments or even cactus gardens (though the latter would require rather careful revelry I suspect!).

All best wishes for the project, I'm really hoping there are no delays in the publishing . . . .I can't wait to become a boarder amongst all those other women's borders – love and many mangoes

Gina

* * *

Postcard from Townsville, tropical Australia – 3

Dear Liz,

Eating all this fruit in a humid climate has made me wax philosophical. Herewith my 'thought for the day'.

It struck me that all feminist endeavour, whether it involves working in a women's refuge or lecturing in women's studies, has a pedagogical component. Fundamentally, teaching is about change. If we're not changing, we're not learning. Feminism too is about learning and change. Our revolutions simply can't take place without them. The development of feminist pedagogies is absolutely vital then, a concern for all feminists, not just those who have traditionally been seen as teachers.

Maybe I drank too many mango daiquiris last night, but I did dig out those letters you asked for . . . see enclosed

love

Gina

* * *

Letters to Maria

Dear Maria,

Well, as you know, I've enrolled in this Graduate Certificate of Tertiary Teaching. It's the first time it's been offered here – strange isn't it, how universities, our great teaching institutions, have only just realised that their teachers might need to be taught how to teach? So I enrol, so keen on self-improvement that I never notice that all these self-improving courses lead me closer to self-destruction than anything else. And, of course, the more courses I do, the less I can get published . . . and whatever the Quality Assurance rhetoric about the value of teaching, we all know the folly of ignoring the publish or perish imperative. It's only crazy women, at the almost-bottom of the hierarchy (over three-quarters of the people doing this course could be similarly described), who try to teach and improve their teaching techniques and research and publish all at the same time – no wonder I sometimes wish I was well-dead rather than well-read!

Saw a comment that made me stop and think the other day, and maybe it will interest you. Did you know that in Australia women make up the majority of clients for both psychiatrists and adult education providers (Wesson,

1975: 9)? So perhaps it's not just me who longs for self-improvement, but a whole lot of other women too. Where does this desire come from? Women from many different places and situations are going to psychiatrists and to people like us, for education. My guess is that they are seeking self-improvement, new knowledges, altered ways of believing and being and, in our case at least, professional training.

So if these seeking women are fortunate(!) enough to journey into our institutions rather than psychiatric ones – they arrive here, seething with desires of multiple kinds, their desires and differences glistening, vulnerable – what happens to them? Have to confess that my experience upon entering university was somewhat akin to the losing of my virginity. A big disappointment. All that build-up about the glory and rightness – but ultimately it wasn't much to tell mum about (and when I did, she said she felt the same). And I suspect that a lot of our grandmothers, mothers, aunts, sisters and daughters would tell us the same story about coming to university for the first time. That is, those of our foremothers who had the right colour of skin and money to be allowed into these hallowed halls. When I arrived at uni I expected liberation, stimulation, gratification, passion and excitement in a community of ego-free intellectuals . . . well it was the late 1970s, and I was only seventeen. OK, so I was a little over the top in my expectations, but was I so very different in my desires from a lot of other women entering tertiary education for the first time? And what did I find? What do the other female clients of this service provider called tertiary education find?

Most often I found narrowness, boredom, frustration, inertia, pain, and a cruel sense of never being quite what I was supposed to be. My desires and interests always seemed to be just outside whatever the subject was, I seemed to be vulnerable at all the wrong times and assertive in all the wrong places. Felt like I'd read the wrong sex manual, I was doing it wrong – all the time – in spite of really wanting to do it right. On top of this I found a pettiness of interpersonal politics unequalled anywhere in my experience.

Here's what Carmen Luke says about what women can expect in the way of 'difficulties' because tertiary institutions position women as 'outsider' readers and reproducers of the masculine canon:

> [making us] feel inadequate in a competitive academic environment where men invariably appear more articulate, more able to sustain rationalist argumentation, and more able to provide the 'life experiences' that professors value and respond to; and finally [where we will experience considerable] . . . emotional and financial strain [as we] . . . attempt to fulfil multiple roles as students, wives, mothers and, very often, part-time workers. The wall of obstacles that many women students at university face is incomparable to men's experiences at university. (1993: 2)

Maybe the psychiatrist and some mind-altering drugs seem the better option? No, but seriously, isn't that true to your experience? How well I remember your honours year, with Fred out of work and the three kids getting so sick . . . and all the rest. I mean, I know that some men aren't exactly given the red carpet treatment at universities either, but do the majority know that awful feeling of never being listened to? For that's what I remember very well from my undergraduate days. Many women in my classes had learnt pretty well how to do the rational articulate routine as required, but somehow our contributions *still* weren't quite right, not quite what Monsieur le Professeur wanted. Listen to this woman's response to having to provide the kind of 'life experiences' that professors value:

> The grey eyes gleam with the razored edge
> of an intellect honed assiduously.
> How she burns! How she listens!
> How she reaches to full stretch . . .
> spaceward, starbound, out to Infinity.
>
> Infinity's a tram-stop to Mary . . .
> Ten kids she has . . .
> What can they teach her, the tutorial books,
> the lecturing pedants and all the wise men
> who confer university degrees? . . .
>
> Astronautical mothers on each birth-bed
> take the space-flight alone to the beyond-dark
> and know it unrecognised . . .
> No Houston call-off for inexpeditious conditions
> no flight-control by the scientific button;
> from blast-off to jettison
> an arc'd journey of too common courage . . .
>
> The full circle scribed ten
> and each only the beginning
> of such a data-collation
> of experience, emotion, practice
> and art – oh, never forget art! . . .
>
> What's in a certificate for Mary
> or conferment of a degree;
> licence to practise skill keened with use
> or permission to fill heart in a wanting place
> that was ten times given free?
> (Wesson, 1975: 85–6)

And so the women come seeking and maybe, just occasionally, find some affirmation in the realisation that their already acquired knowledge is just as important as the knowledge purveyed here. But still the books about mothering, maternal thinking (see Ruddick, 1989) and a zillion other aspects of being a woman are only in specialist, advanced, ghettoised, feminist courses. You know some days I sympathise with Mary Ellman's reference to: 'two literatures like two public toilets, one for Men and one for Women, one men can comprehend, which is elevated to the canon, and one which they cannot, which is just concerned with "women's issues"' (Ellman, 1968: 32–3) Except . . . except, that what are deemed 'women's issues' are everybody's issues. Someone was talking about domestic violence as a 'women's issue' the other day, and I thought, how come it gets that designation? Like, do the women beat themselves up? So really I don't see two literatures like two toilet blocks being such a good idea, no matter how tempting it seems on a bad day.

Bronwyn Davies talks about the need to change more than just the trimmings in educational settings if women are to feel more enabled. She shows how gaining access to education hasn't helped to improve women's educational experience:

> The removal of the more obvious rules of exclusion is of itself insufficient to bring about equity. When female students eventually find themselves in the same classrooms as the male students, studying the same courses, they find that the theoretical frameworks which inform the disciplines they study, the content of the courses they study, the discursive practices through which they are taught, and ultimately the way in which they are located as gendered beings in the social world of schools and tertiary institutions, all militate against the construction of themselves as in any sense equal to male students. Far from being equal subjects with the male students, they learn through the process of schooling that only males have access to non-gendered subjectivity . . . they learn that they are . . . not persons capable of acting powerfully in their own right. (1989: 2)

So is that the effect we want to have on the mother of ten who comes to our doors seeking knowledge, self-improvement, wisdom? Do you and I really want to try to teach her that she is 'not a person capable of acting powerfully in her own right'? And what enormous levels of subjugating force would we have to bring to bear in order to bring about such a 'knowing'? And yet as I write I shiver, because I know such pedagogical feats can be accomplished. And if this sometimes *is* the outcome of education for women, how do we measure the effect of reinforcing that message at yet another level, in yet another setting, and especially a setting which the women enter with such open and admirable desires? What does this do, what has this done to generations of women of potential? And what if we consider the lost potential of all those women who don't even get a look in at institutions like these, because they're not considered to be the right colour or class or age, or they're simply too 'different' to 'fit in'? How are such losses computed in human terms, let alone in terms of the GDP or any other such measure/indicator of 'worth'? I know: I'm waxing loud and rhetorical; and we've all heard it before; and surely things have changed a bit since I was an undergraduate; and maybe Bronwyn Davies is overstating the case . . . except I know she isn't . . . and I know that because of the teddy bears.

Every day when I walk into this university building I am confronted by two 'graduation' teddy bears displayed and advertised in a glass case – their being there is to let everyone know that these bears are for sale at this university (presumably to be purchased by out-of-touch relatives who think cuddling a bear will help with post-graduation unemployment blues). Now one of these bears is a bearish bear, wearing a mortar board and an academic gown. It (note pronoun) really looks like a graduating bear. The other bear is wearing a pink dress, a white lace petticoat and a straw sun-hat with white ribbons. She (note the necessity for a shift in pronouns) looks like a little girl bear off to a Sunday-school picnic. The first bear is the clearest representation Bronwyn Davies could ever want of 'a non-gendered subjectivity', while the girl bear is absolutely subject to a 'gendered subjectivity'. And these charming representations of the gender power imbalance are actively sold by a university which has the audacity to advertise itself as an Equal Opportunity Employer.

How rational or equal is it that my male colleagues and students are represented to the community as serious academics wearing all the insignia of intellectual life, while I and my female colleagues and students are represented as infantilised picnickers in pink frocks and conspicuous underwear? It is not at all equal or rational is the obvious reply – and yet this is an institution which proclaims itself to be founded (traditionally) upon reason and (more recently) upon principles of equity. Have you read Beryl Fletcher's New Zealand novel *The Word Burners*? It's a very interesting exploration of the personal and philosophical issues involved in feminist teaching. Anyway, at one point in the novel a controversial essay is handed in by an exceptional student, causing all kinds of departmental difficulties with regard to awarding marks. Sound familiar? Here is an extract from that essay:

> For too long we listened to the voice of the non-cunt who formulated our identity in tune with His need, His desire, His vision. The muteness of our tongues has been redressed, the silence is silenced. We have regained our voice and have tuned the talk towards ourselves. The Quiet cunt is no more. The talking cunt is here. (1991: 219)

and:

> The contradiction between change and constancy is manipulated by non-cunts to keep cunts in their place. A good example of this is the way that the particular intellectual passion of each age is thought to be unsuitable or even dangerous for the feminine mind. Theology and ontology were the 'in' topics for hundreds of years and were compulsory topics to gain entry to a university. Unfortunately, cunts did not have the highly developed sense nor the intellectual equipment to cope with important questions like whether God wanted us to kill people who said the earth moved round the sun or how many angels would fit on the head of a pin . . . Recently, mathematics has replaced theology and the classics as the correct intellectual pursuit of scholars. Positivism, rationality, evidence and data are the key concepts of our age. Alas little boys race little girls to the lego blocks and develop the superior spatial and logical capacities that ground mathematical ability. Once again, we cunts have missed the bus. (224)

Isn't that a wonderfully irreverent summary of the institutional exclusion of women and women's knowledge from the hallowed halls of tertiary education? When the male lecturer of this Graduate Certificate course gave us a potted history of the development of rational thought, I desperately longed to fax him the essay – for his self-improvement, of course. I mean, he said he was into 'reflective teaching practice' and 'life-long learning' – and yet, in the end, I didn't. Even though my cunt's been 'talking' for many years now, on this occasion I forced it to remain silent. Why? Mainly because I was unused to being placed back in the student role, aware of his power as teacher/assessor, made distrustful of his espoused openness by his closed and authoritative style. Maybe I was also influenced by my gendered subjectivity: he was the bear with the mortar-board and academic gown, the salary and the power (Director of Staff Development), whereas I was the bear befrocked in pink with the pretty hat and explicit lingerie, the half-time lectureship and the contract ending in three months time. And I was there as the vulnerable seeker of self-improvement. I mean, after only ten years as a practitioner of tertiary education, what would I know? Feeling that to speak would be both useless and dangerous, I 'chose' to muffle my rebellious lips.

Carmen Luke and Jenny Gore describe the situation:

> Institutional discourses define the classroom, the teacher and the student. For instance we are inscribed as either student or professor: students take exams, teachers don't; students are graded, teachers grade. Such inscriptions are key in the production of subjectivity, identity, and knowledge in pedagogical encounters. In short we might argue, subjectivity, identity, and knowledge are the work of schooling. Yet, such institutional inscriptions, as well as numerous other (some contradictory) discourses of identity, are embodied by real women and men . . . As feminist educators, we are also women who stand hip-deep in cultures saturated with phallocentric knowledges, in institutional structures ruled epistemologically and procedurally by men and masculinist signifiers [see the graduation bears], and in a discipline which, despite its historical terrain as 'women's work' – a caring profession – remains in the theoretical and administrative custody of men. (Gore and Luke, 1992: 2)

Is it any wonder then that my 'talking cunt' identity was silenced by the shift from grader to gradee, a shift in institutional power further emphasised by the gender of the person who, effectively, held custody over the theory, some of the administration and, therefore, over me? Perhaps even this public exploration of pedagogical theory through personal experience is a dangerous one. Those who wade hip-deep in phallocentric waters are likely to get their ankles mauled by phallocratic sharks, yes? Oh well, it's a risk I need to take in the interests of my self-improvement.

Just had a timely interruption to my unruly flights of rhetoric. One of my PhD students has rung, full of justified rage. There's a shortage of space at the university's other campus, so she and the other five postgraduates based there are being evicted from their offices and told to work quietly at home! She is in the final months of writing a brilliant thesis on feminist writers and theorists and their experiments with fictional forms . . . but no, 'sorry dear, there's no room at the institution for you or your work, so just do it at home, and don't make a fuss, there's a good girl'. Just another unjust example of how women's knowledge is valued here, made to seem as relevant as a tampon dispenser in the men's toilets. Where should we take our desire for self-improvement, I wonder? Would we be better off seeing psychiatrists after all? I know their fees are high, and they don't confer degrees, but at least we'd have the use of an office (shared, it's true) for an hour or so each week and their costs are rebatable through Medicare, which is more than you can say for university fees. I wax cynical again . . . better sign off. I'll write again next week, there's so much on power, pedagogy and the personal that I want to discuss with you.

love from Gina

* * *

Dear Maria,

Sorry if my last letter was emotional and polemical, but it was useful for me to connect these theories with recent personal experience. My main concern was whether it made any sense to you, was it impossible to read? Did it resonate with what you've experienced? See, now I've begun this letter with two questions and an apology, instead of some authoritative statement about feminist pedagogy and changes therein, which is what you said you wanted me to talk about. Mmmm . . .

Catherine Belsey suggests that feminist pedagogy should, by its very nature, envisage teacher/student relationships as 'unfixed, unsatisfied . . . not a unity, not autonomous, but a process, perpetually in construction, perpetually contradictory, perpetually open to change' (1980: 132). I thought about using those last phrases, 'perpetually in construction, perpetually contradictory', as the key motif for these letters, because this is the closest description of my experience in seeking to construct a working feminist pedagogy. But this notion of fluidity, non-unity and the being of a perpetual construction site, sets up some very interesting and terrifying contradictions in itself. As Patti Lather pithily puts it: 'How can such self-reflexivity both render our basic assumptions problematic and provisional and yet still propel us to take a stand?' (1992: 125). In other words, how do I examine and critique my own practices, my own ensnarement in patriarchal power structures, and yet at the same time provide direction, access to information and strategies to others who seek to change their position within those same power structures? Is it in some ways equivalent to a general saying 'Bomb this section of the city boys . . . um . . . I think . . . mmm . . . well, may be . . . what do you reckon, chaps?' while the enemy is battering at the door?

I know I've chosen an extreme example and I don't want to carry the analogy too far. But I chose that kind of extremely hierarchical figure (the general of an armed force) because that is the kind of bogey of Fascist authority against which most feminist pedagogues measure themselves at some stage in their career. It's one of the reasons why feminist teachers have tried for a long time to avoid discussing their power, because the predominant image in our masculinist culture of someone 'with power' is of someone having power over others, having the power to dominate and subjugate. And not wanting to be that kind of person 'with power' has led us into all kinds of contradictions and conflicts, ever since feminist teaching emerged as a cultural practice in the latter half of this century. Though I remind myself that women have been questioning masculinist forms of education for much longer than that. Here's Mary Wollstonecraft's description in 1792 of the Fellows of Oxford and Cambridge as 'indolent slugs, who guard, by sliming it over, the snug place, which they consider in the light of an hereditary estate' (p.159). And here we are, still struggling to get clear of that slime.

Faced with, and very experienced in suffering, the model of masculinist power as dominating, alienating, punitive and disciplining, feminists critiqued this form of pedagogy with effective vehemence. It was what none of us wanted to do in our own classes, but . . . what were the alternatives? Much of the thinking seemed to take the most obvious route: if that was the way of the Fathers, surely the alternative was to look at the ways of the Mothers, and develop pedagogies in line with what we knew about maternal styles of education, which we imaged as being based on more equal distributions of power and a philosophy of nurturance.

Gwen Wesson suggests that 'a teacher must see herself as an equal member of a group of peers' (1975: 10). This and other similar statements sounded so good that many of us believed them and tried to construct ourselves and our teaching practices around such theories, but . . . it never really worked because, for all the beauty of the rhetoric and all the sincerity of the writers, underneath lay the hypocrisy of unacknowledged power. As bell hooks recounts:

> When I entered my first classroom as a college professor and a feminist, I was deeply afraid of using authority in a way that would perpetuate class élitism and other forms of domination. Fearful that I might abuse power, I falsely pretended that no power difference existed between the students and myself. That was a mistake. (1994: 187)

And burying our heads in the sands of talk about equality does not erase the reality of the examiner/examinee, and grader/gradee, equation which underpins most of the tertiary institutions in which we are paid to work. So, no wonder I didn't trust the male teacher's rhetoric about his openness and 'life-long learning' desires, when he was potentially the grader and I was the one to be graded. But more to the point, why should my students believe me if I walk into a class within a patriarchal, competitive institution and suggest that we are equals, that they can trust me, that I'm different to everyone else, that I eschew all authority and that they are free to say what they want? They don't believe me. I don't believe the teacher who says such things to me when I am in the role of student. And they/I would be rather naive and foolish if we did. Most of us as students have an intimate understanding of this power dynamic, just as Gore describes it:

> The institutional location . . . of much pedagogical practice may militate against [empowering rather than repressing students] . . . The pedagogical relation of teacher to student is, at some fundamental level, one in which the teacher is able to exercise power in ways unavailable to students. Teaching remains embedded within a history of moral and cultural regulation. Moreover . . . practices which decrease overt regulation can increase surveillance and regulation through covert and more dangerous means. (1992: 67–8)

We are hip-deep in phallocentric waters, and to try to pretend that we are elsewhere, able to create a 'truly maternal' nourishing space, is a lie . . . and a lie which it is dangerous to feed to ourselves, or to our students, most of whom will recognise it as falsehood, because their legs are wet and cold from years of immersion in phallocentric waters, and they will not and should not abandon their hard-won knowledge of those power structures in order to accommodate our cosy maternal fantasies.

So – this is one of the major differences to develop in feminist pedagogy over the past twenty or so years. Initially, there was the development of what you might call nurturance pedagogy, and it was a pretty attractive model/fantasy which many feminists sought to implement over many (exhausting) years. But more recently we've come to do a power analysis of our own fantasies/theories and have realised that there are intolerable contradictions in them.

Valerie Walkerdine – did you hear her speak at the International Thinking Conference in Townsville a few years ago? In the paper she gave then, and in publications elsewhere, she suggests that from the late nineteenth century onwards, women teachers were exhorted to use their 'natural' talent for 'loving nurturance' to inculcate the right kind of 'natural' development into the children in their care:

> It is love that will win the day, and it is the benevolent gaze of the teacher which will secure freedom from cruel authority in the home as well as the school. Through the figure of the maternal teacher the harsh power of the authoritarian father will be converted into the soft benevolence of the bourgeois mother. (1992: 16)

Maternal methods of structured 'play' and gently loving indirect 'instruction' were seen then (and revived in the 1970s) as the 'best' methods of teaching. The teacher did have power over the students, but if she cleverly disguised it as 'love', 'nurturance' and 'freedom' her power/influence and covert directions would not be resisted by the students. If she had 'discipline' problems it was because she had failed to love them enough: 'women teachers became caught, trapped, inside a concept of nurturance which held them responsible for the freeing of each little individual, and therefore for the management of an idealist dream, an impossible fiction' (Walkerdine, 1992: 16).

It sounds somewhat ludicrous when caricatured in this way, but this was the essence of a particular 1970s style of teaching, and a lot of feminists, reacting against the general of the army model, adopted this maternalised ideology, little realising its coercive history, nor its negative potential. Many individual feminists suffered professional burn-out under this pressure to love and nurture all their students (no matter how repulsive some of those 'little individuals' were), but Jenny Laurence also points out some of the other risks involved:

> It is argued that an alternative feminist educational practice should be based on feminine ways of connecting with the world, ways of connecting which privilege the relational, the contextual, and women's distinctive empathetic and nurturing capacities. However such definitions of feminist teaching practice come perilously close to reinforcing a stereotype of femininity which has helped to confine women to specific sites within education . . . . (1991: 53–4)

But I for one still feel the need to develop 'an alternative feminist educational practice' containing elements of the one Laurence describes, even knowing that it carries essentialist and stereotypic dangers. And it does help my development to recognise some of the problematic aspects of maternal pedagogies. At that Jane Gallop Seminar in Canberra in 1993, the problem with the continuing use of the family model became apparent. Why should

teachers be modelled on either mothers or fathers, as Moira Gatens asked so
pertinently at the seminar (Gatens, 1994: 15)? Why not develop an ethics of
teaching which steers well clear of any romantic, psychoanalytic or New Right
version of the nuclear family? And, like all really good questions, it's so obvious you wonder why it hadn't been asked before. But not before taking in
Gallop's perceptive point, that not only did many feminists embrace maternal
pedagogies, but it was a particularly narrow version of 'the maternal' which
was embraced. In practice there are a multitude of different ways of mothering. But the one that has been lurking, perpetuated in much feminist pedagogy,
is that of the bourgeois all-sacrificing, all-nurturing, well-resourced, power-
sharing, 'good' mother. This mother has no desires of her own, no needs, no
problems, no will of her own except to nourish and empower all her students/
children, whom she loves equally and without reservation!

When Gallop pointed this out there was an audible intake of breath in the
auditorium (1994: 11–12). I and many other women there (fledgling and
fledged feminist pedagogues as we thought) were quite deeply shocked at
what we had unwittingly endorsed in our theorising – especially as this image
of maternity was one we had been actively deconstructing in other arenas. It
is always usefully shocking to be confronted with your own perpetual contradictions, to be made aware when one hand doesn't know what the other
hand of theory is doing. Here we had been prescribing for ourselves an idealistic self-denying, self-abnegating form of maternal practice. The very same
one which we were loudly criticising patriarchal culture for prescribing to
mothers!

Coming to this realisation has been a very useful awareness in terms of
releasing aspects of my feminist teaching practice. For example, when confronted with a particularly odious masculinist student this year, I allowed
myself to indulge (between classes) in punitive fantasies, and then when I saw
him the following week I was far more able to recognise his power ploys and
redirect his destructive tactics so that they lost the capacity to undermine
everyone else in the class – really quite empowering.

Empowering. Now that's a word that crops up ever so frequently in feminist (and other 'liberatory') pedagogies. Yet the power issue is problematic
even in the dynamics of 'empowerment'. As Jenny Gore says:

> my major concern about the politics of empowerment within discourses of . . .
> feminist pedagogy stems from conceptions of the agent of empowerment. Having
> established that the agent of empowerment is usually the teacher, and that the
> subject (or object) of empowerment is Others, a distinction is immediately set up
> between 'us' and 'them'. Even if some teachers attempted to empower other
> teachers, the distinction remains between those who are to be empowered . . .
> When the agent of empowerment [is] assumed to be already empowered, and so
> apart from those who are to be empowered, arrogance can underlie claims.
> (1992: 61)

And the last thing a 'good' mother, 'not-father' feminist pedagogue wants is
to be thought arrogant! So how do we proceed in these marshy arenas of
power called the classroom, surrounded as we always are by hip-deep murky

phallocentric waters? Gore suggests that 'if empowerment is constructed as the exercise of power in an attempt to help others exercise power (rather than as the giving of power), we confront the unforeseeable and contradictory effects of the exercise of power and must be more humble and reflexive in our claims' (1992: 62).

Yes, yes, I see – I must image myself not as the giver (for to give is to assume I have something worthwhile to give – a position of power it's clear), but as a facilitator of others' ability to exercise power. OK, but doesn't the humility and constant self-criticism which Gore so rightly recommends bring us back, perilously close, to the self-abnegating, self-denying humble mother-figure which Gallop so rightly critiqued? And yes, while I thoroughly agree with Gore's notion that we must not promise total liberation in true salesman fashion . . . yet I am also keenly aware of the pressure to promote oneself and one's institution. Wasn't that part of what the recent Quality Assurance exercise was all about? Weren't we supposed to be promoting our teaching, telling the world how wonderful and unique we are? And certainly I have a head of department who keeps urging us to develop courses with 'sexy titles' in order to attract students . . . and I read the Equal Employment Opportunity officer's circulars telling me to promote myself in order to get promoted: don't be too humble, don't be too self-critical, don't fall into the feminine trap of downplaying your achievements, she says. Is this another area in which the left-hand theory doesn't realise what the right-hand theory is doing? If I comply with Gore's call for more humility and self-critique, how then do I successfully negotiate my way around the rest of the university?

Maybe the Staff Development Unit should be offering courses in versatility, so that staff-who-are-student-hermaphrodites like myself can better negotiate these different pressures. Walkerdine raises another aspect of this issue when she discusses the fact that 'female teachers and . . . [female students] are not unitary subjects uniquely positioned, but . . . a nexus of subjectivities, in relations of power which are constantly shifting, rendering them at one moment powerful and at another powerless' (1987: 166). At one and the same time, this is a non-unified, non-humanist being 'perpetually in construction, perpetually contradictory, perpetually open to change' (Belsey, 1980: 132), a curious mix of humility and assertive challenge.

I agree with Clare Bright (1993: 130) when she says that for too long feminist pedagogues have sought to avoid discussions of power and that we really need to examine it, and how it zaps around our classrooms, staff meetings and Graduate Certificate Courses in Tertiary Education. I also think Mimi Orner has a voice worth listening to when she says:

> In education, the call for voice has most often been directed at students. Where are the multiple, contradictory voices of teachers, writers, researchers and administrators? The time has come to listen to those who have been asking others to speak. (1992: 88)

So much pedagogical theory is deeply immersed in an unquestioning quest for the 'good' teacher and I can really relate to Orner's call for us to enunciate and explore our 'bad' teacher fantasies, our problems with power, our desires for power (even if accompanied by our best 'empowerment' intentions). bell hooks slips around and through exactly these kinds of contradictions in her hard-to-put-down book *Teaching to Transgress*. She comments that

> In much feminist scholarship [which is] criticising critical pedagogy there is an attack on the notion of the classroom as a space where students are empowered. Yet the classroom should be a space where *we're all in power* in different ways. That means we [teachers] . . . should be empowered by our interactions with students. (my emphasis; 1994: 152)

Yes, I think we are all in power, like fish in water, and we swim at different levels and sometimes we are sharks, at other times maybe krill. I like the way hooks slides through the binary oppositions of teacher and taught by using this concept. Curiously it was the situation of being a student again which made me aware of some of the contradictions in my own theory and practice. By being made to straddle the grader/gradee boundary for a while I learnt a lot about both sides . . . albeit, the straddling itself was pretty uncomfortable; again, I only wish I'd read bell hooks on this topic earlier, as she so wisely remarks that:

> Not every moment in the classroom will necessarily be one that brings immediate pleasure, but that doesn't preclude the possibility of joy. Nor does it deny the reality that learning can be painful. And sometimes it's necessary to remind students and colleagues that pain and painful situations don't necessarily translate into harm. We make that very fundamental mistake all the time. Not all pain is harm, and not all pleasure is good. (1994: 154)

Does that sound awfully like a promotion for the masochistic desire for self-improvement? Isn't that where I began, lamenting my urgent desire for self-improvement and more learning, regardless of the cost and the consequent development of my desire for self-destruction? Well it may be close, but somehow I don't think so, do you? Maybe all this self-reflective practice has ended not in a learning loop but in a loopy learner! Still, there are an awful lot of other women, good women and magnificently bad, who keep me company on this quest for feminist pedagogies that don't inhibit or prohibit all the potential Marys and Marias and Rubys who come seeking at our doors, their desire for learning so glistening vulnerable . . .

love and contradictions always
from Gina

References

Belsey, Catherine (1980) *Critical Practice*. London: Methuen.
Bright, Clare (1993) 'Teaching feminist pedagogy: An undergraduate course', *Women's Studies Quarterly*, Fall/Winter, 21 (3/4): 128–32.
Davies, Bronwyn (1989) 'Education for sexism: A theoretical analysis of the sex/gender bias in education', *Education Philosophy and Theory*, 21: 1–19.
Ellman, Mary (1968) *Thinking About Women*. London: Macmillan.
Fletcher, Beryl (1991) *The Word Burners*. Wellington: Daphne Brasell Associates Press.

Gallop, Jane (1994) *Proceedings of the Jane Gallop Seminar, 1993* (ed. Jill Julius Matthews), ANU Humanities Research Centre, Canberra.

Gatens, Moira (1994) 'Responding to Gallop: Feminist pedagogy and the "family romance"', in Jane Gallop *Proceedings of the Jane Gallop Seminar, 1993* (ed. Jill Julius Matthews), ANU Humanities Research Centre, Canberra. pp. 13–17.

Gore, Jennifer (1992) 'What we can do for you! What can "we" do for "you"? Struggling over empowerment in critical and feminist pedagogy', in Jennifer Gore and Carmen Luke (eds), *Feminisms and Critical Pedagogy*. London: Routledge. pp. 54–73.

Gore, Jennifer and Luke, Carmen (eds) (1992) *Feminisms and Critical Pedagogy*. London: Routledge.

hooks, bell (1994) *Teaching to Transgress: Education as the Practice of Freedom*. London: Routledge.

Lather, Patti (1992) 'Post-critical pedagogies: A feminist reading', in Jennifer Gore and Carmen Luke (eds), *Feminisms and Critical Pedagogy*. London: Routledge. pp. 120–37.

Laurence, Jennifer (1991) 'Re-membering that special someone: on the question of articulating a genuine feminine presence in the classroom', *History of Education Review*, 20(2): 53–65.

Luke, Carmen (1993) 'Women in the academy: The politics of speech and silence', Women's Studies Seminar, James Cook University, Townsville.

Orner, Mimi (1992) 'Interrupting the calls for student voice in "liberatory" education: A feminist poststructuralist perspective', in Jennifer Gore and Carmen Luke (eds) *Feminisms and Critical Pedagogy*. London: Routledge. pp. 74–89.

Ruddick, Sara (1989) *Maternal Thinking: Towards a Politics of Peace*. New York: Ballantine Books.

Walkerdine, Valerie (1987) 'Sex, power and pedagogy', in G. Weiner and M. Arnot (eds), *Gender and the Politics of Schooling*. London: Open University Press. pp. 166–74.

Walkerdine, Valerie (1991) 'Reasoning in a post-modern age', paper delivered at the International Thinking Conference, Townsville.

Walkerdine, Valerie (1992) 'Progressive pedagogy and political struggle', in Jennifer Gore and Carmen Luke (eds), *Feminisms and Critical Pedagogy*. London: Routledge. pp. 15–24.

Wesson, Gwen (ed.) (1975) *Brian's Wife, Jenny's Mum*. East Malvern: Dove Communications.

Wollstonecraft, Mary (1988: 1792) *A Vindication of the Rights of Women* [(ed.) Carol Poston]. New York: W.W. Norton.

4

Negotiating the Frontier: Women and Resistance in the Contemporary Academy

Mary Evans

For the benefit of those living on Mars I will begin by pointing out that the past twenty years have seen an explosion of feminist work in the academy. A great part of this work has been in the humanities and social sciences, and although the impact has been far from uniform, it is nevertheless the case that many subjects (for example English literature) have been largely transformed by a feminist contribution. Nobody in a British university with any interest in the state-of-the-art of intellectual life could fail to notice this shift. As such, British academic life has, in large part, experienced a paradigm shift not unlike that of previous periods (such as the 1960s) of rapid change and re-evaluation. We can date feminist impact from the early 1970s, with the first women's studies courses on both sides of the Atlantic, and the subsequent establishment in the 1980s of degree programmes and a scattering of academic posts. All this obviously has also been accompanied by the necessary academic baggage of debates, controversies, journals, networks, feuds and friendships.

These considerable achievements, in just two decades of intense activity and furious publication, have been accompanied, as might be expected, by equally intense and furious disagreements. Of the many issues which have divided academic feminists, the status and importance of psychoanalysis and the ethno-centricity of western feminism are two examples. Freud, for example, had a very bad press until Juliet Mitchell effected his rescue in 1976; equally, few western feminists even considered their relationship to the rest of the world before the sharp reminders of Audre Lorde and others (Mitchell, 1974: Lorde, 1984). But whatever the disagreements between the different parties in the debates, there has been a general consensus about the centrality of women's studies in re-negotiating the relationship of women to universities, and, through that newly constructed relationship, the relation of women to knowledge. It is on that issue and the related issue of the relationship of women to the universities – the institutions in our society 'of' knowledge – that I wish to focus in this chapter.

Probably the majority of people reading this chapter will be aware of the long struggle which women had (in all countries of the West) to enter higher education. Whatever re-discoveries feminist history can put before us of the part played by individual women in particular intellectual contexts, the general picture of enlightenment Europe was one in which women were on the margins of intellectual life. Ramshackle, corrupt and largely incompetent as the universities themselves may have been, they were uniformly active in their hostility to the inclusion of women. Organised knowledge kept women out, and kept them out until late into the nineteenth century. On the other hand, and this is the point which has been made at length by feminist historians, women were often allowed to function on the margins of intellectual life (Rogers, 1982). They wrote, they participated in debates and they certainly contributed to debate, but they did not, in any institutional sense, play a part in the construction of what has been optimistically referred to as the higher learning. Again, feminist historians have pointed out the acres of print consumed by attacks on the intellectual capacities of women and equally passionate defences of women's intellectual abilities (Sapiro, 1992). This dialogue, which we can date from the early nineteenth century and the great period (whether we follow Weber or Foucault) of the European codification of knowledge, very rapidly became one of female assertion of equal ability. To enter the sacred portals of the academy, women did not, inevitably, point out their *different* abilities from those of men. The debate, the battle and the demonstration were all about the attempt by women to show their ability to match male intellectual competence. Judging by the standards discovered by Matthew Arnold and other great male reformers of the male public schools, this competence often did not amount to very much, if anything at all. Nevertheless, even if very few people (that is, men) in the universities actually knew anything very much, what they *did* know was how to keep unwanted people (that is, women) out. To this a good deal of attention was devoted at all the élite universities of the West until the First World War, and even then it was often the case that women were only allowed into the academic equivalent of the servants' quarters.

But the place given the women in Oxford, Cambridge, Harvard, Yale or the Sorbonne in terms of actual physical space was in some ways more generous than the real intellectual space. What we can show are the many instances of colleges for women built in the late nineteenth and early twentieth centuries and the many advances which took place in this period of European modernisation in the higher education of a small proportion of white, bourgeois women (and let no one suppose, until the educational reforms in the West of the 1960s, that access to higher education was anything but highly restricted on grounds of class and race as well as gender) (Baker, 1976). Yet in these advances lay important dynamics which have structured the relationship of women to higher education to this day. In the first place, the universities which the small group of white women were able to enter were themselves in a state of re-organisation. Indeed, in many ways the term re-organisation is too strong, since it suggests a degree of existing organisation. What occurred in the second half of the nineteenth century was not, therefore, so much re-ordering as the imposition of a primary order – an order about the status of degrees, the qualifications for entry to the university and the scope and content of the curriculum. Thus women's demands to enter the universities coincided with just that point at which universities were beginning to institutionalise the getting of wisdom. From the point of view of the universities, and their reformers, it is all too easy to see why they did not want their new, fragile, structures threatened by a problematic group.

This brief digression into the late nineteenth century is to make the point that feminist accounts of women's struggles to enter higher education often omit a discussion of the nature and the context of the opposition. When the opposition does appear, it appears as 'men' or 'the universities', and what can then be lost is the complexity of their internal divisions. Between men in the late nineteenth century universities, it is apparent that there were considerable differences of opinion: the scientists had to face the rigid resistance of powerful groups at Oxford (and less so Cambridge) to the inclusion of the natural sciences in the university, and dissenters at both Oxford and Cambridge had to fight endless battles about the influences and control of the Church of England. In this context, it must be emphasised that opposition to the admission of women was only one of the issues which confronted male academics.

But in entering these universities, divided as they were by intellectual and religious difference, women had to decide how to situate themselves in relation to both these debates and the nature of the institution. It is of lasting significance that the pioneers at Oxford and Cambridge of women's higher education chose, on the whole, to opt for assimilation and the unquestioning acceptance of given standards of academic excellence. Having been allowed, grudgingly, to enter the hallowed precincts, women did not then rejoice in the freedom to live and to read as they wished and ignore examination results. What they did instead, as autobiographical and documentary evidence demonstrates, was to work extremely hard. Indeed, women endorsed the academic function of the universities with a zeal unknown to most of their male contemporaries. Hence, of course, the insults about swots, blue-stockings and dried-up spinsters which many educated women, in all cultures, had to endure. The point, however, was that the *tone* of women's place in higher education was set by these early pioneers, and it was set in a way which was largely similar in Britain, the US and France. In memoirs of life at Oxbridge just before and after the First World War, Vera Brittain and Dorothy Sayers both spoke of their intense earnestness about work and their feeling of needing to justify their entry to university (Leonardi, 1989). Even though both women were from middle-class backgrounds, and were only part of an educational experience which was entirely conventional for their male peers, there was nevertheless the sense of the guilty participation in a scarce resource. That feeling, a deadly combination of academic earnestness and refusal of delight in knowledge, were captured forever by Virginia Woolf in her account of the differences between men's and women's Cambridge colleges in *A Room of One's Own* (Woolf, 1929).

Yet for all the tinge of envy which we can detect in *A Room of One's Own* (and inevitably this literary twinge must have been replicated a thousand times in reality by Woolf's perception of her education – or lack of it – and that of her brothers), by the time she came to write *Three Guineas* (1938) the tone has changed. No longer does Woolf envy the glorious buildings and the wonderful food, for she has acquired a perception of what a great deal of this wonder is for. And as the photographs in *Three Guineas* show, the universities are in part about maintaining the power of the military, the established church and paternalistic figures of authority in the culture and the community. Put aside these figures, and the political consequences of the power of these individuals as a group, and the universities are no longer the enviable place that they once were.

Thus by 1938 we can find the most powerful voice of British literary modernism dissenting from the endorsement of organised knowledge. At more or less exactly the same time Robert Lynd published his equally powerful attack on the universities of the United States, *Knowledge for What?* (Lynd, 1940). In Germany, members of the Frankfurt School had begun to ask definitive questions about the relationship between intellectuals and bourgeois society and by 1938 *all* academics in that country had to answer fundamental questions about their part in state-maintained universities. *Critical* knowledge, as opposed to the mere teaching and replication of what is already known and regarded as important by the socially powerful, had moved away from the universities, or occupied only a small space within them. Nevertheless, women by this time were thoroughly established in higher education and had become part of the traditions and the culture of the universities. Woolf's dissenting voice in *Three Guineas* was not one which struck a chord with women in the universities – for them, the issues still largely remained those of increased participation and equality of treatment.

And so, to pass over some thirty or forty years of history, it remained until the 1970s. All western societies massively expanded the numbers of women and men in higher education in the 1960s and 1970s and in doing so offered a limited extension of women's participation as academics. But what is remarkable about this changed situation (and it *is* remarkable that most western university systems now recruit equal numbers of female as male students) is that much of the old pattern of gendered engagement within the universities persists. By this I mean that men essentially control the universities, in that they are the senior managers and the large majority of the professoriat. Thus in the dual sense in which universities are run, that of allocating material resources and deciding on the central issues of the curriculum, it is men, and masculine interests, which prevail. Despite the fact that half the 'consumers' (as students are now termed) are female, the curriculum in many universities remains tuned to the person as male, and the core individual of western liberal higher education as the male citizen. Clearly, ideas are changing, and a collection such as this would not exist if different ideas did not co-exist aside deeply traditional ones. But certain habits and attitudes, developed through a hundred years of a marginal place in higher education, persist in the uneasy relationship between women and knowledge.

The claim that women have been, and to a large extent still are, marginal to higher education, needs little explanation or exploration. The 'facts' are there in those patterns mentioned in the previous paragraph: the absence of women from positions of actual and symbolic power, and the impact which this has on the construction of the curriculum and the very identification of the core issues for any subject. But what *does* require elaboration is a discussion of the implications of women's historical marginality to institutionalised knowledge. First, it has created in women what appears to be a deep sense of insecurity about access to certain subjects. Just as girls' fear of maths has been identified (over and over again) in schools, so women's disinclination to enter the natural sciences, philosophy and mathematics is a commonplace of university statistics (Walkerdine, 1989). Male critics of women students explain this by women's inability (or, more politely, 'refusal') to engage in abstract thought. More determined participants in this blame-the-victim school of explanation simply locate women's talents as descriptive and not analytical. Very seldom in these debates is the nature of the subject brought into view, and even less often (and perhaps more problematically) do women in those subjects speak of their problems for women. Despite the work of a generation of feminist historians and sociologists of science (Sandra Harding, Londa Schiebinger, Hilary Rose, Donna Haraway and so on), the belief is still maintained that certain subjects are simply like that, and failure to understand or engage with them is the fault of the student and not the subject (Harding, 1986; Schiebinger, 1989; Haraway, 1991; Rose, 1994). Given the absolute silence of western philosophy about women, it is still relatively rare for a male philosopher to point this out, or to recognise that, for women, reading Plato or Hobbes has little of resonance. What has to be emphasised here, then, is not that women philosophers (historians or political scientists) are not – now – failing to point this out, but that this work tends to make little impact on the controlling heights of the profession.

But those 'controlling heights' in any academic subject can make or break careers. Thus it is that women's sense of insecurity within the academy is not located only (if at all) in fantasies about male power, but in the actual reality of it. Men do make appointments and judgements about academic work, and what they have at their control is the ability to silence women by identifying their work as marginal. The deeply powerful arguments about key issues of justice and equality being unrelated to questions to gender is just one example of the Everest of assumptions which women have had to challenge. That particular argument in philosophy and politics continues: on the one hand men refusing to countenance the idea of 'difference' in justice, and on the other women, particularly in the US, demonstrating the actual and manifest absurdity of a system of justice which is not gendered (Nussbawm, 1993). Equally, in sociology, a debate has raged about the meaning of social class, an argument which had consistently had as its hidden agenda the extent to which male academics can allow, even for the purposes of academic debate, female autonomy (Delphy and Leonard, 1986). In all these debates, women have had to decide how to situate themselves, and thereby hangs the critical question. To adopt certain views carried the consequence of being described as 'wrong' (or in academic-speak, 'making an inadequate argument'). Being 'wrong' then involves – at the most extreme – a lower class of degree, a lost job and a refused application. At the less extreme, it is about remaining, yet again, on the periphery of the debate.

However, the extent to which the curriculum of the university, and the very culture of the West, is changing is rapid, and it would be misleading to present a picture of all universities hanging grimly on to out-of-date assumptions and rigid refusals of the innovative. Plenty of evidence can be collected for that, but the overall picture has to be presented as one of increasing diversity. But if, as suggested, women are still marginalised by certain subjects, what demands investigation is the nature of those subjects, rather than the differences between the sexes. It is shifting the debate in those terms which now confronts the universities, and it is that shift which it is difficult to see taking place, so great is the entrenched intellectual confidence of disciplines such as the natural sciences, philosophy and history. English literature has had its internal debates made plain to the public, while the social sciences, as 'younger' subjects, possess little of the same social authority. But in the 'old' subjects a sense remains of the implacable and unshakeable confidence of method and subject, a confidence which as yet shows no sign of disappearing.

Thus, in summary of this first point, we find that however considerable the presence of women's studies and academic feminism is, it is still the case that the towering heights of the academy are dominated by men. Now this assertion obviously implies a hierarchical view of the academy, and on this I am prepared to avow publicly to an account of the universities which differentiates between them and within them. Thus, for example, I do think that the 'old' universities (in both the sense of Oxbridge and of universities which were such before the end of the binary divide) offer what is in many cases (if not all) a qualitatively different education from that of some of the 'new' universities. Who and what is responsible for this is another question: the point is that the accumulated intellectual and material capital of the old universities cannot be easily replicated in other institutions. Thus while 'new' universities might be relatively friendly to the idea of women administrators and innovations in the curriculum, the 'old' universities show little such interest. Indeed, from their point of view there is no reason to change: the most academically gifted students are still creamed off by the old universities, and their control on resources is as strong as ever. With this retained and confident privilege goes an assurance (albeit increasingly far from absolute) that what is being taught represents the definitive account of the subject.

If there is to be a slogan for women's studies and academic feminism in the twenty-first century, I would propose that it should be 'Universalism Does Not Rule OK'. I would argue that this is one of the two great battles which has to be fought by feminists in the contemporary academy. Careful readers will have noted that throughout this essay I have distinguished between women's studies and academic feminism, and I do this because it seems to me that, whatever the many merits of women's studies, it is not necessarily and inevitably feminist, in the sense of prioritising the interests of women above all others. In part this is inevitable; step into the academy and a person and/or a subject becomes involved in a way of thinking about the world which is rightly organised around doubt and uncertainty. It is not, it has to be added in parenthesis, that the academy actually always behaves like this, but it should, and its absolute certainties are always its absolute losses. But feminism is about political action, however small the 'p', and it is occasionally difficult to see the political in some of the woman centred, but not necessarily politically motivated, debates within women's studies. The connections are sometimes, although very far from always, some distance from the world outside what used to be called the ivory tower.

But this idea of the 'ivory tower' brings me to what seems to be the second great battle which women now have to fight in universities. It is, in fact, less to overthrow the ivory tower than retain it. By this I mean that the impact of government policies in Britain in higher education (and to a certain extent in the US and France as well) have recently been such as to introduce into the academy the dominance of the market-place view of the world. I would emphasise here that I do not think, quite emphatically, that the universities were ever sites of the pursuit of 'pure' knowledge. I find that view ridiculous, and amongst many people of my generation, whom I imagine also read E.P. Thompson on Warwick University Ltd. and listened to Noam Chomsky on the American Mandarins, there was always a large degree of scepticism about the idealist and romantic view of universities which supposed them to be the homes of entirely unworldly scholars (Thompson, 1970). Universities were always full of personal feuds, envy and malice quite as much as more general betrayals to the interests of the dominant culture and the military industrial complex. So what I wish to suggest is not the invasion of some 'pure' culture by an alien one, but the gradual transformation of many of the liberal assumptions of universities into questionable habits and the values of the market economy. In their brief encounters with the public, politicians sometimes give themselves away, and when Mrs Thatcher remarked to a young man reading history that this was 'a great luxury', she indicated a whole way of thinking about higher education that is inherently hostile to it.

Thus by this point the nature of the second battle for women in contemporary universities should be fairly clear. To put it in terms of dress: I would see conflict emerging (and I would hope it is emerging) between the culture of the power suit and the shoulder pads and that of what I would euphemistically describe as more relaxed modes. It is not, to pursue the metaphor, that shoulder pads necessarily reveal everything about a person, but in this kind of cross dressing, whether literal or not, there lies a willingness to take on the assumptions of a Thatcherite and managerial attitude to education. With this attitude goes a ruthless belief in policing the behaviour and the 'performance' of both students and academic staff and the imposition on the curriculum of unanswerable questions about the 'aims of the course' and the 'learning outcome'.

All this idiot jargon was well known to the old polytechnics, but it is endlessly to the shame of the vice chancellors of 'old' universities that they did not unanimously reject this language of evaluation and the assumptions behind it. Women in the universities might take heed of this particular case: the men who set themselves up as gods in their own institutions could not collectively say 'boo' to a piece of complete pedagogic nonsense. Because of this failure of collective nerve, male and female academics are now increasingly facing the actual erosion of their role as academics as the assessment function of their jobs increases to the detriment of that of teaching and research.

Those in favour of these new approaches to higher education have always maintained that the British system was unique – and apparently uniquely wrong – in giving tenure for life to academics who then sat and did very little for the remainder of their professional lives. Everyone who has ever taught in a university knows of the case of X or Y who, after a promising start, declined into the organiser of the staff football team (this possibility is deliberately gendered). But the point is that we know of so few cases, whereas for most of us the reality is that we are actually surrounded by individuals ever anxious to appear in print and exercise their *autoritas*, not to mention their *potestas*, on whatever is the academic issue of the day. In its typically spiteful spirit of revenge, Thatcherism yet again got it wrong. Moreover, it is difficult not to suppose that Thatcherism got it so wrong because Mrs Thatcher herself had such a miserable, and marginal, time at Oxford. Not only did the university fail to recognise her particular Gradgrind qualities, it also suggested that it had no particular interest in the mere performance of work. To many of us this might be the complete vindication of everything that is great about the non-Protestant and subversive traditions of England, but to Mrs Thatcher it was clearly a rejection of everything that she stood for. 'There is no hell in fury' as the British press is happy to mis-quote every time another woman tells all about a Conservative MP, but the real hell unleashed on the universities was of course that of a woman scorned by the very institution she had probably valued so much.

We have all come to be familiar in recent years with the idea of the 'revenge of the oppressed'. But in Conservative policies towards the universities we find a particularly clear example of the revenge not of the oppressed but of the repressed. The generation which is now in power in the Conservative Party is a generation which was at university in the late 1960s and early 1970s, a time when future presidents of the US and leaders of the Labour Party were learning not to inhale and/or play in pop bands without absorbing information about soft drugs. As such they were at universities which were everywhere in transition. Restrictions on entry were disappearing and the curriculum was changing. It was no longer enough to go to university and hope that it would be an intellectually secure place: for a crucial, if brief, period, universities became more diverse and more open. To return to the beginning of this story: women entered the universities in far larger numbers and brought with them what was at the time a unique refusal to accept the male definitions of the curriculum. For a brief period – perhaps about 1968 until 1975 – it seemed as if women, now at university in considerable numbers, could begin to challenge universalism, move out of the attic and engage centrally in debates about the organisation and distribution of intellectual power.

Some twenty years later what we have to observe, at least in Britain, is that while the first part of the description above is still true (in that women and men undergraduates are now numerically equal), the challenge to universalism and the engagement in debate about the organisation of the academy is largely absent. Thus I would argue that women academics face two crucial questions: first, the need to retain – in the face of post-modernist pluralities – that sense of the abiding power of universalistic judgements which makes it possible to contest them, and second – and very importantly – a concerted critical and resistant evaluation of the new processes of control and evaluation now shaping academic life. Again, let us return to a contrast suggested earlier: that between *A Room of One's Own* and *Three Guineas*. In the first essay we can see, and read, of Woolf's envy at the spacious privilege enjoyed by male undergraduates, a spaciousness which is both material and intellectual. But in *Three Guineas* we see a new scepticism and a degree of contempt about the universities. Woolf, in fact, had lived through much of the same kind of intellectual shifts that the West has known in the last thirty years. The Cambridge which her brothers attended just before the First World War was one infused with the novel ideas and uncertainties of modernity: heady stuff to plunge from Edwardian England into psychoanalysis and Impressionism. To view Cambridge from the point of view of the restrictions of the Edwardian school-room, even if it was a school-room dominated by Leslie Stephen, was to see it as a place of intellectual excitement, social radicalism and political dynamism. But with the hindsight of maturity, and in Woolf's case the experience of living in an intellectually rich milieu, the formal academy must have had less appeal. Indeed, by 1938, the universities of Oxford and Cambridge appeared to many critics as part of that 'dying culture' which Christopher Caudwell (1971) identified. What Virginia Woolf had seen is what many people see simply through the experience of getting older: that as much as they examine and inspire the novel and the innovative, universities also reinforce and uphold the conventional and the established. Given that the culture which the British ruling class was visibly upholding in the 1930s was the Empire, class hierarchy, appeasement with Fascism, and a general resistance to modernity, there was little reason for Virginia Woolf or anyone else with radical political and intellectual sympathies to feel a continuing sense of loss at exclusion from the universities.

Since 1938 British – and western – universities have moved slowly in the direction of a greater cultural pluralism and a greater social diversity. But degree-granting processions in many universities do not, in many cases, look vastly different from those in *Three Guineas*. The 'old orthodoxy' of church, local politics and the military has largely been replaced by a new orthodoxy of local politics, university administration and management. But it is still an orthodoxy and it is still male. Looking at these processions, and listening to the public orators for the award of honorary degrees to (literally) civic fathers, it is quite possible, indeed entirely reasonable, to suppose that little or nothing has changed in the universities. It is still a largely masculine hierarchy which dominates these events. But in saying this, there is a real danger that women academics of a feminist persuasion simply see men, and do not see the particular kinds of men, or the interests of particular kinds of men, which are now predominant. The old oligarchy of Conservative Party, Military and Church of England has, on the whole, been replaced by a less differentiated but more ideologically coherent class: that of the managers of the 'new' market-led public institutions. The snobbery and the social exclusivity which kept money and trade out of British universities has now disappeared in the face of a culture which wholeheartedly embraces private and public sector managers. Given that a major political programme has been fought by the British Conservative government on the need to privatise all sectors of the economy, it is hardly surprising that the worthy figures in borrowed academic robes following vice chancellors in procession are those of figures central to this politics. To illustrate this shift and this point, let me refer to one example. In the late 1960s, the University of Kent at Canterbury was offered a large sum of money by Marley Tiles Ltd. The then vice chancellor turned down this possible gift on grounds which included the problematic nature of financial gifts to universities from private industry. Some twenty years later senior figures at the university appointed to the symbolic post of chancellor Robert Horton, a man with, to say the least, a mixed reputation in business who had been ousted from British Petroleum in a bloody board room coup.

It is the scale, and radicalism, of this shift which is important here since we can see a movement in less than twenty years from a climate in which universities and private money only problematically co-existed, to a situation in which universities will apparently do almost anything to publicly endorse private ownership and the values of the market-place. Thus just seeing men and the problems of the deeply gendered hierarchy of the universities is to see only part of the problem. Obviously, a discrimination against women is real, to be deplored and to be fought. In addition, however, there is increasingly a point in contemporary universities at which women have to ask questions about promotion and appointment to what, and for whom.

Thus Virginia Woolf's loss of faith in universities seems entirely just and entirely modern. We all know that universities are not merely degree factories, and that work of real and lasting value is still done within them. Yet at the same time there might also be a sense in which feminist academics, women in women's studies and feminists in women's studies (however the particular coalition is made up) might think – from the relative freedom of the margins and frontiers – of women's relation to the management culture and to the implicit assumptions of it. Three questions could then be identified as core questions of the new reality of gender and power in British universities.

First there is the issue of the degree to which feminists in the academy should endorse the new management culture of the universities and, moreover, if they do not wish to endorse it, how forms of resistance can be organised.

Being 'on the margins', as women's studies has been described, is some assistance here, in that a marginal subject has little to lose from developing a position of dissent rather than collusion.

The second point is that of the complexities of the relationship between women in women's studies. At present, the shift in British universities is towards introducing ever greater competition between universities and departments. This puts individual departments or centres of women's studies in the situation of having to fight against (rather than with) each other in bids for externally valuable recognition. Becoming 'just' another academic subject, with the endless implication of academic feuds and competition, was always a warning voiced against the integration of feminism into the academy. And in the pressures of the last fifteen years this doubt seems to have acquired a real meaning, made all the greater by the insecurity which the academy itself creates in some women. The sense of being 'allowed' space in the university, rather than owning it as of right, still seems to me to be of fundamental importance, both in the literal sense of controlling and organising the material space of universities and in the more metaphorical sense of the refusal of the patriarchal university to allow and to recognise women's knowledge.

The third issue, relating to both of the above, is that of the ownership and control of knowledge. Women's achievements in demonstrating the many inadequacies of universalistic modes of thought are there for all to see, but they are likely either to disappear or to remain marginal if women fail to engage with that very culture of the apparently universally validated value of the market economy, which is now transforming not just the universities but the social world in general. As a person old enough to remember 'society', my conclusion is therefore one of an argument for, yet again, a double shift by women. It is, of course, to engage with the false and limited premises of patriarchal universalism. But it is also to recognise that these values are part of a social system, and one which is at present moving towards an ever closer identification with, and legitimation of, the priorities of the capitalist market. That market can allow (indeed encourage) some women in the West the heady experience of personal autonomy and individual fulfilment, but it cannot provide, indeed does not provide, anything other than exploitation and subordination for women globally. Thus the personal and cultural freedoms apparently allowed by capitalist post-modernity are limited, I would argue, and the real and lasting radicalism of women's studies would be to recognise and question this false freedom. Since women's studies now has something of a room of its own, its strategic use of that position could be to barricade the door against managerial intervention and develop what universities in the West now so strikingly need, which is coherent resistance to the ever closer fusion of the university and the interests of the market economy.

References

Baker, Liva (1976) *I'm Radcliffe, Fly Me! The Seven Sisters and the Failure of Women's Education.* London: Macmillan.

Caudwell, Christopher (1971) *Studies in a Dying Culture*. New York: Monthly Review Press.
Delphy, Christine and Leonard, Diana (1986) 'Class analysis, gender analysis and the family', in
    R. Crompton and M. Mann (eds), *Gender and Stratification*. Oxford: Polity Press. pp. 57–73.
Haraway, Donna (1991) *Cyborgs and Simians*. London: Free Association Books.
Harding, Sandra (1986) *The Science Question in Feminism*. Milton Keynes: Open University
    Press.
Leonardi, Susan (1989) *Dangerous Degrees*. New Brunswick: Rutgers University Press.
Lorde, Audre (1984) *Sister Outsider*. New York: The Crossing Press.
Lynd, Robert (1940) *Knowledge for What?* New York: Harcourt, Brace & Co.
Mitchell, Juliet (1974) *Psychoanalysis and Feminism*. Harmondsworth: Penguin.
Nussbawm, Martha (1993) 'Justice for women', *Women: A Cultural Review*, 4: 328–40.
Rogers, Katharine (1982) *Feminism in Eighteenth Century England*. Brighton: Harvester.
Rose, Hilary (1994) *Love, Power and Knowledge*. Oxford: Polity Press.
Sapiro, Virginia (1992) *A Vindication of Political Virtue*. Chicago: Chicago University Press.
Schiebinger, Londa (1989) *The Mind Has No Sex*. Cambridge, MA: Harvard University Press.
Thompson, E.P. (1970) *Warwick University Ltd*. Harmondsworth: Penguin.
Walkerdine, Valerie (1989) *Counting Girls Out*. London: Virago.
Walsh, V. and Morley, L. (eds) (1995) *Feminist Academics: Creative Agents for Change*. London:
    Taylor & Francis.
Woolf, Virginia (1929) *A Room of One's Own*. London: Hogarth Press.
Woolf, Virginia (1938) *Three Guineas*. London: Hogarth Press.

5

In Law and Outlaw?
The Tale of a Journey

Angela Montgomery

I have been a feminist academic who has developed a particular view of a number of issues which I have experienced by virtue of being a feminist, in a particular discipline, and also in a number of different academic departments and institutions. But my profession is primarily one based outside of academia: the legal profession. There are many people like me, who are 'in academia' but who have a lot of professionally-necessary dealings with a related professional group 'outside' and indeed who have at one time belonged to 'outside'. I have been an academic in a number of institutions around a discipline area which is both 'outside' and 'inside' in this sense, but I later made a choice to return to 'outside'.

I have been a feminist academic, but I am no longer. At its most simple, the question which I shall consider in this chapter is, did I leave academia because I did not feel at home within it, or was I pushed out of it by forces and processes outside of my control? As I shall show, providing an answer to this question is by no means easy or straightforward.

Starting off

While an academic, I moved between four different institutions. I started off my teaching career in the 'old' university sector, in a law department which was, and still is, quite traditional. When I started, I was part-time; there were only three full-time female members of staff out of the staff complement of twenty-two or twenty-three. At that time I never intended to go into academia as a career. Indeed, I did not choose to go into it, in that positive sense. I did my degree, then went off and did something else, and I ended up teaching part-time primarily for the money. I imagined that the people who taught in universities were people who had gone to Oxford or Cambridge and then took up high status jobs within similar kinds of institutions, not people like me.

Law departments are quite strange places. Generally there is a very strong tradition within them, which is very much more about the narrowly academic and far less about teaching around the theory of law. In the first department

I joined as a staff member, there was a line drawn around those who were seen as involved in legal theory. It was the philosophy of law and the jurisprudential lawyers, those who had a theoretical base to their teaching and their research, who were the oddities on one side of a divide, and there were those who did not on the other. This was not quite so true of the next institution I worked in, which was at that time a polytechnic. It was in many ways anti-intellectual and prided itself on being more practice-oriented. This – the separation between those interested in thinking through theory, and those immersed in legal practice – has been one of the important divides within and between law departments.

Law departments are also odd perhaps because of the split between the vocational and the academic and, because of the particular vocation concerned, they are quite traditional in their activity and outlook. They are situated both 'on the border' of the academic and the outside and they are absolutely and traditionally 'academic'. They are also typically incredibly well run. Administratively, every law department I have been associated with has run like clockwork. When I moved into the social sciences it was chaos by comparison, but whether that comes from the people who choose to go into the law being orderly, and law being about order and moving away from conflict, is a moot point. In addition, in my first academic department there was, in the whole institution really, a tradition of public school as well. The Senior Common Room was like a public schoolboys' tea party: they would read the *Times* and it was clear that they did not want to be joined and that this was very definitely their territory. There was the tradition, and then there were people who were seen as different from that tradition. The women in the department were never really incorporated, and if you were seen as a feminist woman, and black as well, then it was as if you did not exist. Looking back, they were probably quite frightened by what they conceived as newcomers coming into something that they had always had and controlled. However, ironically, that once-mainstream has now been marginalised because the university became very involved in teaching overseas students, where the first year of a degree course was taught in Singapore or Cyprus and then the students came straight into the second year, and a large number of new and very different members of staff were employed as a consequence.

I started off as an undergraduate doing politics, social work and law. Professionally, I thought about social work as a career; I was not attracted to politics, because the politics department in that institution saw politics as really for men and believed that women were not 'up to it'. My parents, however, were not very happy with the idea of social work because they saw it as an unsuitable profession for a woman. Their ideas were based on their perception of the types of people who would have to be dealt with, the kind of people they thought would have committed offences. The law is of course centrally concerned with criminals, but the crucial thing was the distance involved in the different professional relationships. My parents would not have liked me to go into the criminal law; however, criminal law is only a small part of 'the law', and the rest of it takes place in private and is therefore largely unseen in public perceptions, although this is the law that has a publicly high profile. My parents had really quite sophisticated ideas, seeing social workers as 'hands on' with the rough end of society, while seeing the law as removed from this sector, thus making an important status difference. My parents were also quite concerned about safety issues – they saw social work as unsafe for a woman and therefore as unsuitable for me.

In the law department where I was an undergraduate student there were quite a lot of women teachers, and on the particular degree course that I took about a third of the students were women. It was also one of the very few university law departments that had a reasonable number of black students as well, while the politics department was largely white, male, and public school. Looking back on it, it was not dissimilar to the first department I moved into as a teacher in this respect. That kind of culture was quite strong in both. This white, public school, male composition produces a particular kind of departmental culture, a particular set of students, and also – closely associated with this – a particular set of intellectual interests. There is a concentration of power in a sense. The ability of these people to hang on to control comes because they have all three – class, gender and 'race' status – and the way these interact with each other compounds the situation.

In my undergraduate department there was the clear acknowledgement of difference: women were different, black people were different. We were certainly marginalised, but at the same time at least our difference was recognised. In the department I then entered as a member of staff, they were so apparently 'right on' that there was no difference acknowledged, and this became more of a problem than the earlier marginalisation had been.

On Boys' Clubs

Public school, male, white: the fact of these three factors overlapping in many academic departments and institutions is often disguised. Whether someone is a man or white can be seen, but it is not visibly available to onlookers that they may also be a member of a particular class grouping. I frequently have been shocked that men who present themselves as though they came from a council estate and the local secondary school have in fact actually been to Eton, Harrow, Oundle or one of the other high status public schools. Being a woman, black and certainly not upper class, what motivated me to become involved in academia was primarily the learning relationship that exists between students and lecturers. I became a law student, then I did a Master's degree; while I was doing it I was very short of money, so when I was asked to do some teaching I agreed. My aim at the time was to practise welfare law and to work in a law centre. Ideas about criminal justice and equality underpinned this. At that time, it was quite difficult to get jobs in the law centre field and the competition was extremely keen, so I registered to take a Master's degree, then the only one in the country on welfare law. However, I was surprised and disturbed to find that there was little room for analysis or politics; almost nothing like this was in the syllabus. It was ironic that this was a welfare course, and that although ostensibly it was run by people motivated by a commitment to equality, its organisation was in fact one grounded in hierarchical relationships and patterns of *in*equality. The people who ran it were immersed in teaching the details of, for example, immigration law, but they failed to consider the nature of the state, who is a full citizen within it and who is not, who has rights and who has not, whether the citizen is 'raced', classed and gendered and so on.

Gender patterns and hierarchies within this department were very clear, even to the graduate students within it. As largely women graduate students, we were reluctant to criticise anything that we were unhappy with about the teaching of the women in the department. Whichever way we did it, the male members of staff would have used this against them and they would never have had the space to change. One of the really difficult things in academia is that, for women, there is very little room to develop and to make mistakes because someone is always waiting to get you, always waiting to measure you against a man and find you wanting. You are always on the edge, always on the boundary. You feel you cannot get anything wrong because there is no room for error and there is also consequently no room for taking risks. People develop by taking risks and by trying out new things, and if these don't work out then this is chalked up to experience. Men do this all the time in academia and when things go wrong, even when they go badly wrong, it is never seen as a gender issue. However, if a woman changes her teaching method and it goes wrong then this is seen much more negatively, as not only the fault of that individual, rather than of other factors such as the students or whatever, but more particularly as the fault of her being a woman. This removes from women the space in which to make the mistakes that are necessary within a learning process.

Men are given the space to make such mistakes within academia, but at the same time and in spite of this there is little outward perception of men shifting and changing in academic life. It is the women who are doing this, in spite of not having the room and in spite of being judged extremely negatively when they make mistakes. In a way women do not have much choice about this, because students treat women differently, porters treat women differently, the women who serve in the refectory treat women members of the teaching staff differently, the secretaries do so, everybody treats women members of staff differently from men and so everything you do involves taking a risk whether you try to play safe or not. But it remains the men who get on. The mistakes they make are rarely held against them. They are often as dull as ditch water and this is seen as a virtue. In a sense it seems that whatever men are is seen as virtue; and whatever women are is seen to detract from the processes of getting on. The women who do get on do so against the grain, while the men slide along it. My sense is of the onward and upward march of mediocrity in academic institutions, of which a manifestation in the new university sector is the proliferation of professorial Chairs – Ratner's Chairs.

In the second department which I joined as a member of staff, being intellectually able was seen quite negatively unless judgements about this could be made around people's politics. One member of staff was seen as academically very able, someone who would go places. The head of the department saw his articles as wonderful, while I thought they were alright although not that special. But the politics were right for this man, for he was on the Left in a department which was generally on the Left. His problem was that he slept with a lot of female students, but that was never seen as a negative thing by 'the department', only by the women involved in it. This supposedly leading light of academia was sleeping with a number of female students in the department and received complaints from their husbands or partners. The man was a complete mess but he was encouraged and praised. Behind this was a one-dimensional way of thinking about being right-on. The political culture of the department depended superficially on intellectual criteria, but actually on left-wing credentialism. Although recently academic feminism has been accused of 'political correctness', in practice enforcing this requires considerable organisational power and 'clout', and to have this you need to belong, to be an insider. Anything seen as being 'different' decreases the ability to gain power within such a system, and political correctness is in fact a characteristic of the boy's club, not of any women's involvement within academia.

New male members of staff in this department were given a good deal of support from the other men in the department. Two women who started their employment within it at the same time as a man were treated very differently from him. He had a good deal more choice in terms of who he could go to for help, but the women were in a quite difficult situation, dependent on the women already there but mainly on men who were not at all keen to help them. One or two were helpful about not taking it all too seriously, but this is most definitely not the same thing as showing someone how to produce an academic CV or introducing them to the dean or to senior members of the discipline in their area of specialism. This never happened to the women, but it did happen to the male members of staff. However, the key things we women were excluded from concerned writing and research. Access to commissioned and funded research is very much based on whether you are involved in a junior capacity and the reputation you gain from this; and being involved in this junior way is based on your relationships within a department. By and large the women members of staff in this department never got a look in here. The men did not make those opportunities available to the women, but they did for the men. The women staff were relatively new and junior, so there was not really the opportunity for this to occur via other women within the department. If one was to get on, then this necessarily involved the more senior men. But even if there had been senior women members of the department, there are problems here in feminist terms with this notion of a women's system of patronage and the opportunity to get on within it. These are very hierarchical relationships: I am daddy, you are baby, I will offer you patronage; but in order to offer patronage you have to be in a hierarchy in which some people are at the bottom as well as others being at the top. I don't think it is possible to have a girls' club, like the boys do, which is not hierarchical.

These issues revolve around networking and knowing what is going on, and finding this out always takes a considerable amount of time. When I first joined the department I was seen as a novelty. Certainly I was the first black member of staff that had been appointed, and, although I did not realise this until later, I was the first black woman to be appointed into an academic department in the whole institution. Other women had been appointed, but not in academic posts. In my first teaching department there were a lot of black students. I remember feeling that difference as I moved from one institution to the other. I came to realise that I am a kind of anomaly within the system, because if you are a black woman then the qualification most likely to get you into academia is to be upper class and I most certainly am not that. Other people have a sense of me as someone who is very highly motivated. However, I was not very directional in this regard when I started my academic career. I simply wanted to obtain a law degree and then to work in a law centre, and it was this that got me through my first three years of an undergraduate degree and then also got me through my Master's degree. But there were no jobs available by the time I finished, so I went into teaching, and here it was the students that kept me going, for I saw the benefits of the job solely in terms of them, in terms of the relationship I had with them and the way in which I learned from them as well as enabling them to learn. After about a year and a half of teaching I had concluded that I didn't really belong. I could not stand it, could not stand the way the boys' club operated and the way that it positioned people as either insiders or outsiders. But the plus side was that I liked the teaching and I liked the students.

I first experienced the fact that I was not at home, that I did not belong, in a strange way. My first teaching post was in a clubable department and I was in a way a part of the club when I first started. This came about because I was such a novelty – I was invited into the club, and it was extraordinarily ironic that quite a few of the men said to me that 'we don't really see you as a woman, you know', but they never said to me that 'we don't really see you as black'. In that job and various subsequent training work, a lot of the men said 'we don't see you as a woman really, but we see you as black', as though being black is the primary thing that they can see and that it is this that they necessarily relate to rather than any other characteristic of me as a person. The anomaly here, and the strangeness of my position, was that the men in the department related to me as a sort of token bloke, a token black bloke. However, it rapidly became apparent that I was not as 'clubable' as they had thought, that I was in fact a woman rather than a bloke in drag, because there were differences of opinion over students, one case in particular where there was an appeal. I was asked to say that the case of the woman concerned had been fully discussed at an examination board when it had not been.

The knock-on effect of this was quite large in terms of how I was treated afterwards; 'you are obviously not one of the club because you are difficult and you are not prepared to bail out other club members.' Part of the issue, something which I do not think would happen now, was that the woman was Asian and the problem concerned her treatment by men in her local community. The department had had very few black students when I first started, and the other staff members could not conceptually understand what the issues involved were for women members of ethnic minority communities.

The most noticeable of the changes afterwards were that the men in the department were distant and, although there were no formal sanctions, things 'just happened' to me as the result of being a difficult woman. I ended up doing almost all the administration in the department at one point; it was a case of 'we will drown her'. It was a punishment like writing lines. If you were going to be difficult, you would get more and more admin but not the help that other people got, like study leave or the time of a good secretary in the department, and so on.

By contrast, in my second teaching post it was difficult to get any administrative responsibility because this was seen as high status. In the polytechnic context, the men who wanted promotion wanted all the administrative tasks because this would be 'counted' as part of their claim for promotion. The structure of management and control within the now ex-polytechnic sector was one which took people out of academic life, for in these institutions heads of departments and deans were – and still are – administrators rather than academics, in spite of all the Chair titles about. The people who ended up with the high status administrative tasks were the ones who the head of department felt would bail him out in difficult circumstances. None of the women would do this. Even though we were all very different from each other, all four of us believed that he had got himself into a mess and that it was his own fault. We felt we were outsiders and things worked so as to exclude us, so the dynamic was one in which we did not have any loyalty towards him.

These divisions also took place in the context of differences about teaching. There were two things in particular. Following the change-over in staff, I asked to take over lecturing on constitutional law in the department, as I was a public lawyer first and foremost. This in fact went to a new member of staff, a man who had a lot of experience in teaching constitutional law, and so a decision which I could accept as fair enough. However, then my request to teach constitutional law on a part-time degree course was also rejected and this went instead to someone who had just finished being a student in the department and who had never taught before at all. In order to establish any kind of reputation in this department it was necessary to teach in one of the six core areas, and from this also came security of tenure as well as high status activities as part of cases for promotion. However, if I had taught in one of these areas this would have made me more central in the department. It was clear to me that the head of department wanted me to remain peripheral. The second difference concerned three senior lecturer posts, which some very junior members of staff were informally invited to apply for while I was not.

In the end the consequence of these differences – over the treatment of students and the operation of 'the club', and around the way in which I and other women were treated as more peripheral than junior men who were not so well qualified – was that I concluded there was no point in remaining. I applied for a number of other very different kinds of jobs, including one which was a research job to investigate the position of women in the further education sector across the ten further education colleges in the county. To my surprise, I was short-listed and then appointed, and I asked for a secondment for the two years of the contract. This was opposed by the head of department and it was only when I made an appointment over his head with the assistant director of the institution that he agreed. But although I was seconded, I never went back. I enjoyed this new job and I also started some part-time lecturing at another university while I was doing it.

Thinking about these matters now, with benefit of hindsight, the dynamic at work seems to have been one in which I became a staff member of an academic department which had a 'club' characteristic and which was run by men who had tight notions of who was in and who was out. In the main, the people who were in and thus clubable were those white male members of staff who were from public school or 'good' boys' grammar school backgrounds. This was true to one degree or another of both the academic departments I had taught in thus far. There was greater lip service paid to radicalism in the second department than the first, but the structural features of both departments were the same. When I arrived, I felt at odds with some aspects, but because there were other people who were also outsiders I felt more at home in the second department. However, over time I developed a practical critique of how things were done there which led people to conceptualise me as difficult and problematic, which then led to my being more and more pushed out and excluded, to the point where I wanted to remove myself. To my mind it says a lot about academia that I could experience two ostensibly very different kinds of institutions as having exactly the same kind of structural mechanism, but a structural mechanism which absolutely did not exist when I was the deputy director of the further education research post. Here I worked for the local authority, not for the colleges, and I was not actually based in a department: because of the research, I was always going somewhere else.

From these two initial experiences of being employed in academia, I had become unused to being part of an institution or department, and I had developed a positive need not to be a part. This was the crux of the problem in the third lecturing job that I had, where much of the department's organisation was centred on a very specific kind of club. I arrived being very clear that what I liked was the autonomy and independence of the lecturing role, but I joined an organisational context that was more club-like than either of my two previous departments, a characteristic emphasised by the geographical isolation of this particular institution, and which undermined a sense of institutional procedures and rules being of primary importance. It was a club which was much less about being part of the male public school class and very much more about male left-wing credentialism. In the other two institutions where I had worked, it was clear that certain things were acceptable and certain things were not, and so things were done in a reasonably consistent way, whereas at this third institution, a college located on the boundaries of the higher education sector, people 'did their own thing' – people further up the hierarchy more than others, but everybody to some extent or another.

Analytically it is useful and interesting to compare the dynamic at work here with the earlier one I have summarised above. At the college, it seems to me the 'club' was not based on institutional hierarchy and a form of masculinism which simply excluded 'troublesome women', but was rather a personal and interpersonal one, dependent on one person's particular credibility in the rest of the academic world, which then provided internal kudos within the institution. Some people in all grades above and below could become a part of this; others, again at all levels in the institution, could be excluded. Because of the size of this institution, a comparatively small one, people's personalities and their interpersonal wheelings and dealings had and still have very much more effect than in the larger, hierarchical and relatively rigid institutions.

However, this kind of highly personalised way of working, in which the getting of power can involve harassment of all kinds, including sexual harassment, is something which is generally tolerated across the very different kinds of institutions involved in academia and in spite of the size differences between institutions. In the larger more formal ones it is combined with 'superior' position in the institutional hierarchy. Such men get away with it because they are 'successful' in the terms that the institution's managers, largely other men, want – it is only when such behaviour adversely affects other things which 'count' that there is any question of control or disciplining. Morality and ethics seem to be irrelevant so long as academic status and the flow of research money stays intact. What counts is status in the outside world, with money and publications being two of the most important kinds of institutional currency for measuring this. The behaviour of the 'in group' is tolerated and colluded with, and behind this there is the club, which is about being male, being white and, still, being public school. 'They' see the rest of us as interlopers who really should not be there.

This institutional collusion in academia in sexual and other forms of harassment is linked to whatever is seen as 'politically correct': club members can behave completely unacceptably, be drunk, beat up girlfriends, sexually exploit students, bully colleagues, so long as they pay lip service to the standard of political correctness that prevails in that department, faculty or institution, that is, in the sense of their positioning around the local political culture. The very overt forms of harassment that I experienced in the college are not in fact central to maintaining the status quo. The 'club' means patronage, which means that those at the top can make use of the labour and ideas of those below. Harassment also does that. These are simply different mechanisms for achieving the same result, which is that those at the top of the hierarchy can 'make use of' other people in supporting and maintaining their superior power position.

In an institution like the college, those lower down the hierarchy and on the receiving end of patronage and harassment are experiencing two varieties of the same dynamic for producing and maintaining superordinate status. Harassment involves another version of 'the club', preserving silence and thus protection for a member who is 'alright except for this minor problem'. The net effect is similar to that in a well-run mainstream department headed by white, public school and middle-class males who offer patronage to young white public school males and help them into publication, success and promotion. There is a different set of mechanisms, but the structural features are almost exactly the same, as indeed is the outcome. However, and it is an important 'however', it is easier for women to challenge the traditional white male public school hierarchy, particularly because here there is little pretence at being pro-woman or pro-feminist, but mainly because in the conventional kind of academic department, no matter how appalling it might be, there is some notion that it is possible to disagree.

An important issue here is that in a context like the college there is no line drawn between the professional and the personal. Feminism too questions that line. But when that line is maintained in an academic institution, it seems to be associated with the view that people do not have to agree about absolutely everything and that it is possible to disagree even though someone may not be liked for this. There is some kind of basic recognition that people have a right to think differently and that people will be different. Whereas when the line is abandoned, with an 'operator' in a personal hierarchy as in the college, or indeed within in a formal one, such people operate beneath the formal structures of the institutions and through interpersonal networks. It is salutary to contemplate here the idea that feminist networks are similarly 'extra' to the formal hierarchies of higher education institutions and operate using equally informal ways of behaving, and so feminists of a similar cast of mind to the male 'operator' I had to contend with in the college could conduct themselves in similar kinds of ways. What is central are the currencies of exchange and getting on and getting up by informal interpersonal – indeed totally personalised – means.

The 'club' may be integral to institutional hierarchy and processes in academia, but these 'operators' are not. They are the spaces between things; they are on the margins and in the gaps between the formal structures and they operate within this set of circumstances through purely personalised ways of behaving. To date, academic feminism has *had* to work in similar ways, operating in the spaces and gaps in order to create some kind of networking with other women who share a gender analysis. If there aren't formal mechanisms of control constituted by notions of morality or ethics, then feminist operators could misuse and abuse these relationships in the same way that the male operators presently do. There are, however, two saving factors here. One factor is that, even informally, feminism is informed by morality and ethics, and this checks excesses because of internal sanctioning; the other factor is that in the last resort 'operators' have to be able to 'deliver' within an institution and still relatively few women, let alone feminists, are in this position, at least in the UK. However, I am clear that ultimately academic feminism must constitute and work through formal mechanisms: academia is definitionally about structured inequality, that of students in relation to teachers, and we must adopt mechanisms which help 'them' by controlling 'us' and our ability to use and abuse this.

Racism, while discussed at great length in terms of what occurred 'out there' in society, was never acknowledged as something which occurred 'in here' in academia in relation to the students who were taught or the staff that were employed. The underlying assumption was that because academia is a space for intellectual thought, those within that space are incapable of discriminating on the basis of colour or 'race'. In many ways the unacceptability of racism on the outside has crossed over into academia as something which does not exist within its ivory towers, and should those ivory towers be based on left-wing credentialism then this itself negates the existence of any possibility of racism. I would say that the refusal to apply critical analysis in the area of in/equality within academia is based upon the belief that academics possess a heightened intellectual and moral status, and as such could not possibly possess any elements of racism. After all, isn't racism based on ignorance, and surely knowledgeable academics can't be ignorant?

In the college there was a women's network, but it guarded itself against women who were seen to have been co-opted as 'one of X's women' and who were therefore a part of the informal system of personal influence and control operated by this individual. Because I had joined a bit of the formal structure over which this man had informal as well as formal influence, for over a year I remained entirely outside the women's network until I made a formal institutional level complaint about harassment. The women who had not spoken to me before then started to do so, and in a sense I thought this was far too late to be practically useful and supportive, although I was still glad that it had happened. One of the women involved said she felt that if I had been white then the women's network would have made more of an effort at an earlier stage; whether they were willing to admit it or not, because I was a black woman there was a real reluctance to come forward, perhaps because they were unable to make an evaluation of how I was likely to behave with regard to the male operator involved. They had in fact more quickly come to support others in that department who had also experienced how it was organised as dependent on quasi-sexual relations to which any resistance was responded to by overt harassment. I was just 'other' and they did not know how to respond to me or how I would respond either to them or to the circumstances. There was no sense of solidarity because perceived colour difference ruled over assumed gender similarities in that setting. Central to these informal interpersonal structures is the way they mar all relationships for newcomers: as people join that part of the institution, they are cut off from everybody else and aligned with the power centre and nobody and nothing else.

Standing back

Law departments are, I think, different from other academic departments in the particular sense that they are organised around a much clearer version of the typical academic structure of control by public school white males, and with a hierarchy between the theoretical and the applied. While this may be disguised by the way that in some institutions it is the applied aspects which bring in money and this kind of status, nonetheless overall there are still these divisions. Another variation is that in the 'old' universities and the former polytechnics, this structure is mediated by an acceptance of the right to disagree but an intolerance of difference, whereas the smaller scale non-university part of higher education is organised more around personalities and personal power, with the consequence that acceptance of difference can be completely removed.

Over the years of my employment within higher education, I developed first an unwillingness and then later an inability to be part of 'the club' – men in the hierarchy, with older men co-opting predominantly younger men, clones, so that these men reproduce by themselves in academia without women being involved except as 'underlings', as secretaries and support staff, including contract researchers. Sometimes, of course, they may offer these bonds of patronage to women. This happened extensively in the last academic institution I worked in. Although there were completely unacceptable things about the way that sexual harassment was used to control dissent here, the structural aspects of this were perhaps surprisingly similar to those of the boys' clubs that operate in the older and bigger institutions further up the status hierarchy of higher education. I did not want to belong to 'the club' in any of these institutions, perhaps because I was 'other' to it, in part because of my own biography, for I am not an upper class woman, and have made it in academia as a black woman without benefit of such class status. But I also have what some people call an independent cast of mind, and what others call bloody mindedness. Coupled with this, I don't take it all absolutely seriously – there are more important things in life than universities and colleges and what goes on within them. So there are personal things about me as well as structural things which fit together and encourage me towards what I hope is a coherent critique that joins together the interpersonal and the structural around gender, 'race', class and the dynamics of inclusion and exclusion in academia. So why is it, then, that at times I contemplate 'going back'?

I now have not only a professional position outside of academia, but I have come to the realisation that I actually enjoy both being outside and also moving in and out of the organisation I work 'in' but I am not entirely 'of' by virtue of the kind of job that I do. But still, periodically, I apply for academic jobs, so it is interesting to consider what, in spite of all that has happened, still attracts me to the idea of the university. Crucial to understanding my continued attraction to the university is the fact that I continue to have an interest in doing research in the fields of equal opportunities and criminal justice, something which I am unable to do satisfactorily in the kind of job that I am presently in. Of course, knowing about the absence of a decent research culture in almost every institution I might obtain a job in considerably puts me off: fighting each other to have time to rip off other people's ideas and work so as to be seen as 'research active' is not an attractive proposition. I like 'the university' as an idea, then, while knowing that the practice is often appalling and repellent. But, contemplating 'the university' as an idea, I am drawn to its good and attractive aspects because I have a high degree of motivation and commitment to some of the features of the ideal of academic life, and in particular a sense of the importance of justice and equality, space for those of a reflective frame of mind, and encouragement for those with a capacity for critical thought. These are the things that still attract many people to 'the university' – not just people who want 'a job', but also those who retain a commitment to these ideals.

Although in my non-university present employment I have been able to pursue these three aspects to an extent, I have not been able to do so to the degree I would ideally like. However, it also has to be said that it has been easier outside because there have not been the other worries, for these are considerably less individualistic and competitive workplaces, and much readier to contemplate change. For example, a review is now being undertaken around equality issues in the organisation I presently work within. Thinking about this and recommending courses of action is seen as my legitimate role, and there is a considerable willingness to consider options to change things. The strange structures of higher education actively militate against doing anything like this. The boys' club still rules, even if this is not quite as OK as it once was.

At a recent academic job interview which involved five candidates, of whom I was one, one of them was a white man, one a white woman and the other three of us were black women. All three of us black women were involved in the process of taking a higher education institution to an industrial tribunal. This says something very powerful about the types of institutions these are, and the vulnerable position of all women, particularly black women, within them. Things have got to change a very great deal for these to become safer institutions for women. Higher education is much more discriminatory against women than any other kind of professional employment. Most kinds of professional employment outside of academia have changed massively over the last two decades, whereas it seems to me that universities have not changed significantly with regard to patterns of exclusion and discrimination in employment. This is perhaps particularly the consequence of the intellectualisation that occurs around discrimination within higher education – all kinds of spurious academic reasons are used to justify the continuation of discrimination by hiding it behind calls to academic freedom and a concern with standards in intellectual life.

The reasoning here is that some candidates 'just happen' not to be up to high status academic jobs, and these 'just happen' to be women, to be black and so on. Within academia appointments and promotions processes are described in 'objective' and apparently plausible ways. But what is meant is that Y is not going to be promoted because they are a woman, nor is Z going to be appointed because they are black or because it is apparent from their publications that they are a lesbian. These reasons are dressed up to sound like an intellectual case against their capabilities, so that what is actually discrimination is instead turned into the personal characteristics of those found wanting, the intellectual lack of particular candidates which 'just happen' to have particular characteristics. This is thoroughly built into the institutional processes which seemingly justify and confirm these evaluations of the people who are 'other' to the boys' clubs of academia. Equal opportunity policies do not seem to be making any inroads because there is no monitoring of the working of the internal labour markets involved nor of the processes of short listing.

The result is that the system continues to appoint and to promote grey boys who join the club of other boys just like them and then climb its hierarchy through its formal and, even more important, its informal systems of patronage. Women, particularly black women, are always 'other' to this and are either incorporated as subordinate members or, more typically, simply abandoned to find their own way if they are appointed. Even more typically, of course, they are not appointed at all. The reality of 'the university', I have to keep reminding myself, is very different indeed from the ideal which exists in my mind.

References

Bhavani, Kum-Kum and Phoenix, Ann (eds) (1994) *Shifting Identities, Shifting Racism: A Feminism and Psychology Reader*. London: Sage.

Carter, Pam and Jeffs, Tony (1995) *A Very Private Affair: Consensual Sexual Relationships In Higher Education*. London: Education Now.

Collier, Rohan (1995) *Combatting Sexual Harassment in the Workplace*. Milton Keynes: Open University Press.

Donald, James and Rattansi, Ali (1992) *'Race', Culture and Difference*. Milton Keynes: Open University Press.

Dunant, Sarah (ed.) (1994) *The War Of The Words: The Political Correctness Debate*. London: Virago.

Hull, Gloria T., Scott, Patricia Bell and Smith, Barbara (eds) (1982) *All the Women Are White, All the Blacks Are Men but Some of Us are Brave*. New York: The Feminist Press.

Mohanty, Chandra T., Russo, Ann and Torres, Lourdes (eds) (1991) *Third World Women and the Politics of Feminism*. Bloomington: Indiana University Press.

Morrison, Toni (ed.) (1993) *Race-ing Justice, Engendering Power: Essays on Anita Hill, Clarence Thomas and the Construction of Social Reality*. London: Chatto & Windus.

Ware, Vron (1992) *Beyond the Pale: White Women, Racism and History*. London: Verso Press.

6

Nursing the Academy

Jean Orr

I returned to Belfast in 1991, after spending ten years at Manchester University, to the foundation Chair of Nursing at the Queen's University, Belfast. My role was to establish a School of Nursing. There were few resources. As the vice-chancellor said when I tried to negotiate the dowry which usually goes with a new Chair, 'there isn't even a pencil.' At first I had dismissed the idea of returning to my home town of Belfast, but when the Chair was advertised I saw it as a challenge, both personally and professionally. In taking up a post as a professor and head of department, there were many questions in my mind. How could I do the job and make a difference to nursing? Would the school differ in ethos, focus and ambience from others? To what extent could or would I have to compromise my hopes for a woman-centred school?

My main concern was in starting a totally new venture in a climate of economic stringency in the university sector, in a time also of uncertainty about the future direction of nurse education. As a senior lecturer in Manchester University I was, of course, familiar with the academic aspect of university life. What I was not experienced in was the business planning and budget meetings which were a feature of the post. Going to my first budget meeting I debated with myself: had I asked for enough money, should I inflate the figures in the expectation of getting less, how would the system work, and how did the boys negotiate? I did get what I asked for at this budget meeting and on the way out the dean said to me 'you should have asked for more', but that, of course, was not the time to tell me.

When I joined the medical faculty I found it quite formal, with tea and coffee being served to me in china cups. This was not what I was used to at Manchester. I was conscious that the secretarial and administrative staff, while being very polite, were rather wary of me as a female professor and also wary of me as someone who had no support services, just a table, a chair and a phone. They were, quite rightly, anxious that I might ask them to do typing etc. I couldn't help but feel that, had I been a man, that would not have been an issue. Gradually, over a number of weeks, they did recognise that I would wash my own cup and indeed make my own coffee and offer coffee to them, a situation which was not the norm. I was determined to have a school which reflected my beliefs and values about non-hierarchical structures, as far as this is ever possible, and a valuing of the contribution of all staff, not just that of academics.

My observation of university life led me to see that women, however they relate to the male academics, are truly invisible, the hidden infrastructure which keeps the system going. The concept of interdependence is one which is not familiar to many men in the academy. I wanted the school of nursing to be somewhere where everybody felt valued and happy, and women would not be exploited at all and certainly not as a result of gender. In many departments and schools in universities, it is common for women academics to do the nurturing and supporting work and be responsible for the pastoral care of students and staff, while men, quite single mindedly, do the work which helps their career. It would of course be arrogant of me to say how I thought the school had turned out without asking the people who work in it and, in order to write this chapter, I did ask their opinion. Of the thirteen staff, all but one are women and all said the atmosphere is very different from that they have experienced in other universities or in other schools. We care about the environment in which we work and have spent some considerable time and resources in making it pleasant by putting up pictures, having flowers, plants and decent cups and saucers. It is sometimes the small things, the minutiae of everyday life, that makes a difference to work.

My approach is to raise the consciousness of women I meet. In Ulster, men are still very much in control and men and women still call women 'girls'. I find it surprising that feminism and women's issues seem such strange concepts to many. I try to focus the nature of the discourse in the school and examine the way the questions about the everyday work of academia are framed, and I challenge the 'taken for granted' assumptions about how academic departments work. However, there is a growing tension in the university system, because as it becomes more bureaucratic and more controlled from the centre it takes more effort to maintain this approach at school level.

It is important to give confidence to the people who are working with me as women and as academics in a subject such as nursing, so that we can give confidence to the students who study with us. According to Adrienne Rich (1979: 126), the idea of a women-centred aspect of a university may sound biased or improbable until we try the sound of its opposite, the 'man-centred university', to see what universities are really about. For the first three years of our Master's in Nursing Programme we had no male students, and this caused considerable questions and comment. I had difficulty with the concept of 'Master' in a female subject, but no doubt a Mistress of Nursing would have run into difficulties. We did not discriminate against men; few men applied, and those who did apply did not turn up for interview. Nevertheless, what was interesting was how uncomfortable some of the female students felt at not having men in the class. I wondered how many classes in engineering and science had men asking why there were not more women. Nevertheless, at the end of the Master's course many of the students expressed their enjoyment of having space to discuss and raise issues about nursing without men being present.

It is very difficult to straddle the two worlds of the university and nursing.

At times I am extremely irritated by the resistance that nursing has to academic issues and the extent of the anti-intellectualism which exists. I feel almost defeated by the complexity of nursing and the difficulty in changing a large and disparate group with its many divisions and traditions. Nursing academics are frequently seen as the enemy, having sold out to theories and not having enough creditability in practice. It is equally isolating to be part of the university as a woman, and I am not sure if women ever can feel fully at home in an institution which is so male dominated. Part of the problem is the difficulty in actually locating the locus of power and determining how that power is exercised. It may be different for women who are in powerful subjects which are prestigious and have access to research monies, but such subjects as medicine and science have men at their head. Although there is a commitment to anti-sexism in Queen's, I suspect that some men go through the motions but are still quite uncomfortable about it. They turn it into a bit of a joke and never miss an opportunity to demean it. It also depends on the level that one is operating in the university whether it is possible to feel comfortable, to feel part of it. In smaller committees and working groups it is much easier to feel part of the system. It is difficult in the larger committees where one may be the only woman and the subjects may be ones I am not so familiar with, such as financial planning. There is no doubt that the issue of language and speaking out becomes a problem in that kind of setting and it is comforting to know the work of Dale Spender (1980) in identifying the issues of man-made language. I see the problem as not all to do with me but as part of the structure. I have tried hard to make nursing acceptable in the university, but the nursing bodies and institutions have unrealistic demands and expectations of the university, largely because they don't understand the system. In addition, very frequently they want high status people such as the dean or provost to deal with them, as it seems to reinforce their own status. Perhaps this is because many of the senior people in the nursing world are men and seem more comfortable in dealing with men from the university. But despite the problems of being part of the university, this is where I want to be. I am more in tune with the ethos of the university. I find that part of my work understandable, if not always easy, and I feel increasingly removed from the world of nursing, yet committed to it. I am in the university but not of it and of nursing but not in it. In my life I have crossed a number of boundaries, spatially and intellectually, in moving from nursing to academia, and from Belfast to Manchester and back again. My experience as a nurse raised my consciousness about women's lives and this has been reinforced by my work in the academy. Feminism is the lens through which I view the world, an optimist by theory and sometimes a pessimist in reality.

Being a feminist

I became a feminist before I knew the word. While training as a nurse in the 1960s I became aware of the oppression suffered by women. There were many examples, not least the woman coming into casualty, bruised, beaten and ashamed. Excuses were made about falling or having an accident. The staff colluded, knowing the woman had been beaten up by her husband/partner. The explanation was that she must have asked for it, he must have been drunk or, it was said, 'that's typical of working class lives'. Any superficial examination of these explanations was found wanting by me. After all, why would a woman seek pain – was she so different from me who had no desire at all for pain? The explanations acted as excuses and left many like me feeling uncomfortable, puzzled and disturbed.

Another example of the condition of women's lives was highlighted when I undertook a psychiatric hospital placement and read the male and female patients' notes. The male patients had labels such as 'paranoid schizophrenic', 'manic depressive', 'psychotic' – in other words, real illnesses. The notes of the females contained labels such as 'inadequate personality', 'temperamental', 'not accepting her role', 'anxious' or 'depressive personality'. These were labels which made the illness the women's fault.

The majority of these women had a history of sexual abuse, rape or violence, mainly within the family. This was startling, as the existence of violence on children was, at that time, not publicly or professionally debated or addressed. When I asked the male psychiatrist about the possible relationship between the history of the women and their mental illness he said, 'Don't you know Freud? These women imagine it.' So, despite the evidence in the notes, a layer of meaning was imposed which denied the reality and made life more comfortable for the professionals. We now know it is likely that the earlier experiences of abuse had an effect, as did the role women had in society. Yet to show they were getting better and able to go home, these women were judged on their performance of 'female tasks', such as giving out meals or cleaning, and they had to make an effort with their appearance to show they were rehabilitated. And so the aspects of their lives which brought them into the institution had to be emphasised and embraced before they could go home, 'cured' by those very things that had brought the problem into being.

I had many similar experiences during my work as a nurse and health visitor, and the discovery of feminist literature in the 1970s provided a framework for understanding and guiding my practice. Feminist analysis helped me place women's health within the wider context of society and helped explain the discontent women had with their lives, which Betty Friedan (1963: 13) calls 'the problem with no name'.

More recently, being in the academy has provided me with the opportunity to observe those who shape the debate by their research and writing. The public persona is often at odds with what one sees in private or at conferences. Thus, at a conference in Rio on child abuse and neglect, I observed session after session on the diagnosis of abuse. What this meant was room after room full of doctors, psychiatrists and psychologists (mostly men) looking at slides of damaged genitalia. It was voyeuristic, and the atmosphere in the sessions I attended left me feeling very uncomfortable. There was little emphasis given to prevention of child abuse and any reference to a feminist or power analysis was dismissed or, on a number of occasions, shouted down. Some of us who were unhappy with this then organised a day which involved local social and community workers. This was the only real experience of the conference, for to be in Rio where street children are abused and murdered and not discuss this as a key example of abuse was more than surprising. The key speakers moved on to another conference in Argentina, while I was left wondering how much money had been spent, how many children had been helped and how many slides of damaged genitalia does anyone need to see.

The way men in power treat others still shocks. Recently I saw a letter from a leading doctor about setting up a multi-disciplinary research study. The letter was full of references to the importance of getting enough 'Indians' to do the work but not to have their name on papers. The numerous references to 'Indians', referred to as 'she' throughout the letter, included nurses, research assistants and psychologists. Presumably the doctor did not realise the racist and sexist nature of his remarks, or he was arrogant enough to not care. In both these examples the people involved are highly regarded as caring and dedicated.

Even at its best, for me there is a conflict which remains. And this concerns the tension between the theoretical or 'academic' understanding of women's lives and the slowness of practical progress, within and outside of the academy.

Returning

In 1991 Northern Ireland was still in the grip of 'the troubles', and this affected the daily life of the province. There were army patrols, centres of towns were ringed by security and people were searched entering shops and buildings. The atmosphere was tense, with bomb scares, explosions and shootings. Whatever the local people said, Belfast was a city which was a product of twenty-five years of violence. Northern Ireland is a conservative society and the main institutions are dominated by male élites. There are no Northern Irish female members of parliament at Westminster or in Europe and little hope of any coming through the system. The churches maintain power and veto legislation such as the introduction of abortion. Key organisations such as the Orange Order and Hibernian Order are male, and the paramilitaries on both sides epitomise the maleness of terrorism.

In Northern Ireland one is constantly reminded of the divisions between its people and the position of Ulster itself, divided from the rest of the UK by more than the Irish Sea. There is constant reference to the sectarian divide or the divided community or the two communities. There are, however, *many* communities in Northern Ireland – for example, Chinese and Indian, male and female – but Ulster is so dominated by religious divisions that any reference to 'race' or gender is largely absent from the debate. There is no reference to class politics even though the working class on both sides have more to unite than divide them. The debate is structured so that there is no room for people to unite on social or economic issues. People have lived with this polarisation for so long that they have a mind-set of division and continually structure many aspects of life in conflict terms. For example, I was conscious of people trying to 'set me up' against the nursing department at the University of Ulster in a way which would not have been the case in England. This happens in many aspects of life here. The only issue that the extremes of both religious groups have united on has been their opposition to the establishment of a Brooke Clinic in Belfast. This is a clinic offering young people advice on contraception and relationships. Since it opened two years ago there have been daily pickets by both sides – united not by twenty-five years of killing but by opposition to young heterosexual people having control of their sexuality.

Queen's University was founded 150 years ago and would be seen in Northern Ireland as a bastion of the establishment. Incidents of religious discrimination have damaged its image and the university has implemented a range of measures to meet the requirements of the Fair Employment Agency, set up under the Fair Employment (NI) Act (1976), which legislates against religious discrimination. Interestingly, there is no similar legislation in the rest of the UK. The Fair Employment Act (NI) (1989) requires employers to notify the Agency of the perceived religious make-up of their workforce. For those people who were born in Northern Ireland, this is determined by the primary school they attended. People born elsewhere are not counted. Not realising this, I was angry to get notification from the university that I was a perceived Protestant because I had attended a local state primary school. In the intervening years I could have become a Hindu or a Catholic, but for all time I am perceived Protestant under the legislation. On writing back to say that if I had to have a label then I wished to be a Feminist Socialist, I was told 'you have to be a Protestant'. It is difficult, even impossible, to be seen as religiously neutral and to leave aside one's tribal/religious label, even for someone like me who holds no religious affiliation.

In order to meet the requirement of the Act, all appointment boards and promotion boards have to contain both Protestants and Catholics. The university also insists on a gender balance. University members have to consider religion in a wide range of activities. Of course it is crucial to be fair and seen to be so, but I felt uncomfortable with the emphasis on religion. It can be argued that the Equal Opportunity or Fair Employment legislation may provide access, but it does nothing to challenge the existing organisational hierarchy. There is a conflict between the Equal Opportunity legislation and the Fair Employment legislation which affects women (and men), but mostly women in secretarial and clerical grades. I also observe that when committees are more representative, then the power simply shifts to new smaller structures still controlled by the élite.

Two different worlds

The long term aim of the school is to integrate nursing and midwifery education into the university following the introduction of a new form of training called Project 2000 (UKCC, 1986). The establishment of a school of nursing posed particular problems for me. Firstly, I had to straddle the world of the university and the world of nursing, both with their factions and divisions. As a director of a school and one of only eight women out of a total of 129 professors (QUB, 1991), I am on a range of major university committees. I would like to think this is because of my expertise, but I know it is also to improve the gender balance. One has to straddle two very different worlds, representing the world of nursing to people who are not necessarily sympathetic, and negotiating with the nursing world on behalf of the university. Neither position is comfortable.

My appointment disturbed the existing power bases in nursing, while the establishment of the school posed challenges for other organisations involved in nursing education. At the time I was appointed, men were in charge of the major institutions of nursing, including the Department of Health and Social Services, the National Board for Nursing (the statutory body responsible for validating and approving courses), the Royal College of Nursing and three out of the five colleges of nursing. I was seen as a feminist, and indeed the school is known as 'the feminist school'. There were a series of battles with the statutory body over issues of control and validation, and the university was bemused to experience the politics within nursing. As one academic said, 'if you thought medical politics was bad, try nursing.'

Susan Roberts (1983: 21–2) argues that nurses can be considered an oppressed group because of control by forces outside nursing that have had greater prestige, power and status and that have exploited the less powerful group. Therefore, as an oppressed group, nurses are given to intra-group conflict and do not speak with one voice. As Celia Davies (1995) states, the development of nursing in universities has generated division and defensiveness among nurses. The debate still rages about the necessity for an 'educated' nurse at degree level.

Both 'worlds', nursing and education, need convincing of the merits of nursing in the university for different reasons. The university was unsure about the academic credibility of nursing – was it a *bona fide* university subject? Had it a body of knowledge which could be professed? What is nursing research, how can a practice discipline be academic? Such questions are never asked of medicine or engineering: they are automatically assumed to be part of the academy. As Susan Reverby (1987: 207) says, 'Nursing has always been a much conflicted metaphor in our culture, reflecting all the ambivalence we give to the meaning of womanhood.'

Nursing is not seen as 'scientific' or 'academic', whatever those terms mean. Because 'nursing' is so familiar at one level, there is a denial or lack of recognition of the range of nursing roles and responsibilities. The devaluing of practice has its roots in the western tradition of valuing the theoretical and abstract over the practical. Real knowledge is seen to lie with others, and nursing knowledge is overlooked because it is informal and particular. It is not easily formalised or generalised. It is, however, through repeated experience that nurses build up the particular knowledge rather than the typical. The differential status in legitimisation which is given to formal knowledge that can be stated in laws and mathematical equations overlooks and discredits skilled nursing knowledge.

My first course to go through the university system was a Master of Science in Nursing. It was nearly rejected because the dean of science objected to a science degree being taught outside the science faculty. When the MSc in nursing got to academic council, someone else from science said he had never heard of such a thing as a MSc in nursing – whatever next? The course was stoutly defended by one of the pro-vice chancellors who started off by asking if science was a subject or a method, and then went on to talk about the importance to the university of discipline-based subjects such as education and nursing. Nursing was in the academy and therefore had to be defended in public, whatever was thought in private.

Adrienne Rich's (1979: 136) observations that 'the real curriculum is the male-centered one; women's studies are a "fad"; that feminist teachers are unscholarly', can be applied to nursing studies. Rich highlights the hierarchical image of the university, including the structure of relationships, the style of discourse including theory and practice, the ends and means, process and goals, being invisible and less amenable to change. She goes on to say that 'each woman in the university is defined by her relationship to the men in power instead of her relationship to other women up and down the scale' (137).

As a woman, these are issues which I have to think about and negotiate in social as well as business settings. In my very early days at Queen's I was invited to a summer lunch party which was attended by the senior staff (all men) in the medical school and university. As is common in Ireland, the men gathered together. They stood in a circle at the bottom of a very long garden while I stood at the top. The dilemma was whether I should join them and face a very lonely walk and an uncertain welcome, or stay and talk to the women. A man in my position would not even have hesitated. I had to choose and I chose to stay with the women, which I preferred. But was it the 'right' decision? Because I am now more familiar with the men the outcome of the decision might be different, but the question would still have to be asked and probably will always be asked until there are more women 'at the bottom of the garden'.

On the nursing side, there was concern that the school of nursing was in the medical faculty, with all the resonance of the unequal relationship between doctors and nurses (Bunting and Campbell, 1990). In reality, Queen's had set up the school of nursing as one of four in the faculty equal in organisational terms, if not size, with the schools of clinical medicine, biomedical science and dentistry. The dean of the medical faculty was extremely supportive, and this was a key element in the success of the school. In addition, there was a general feeling of welcome. Queen's had rejected taking on nursing in the past, and there was some scepticism that they were serious about it now and would resource it adequately. Overriding all of that was the ambivalence about the need for educated nurses.

Regarding this, probably both parties were agreed. Davies (1995: 116) says the comments from some doctors following the report recommending Project 2000 was that 'The work of the nurse is . . . practical and personal; it is something that requires a fairly brief training without a strong theory component.'

While nurse academics strive to develop a strong theoretical base of nursing knowledge which emphasises individual professionalism and autonomy in practice, there is a correspondingly strong political drive among nurses to increase nursing's public identification as a workforce with group power and solidarity. Recognition of nursing's theoretical contribution is often diminished by consideration of nursing as an employee group engaging in practice that does not require a specialised knowledge base. Feminists would believe that this kind of traditional discrimination serves to lessen the threat of women's social and professional contribution to those in power. A problem basic to nursing administration, practice and management is the perceived division between the leadership group in nursing, including educators as well as managers, and the nurses who do the work of nursing. Practising nurses do not relate well to nursing leaders and academic nursing issues. Those activities which are necessary for the evolution of the discipline seem distant from the high technical and crisis orientated world of the working nurse (Neil and Watts, 1989).

Reverby (1987) argues there is a crucial dilemma in contemporary nursing, in that it is a form of labour shaped by the obligation to care but existing in a society that refuses to value caring. Witz (1994) similarly proposes that the history and identity of nursing cannot be understood unless the bond that has wedded it to womanhood is also unravelled and revealed. She sees the daily reality of nursing work as needing to be contextualised within hierarchies of power and authority in care settings that are structured by gendered and sexualised relations of domination and subordination. The challenge to medicine posed by nurses who want to develop their roles translates into women's challenge to men's authority, for, as Witz states, 'it is difficult to imagine a workplace situation where women are treated as autonomous knowledgeable doers in a society that systematically constructs women as subordinate and inferior to men and degrades work whose content is gendered by its association with women' (p. 38).

Similarities and differences

Where the two 'worlds' are similar is in their control by men and their conservatism. Nursing has been dominated by male doctors and administrators despite having had formidable female leaders; in addition, over the past five years men have taken a share of the top posts which is disproportionately large in relation to their numbers in nursing (Davies, 1995: 44). As Davies says, 'Men when schooled in masculinity will reproduce their world in ways that are gendered masculine. This is true at a practical level of the institutions and organisations they found and populate and at the level of the theories they offer to represent, explain and justify the public worlds they inhabit of work and politics' (1995: 30–1).

There are unexpected differences between the two 'worlds'. In the university there is a code of gender-neutral language which is implemented throughout the institution. At committee meetings men pour the coffee. At first this came as a welcome surprise, but then it occurred to me that they had to pour the coffee because there would have been no women present at many of the meetings. All staff at Queen's must attend an equal opportunities workshop and additional workshops have been laid on for all senior staff. In contrast, the United Kingdom Central Council for Nursing, Midwifery and Health Visiting (UKCC), which is the statutory body regulating the professions, voted not to implement gender-neutral language despite the fact that nursing is 91% female. The most vociferous opponents to change were the midwives, one group that in my view should be feminist revolutionaries. So, I still remain the chair*man* of a committee, although I continually refer to myself as 'chair' or 'chairperson'.

A function of UKCC is to consider cases of professional misconduct such as ill-treatment of patients, sexual abuse and theft, and to remove nurses, midwives and health visitors from the register if necessary. It has taken ten years of lobbying to get UKCC to break down the figures for those coming before the professional conduct committee into male and female, surely one of the most accepted categorisation of statistics. Men in nursing make up 8.9% of the 600,000 nurses, midwives and health visitors registered with the Council, and yet 51% of those nurses whose names were removed from the register were men (UKCC, 1992). In 1995 this figure was 48% (UKCC, 1995). At the Council meeting where these figures were reported, I was the only one of the sixty members present who commented on this finding and asked for further research to be undertaken in the public interest. No one supported me. The *Nursing Times* correspondent at the meeting said she wanted to run the story but was reluctant because when they reported anything which placed male nurses in a bad light they received abusive mail. They did run the story after I spoke to the editor and they subsequently did receive abusive mail, as I myself have done when writing about issues of pornography or sexual violence.

These two examples demonstrate the lack of awareness of gender issues and the conservative nature of nursing. The use of language in the first example helps make women invisible and the reluctance to identify men in the statistics in the second protects guilty men from public scrutiny. In both of these instances women are implicated as well as men.

Nursing in the academy

What will it mean for nursing to be in the academy? On good days it is possible to believe that the academy wants nursing in the same way as any other discipline and that the sheer scale of the enterprise, when nursing is fully integrated, will be viewed positively. A university climate, when numbers are important, is good news for nursing, particularly when there is a large pool of potential students who want to undertake top-up degrees and post-graduate courses at their own expense. If the integration of nursing and midwifery takes place, then the school will be one of the largest in the university, with 600–700 full time pre-registration students and continuing education and post-registration courses for 7,000 students. There will be 90–100 staff and a £6 million budget.

But to provide nurses with an education in the university is not the same as providing a university education. The new preparation of nurses, called Project 2000 (UKCC, 1986), is at pre-degree diploma level. This poses problems for nursing in the academy as it will be seen as sub-degree and represents a major and ill-judged compromise by the statutory body of nursing, midwifery and health visiting, who did not push for an all-graduate profession. There are degree programmes in the UK which represent a university education in the accepted sense, but the bulk of nurses will undertake a three year diploma with students receiving a non-means tested bursary. With integration, the transfer of nurse tutors from the colleges of nursing into the university means that much of nurse education may be very much as before. The transfer of large numbers of staff who are not involved in research will weaken nursing's position, especially when funding is fully related to research output. Schools of nursing in the academy may become ghettoised and marginalised because of these factors.

Nursing must be the last group in health care to continue to shy away from graduate status. This means that able students are lost to nursing. The perception persists that nursing is for young women who have no hope of a university degree. There is also the conflict of volume over quality, in that the intakes to courses are controlled by workforce needs and very tight targets are set for recruitment so that entry criteria may be driven down. Nursing in the academy may very well be on the borders of the institutions, spatially in that the campus may still be located on old College of Nursing sites on hospital premises, and intellectually, as nursing is not seen as research active and is regarded as 'women's work'.

Alison Tierney (1994: 598) showed that nursing was rated lowest of all seventy-two subjects reviewed in the 1992 assessment of research in British universities. On the twenty-nine departments assessed, seventeen received the lowest possible rating and five were given an average or above average rating. Tierney argues that the twelve larger, longer established departments based in research-strong 'old' universities have more research active staff and therefore did better than the small, recently established departments in the 'new' universities, formerly polytechnics, which could not have expected good results. Nursing in the academy in the UK is relatively young: the University of Edinburgh established nursing only in 1956 and the University of Manchester in 1959. In Tierney's view, any new nursing department should be strategically placed in research-strong universities, but with nursing integration this is not happening as many of the 'new universities' are taking on nursing.

Conclusion

My work has been shaped by a commitment to helping women develop through education. Adrienne Rich writes eloquently of what I believe in her poem 'Culture and Anarchy' (1981: 14–15). Here she quotes from Elizabeth Cady Stanton's speech 'On Solitude of Self' (Anthony and Harper, 1902):

> The strongest reason
> for giving woman all the opportunities
> for higher education, for the full
> development of her forces of mind and body . . .
> the most enlarged freedom of thought and action
> a complete emancipation
> from all the crippling influences of fear –
> is the solitude and personal
> responsibility
> of her own individual life.

References

Anthony, Susan B. and Harper, Ida Husted (1902) *The History of Woman Suffrage*, Vol. 4. New York: Fowler and Wells.

Bunting, Sheila and Campbell, Jacqueline (1990) 'Feminism and nursing: Historical perspectives', *Advances in Nursing Science*, 12 (4): 11-24.

Davies, Celia (1995) *Gender and the Professional Predicament in Nursing*. Buckingham: Open University Press.

Department of Economic Development (1976) *Fair Employment (Northern Ireland) Act 1976*.

Department of Economic Development (1989) *Fair Employment (Northern Ireland) Act 1989*.

Friedan, Betty (1963) *The Feminine Mystique*. Harmondsworth: Penguin.

Neil, Ruth and Watts, Robin (1989) *Caring and Nursing: Explorations in Feminist Perspective*. New York: National League for New York.

Queen's University (1991) *Equal Opportunities Report*. Belfast: Queen's University of Belfast.

Reverby, Susan (1987) *Ordered to Care: The Dilemma of American Nursing 1850–1945*. Cambridge: Cambridge University Press.

Rich, Adrienne (1979) 'Towards a woman centred university (1973–74)', in Adrienne Rich (ed.), *On Lies, Secrets and Silences*. New York: Norton & Co.

Rich, Adrienne (1981) 'Culture and Anarchy' in *A Wild Patience Has Taken Me This Far: Poems 1978–81*. New York: Norton & Co.

Roberts, Susan (1983) 'Oppressed group behaviour: Implications for nursing', *Advances in Nursing Science*, July (5): 21–30.

Spender, Dale (1980) *Man Made Language*. London: Routledge and Kegan Paul.

Tierney, Alison (1994) 'An analysis of nursing's performance in the 1992 assessment of research of British universities', *Journal of Advanced Nursing*, 1.9 (3): 593–602.

United Kingdom Central Council for Nursing, Midwifery and Health Visiting (1986) *Project 2000: A New Preparation for Practice*. London: UKCC.

United Kingdom Central Council for Nursing, Midwifery and Health Visiting (1992) *Statistical Analysis of the Council's Professional Register April 1991–92*. London: UKCC.

United Kingdom Central Council for Nursing, Midwifery and Health Visiting (1995) *Statistical Analysis of the Council's Professional Register April 1994 – March 1995*. London: UKCC.

Witz, Ann (1994) 'The challenge of nursing', in Jonathan Gabe, David Kelleher and Gareth Williams (eds), *Challenging Medicine*. London: Routledge and Kegan Paul.

7

Bordering on Change

Chris Corrin

I have decided to begin with 'learning'. I have learned and continue to learn as a student, a teacher, a researcher and a political activist. Feminist thinking has guided me in many aspects of my learning. Feminist thinking for me is about seeing things from women's perspectives and challenging male privileges and abuses of power, and has served as a guideline in how I have endeavoured to live my life. My mother, Eva, always taught me my right to question and that also has served as a guide in my learning. Of course, the processes by which we learn differ greatly, and translating such processes into 'academic' contexts and across various real and imagined borders is by no means straightforward. In assessing how my thinking and involvements have changed in different modes of action, I have attempted to understand what the consequences that a shift in one perspective has for developments within others. This chapter is one element within this continuing process of assessment and reassessment.

My research from 1984 centred upon women's situations in Hungary and I shall say something about the development of this work, which began as an Oxford D.Phil thesis, how it changed over time, how my views of it shifted, and then how the thesis became something different when finally published. The period 1984–94 was very much a time of shifts in perspective for me with regard to my knowledge of the impact of changes in nation-states in East-Central Europe and how such knowledge informed my thinking and my choices of action.

Within this process of assessment, questions of boundaries or borders to change immediately arise for me, specifically in terms of what sort of 'academic' and indeed what sort of 'feminist' I am, as well as concerning the consequences for women's lives of the socio-political changes in East-Central European countries and feminist perspectives on these.

The choice of my research topic took much deliberation on my part, in that I had to come to terms with my confused notions about 'writing about women', which seemed parasitical and somehow unethical. I had previously only tackled theoretical approaches which attempted to explain social change. Thinking about how to write of women's lives without objectification meant that I had to decide on a methodology and a way of working that would privilege Hungarian women's voices and feed something back into their lives.

These were my aims when I began my research work. By living in Hungary for eight months in 1986, I planned to spend time with women in various ways and to discuss with them how they viewed their lives and their opportunities and how they perceived potential changes. I wanted to learn more and hoped that my work could be of some benefit to other women in Hungary and elsewhere. It was a daunting time for me – an initial leap of faith – and I was very naive about what a UK graduate student could expect to accomplish.

In the transition from working on aspects of Hungarian sociology and critiques of 'actually existing socialism', highlighted by Konrád and Szelényi's (1979) *The Intellectuals on the Road to Class Power*, to deciding to work with women in Hungary, I wrestled with many questions. How does a feminist student write of other women's lives? In what ways could I highlight some aspects of Hungarian women's situations? How were their lives affected by the political/cultural milieux in which they lived? How were these issues related to ideas and questions about 'socialism' and 'feminism'? Many other issues arose from these questions, not least in terms of feminist analyses of 'socialism' and of how 'socialist' politicians and policy-makers in East-Central Europe viewed 'feminism'.

I moved to England from the Isle of Man at age twenty-two and consequently my historical knowledge of feminist debates was poor and my ways of learning seemed somehow 'underdeveloped' in the academic environments in which I later became involved as a mature student. From age eleven I was a pupil in a harsh school environment and was severely disciplined for 'trying to fight the system'. It was then that 'me' (or sometimes 'us') and 'them' categories came into play in my life. Such distinctions have seemed ever-present to me: not 'fitting in', first within the southern English university environment, then later at an Oxford college, and also as an 'outsider' in Hungary, a country then somewhat at odds within feminist groupings in Western Europe, and again becoming an 'outsider' within an all-male university department. This has been a condition of my life. Feminist thinking became a lens through which I attempted to clarify my shifting perceptions and from which to test out boundaries and borders in the development of my research and analyses of change.

In terms of feminist analyses, I have never fully understood the battles between Marxist, socialist and radical feminists that seem to have waxed over time within the UK. As a lesbian activist I was often 'presumed' to be a radical feminist, yet anti-racist struggles within the perceived racialised states in the UK and Ireland were also a big part of my life. I always felt an 'outsider' when socialist feminists talked of the problems of radical feminist analyses, and in the same way when some radical feminists critiqued what they perceived as the blinkered narrowness of socialist feminists' focus on 'the state'. What 'sort' of feminist was I, am I? Perhaps this lack of understanding meant that I was more shocked than others would have been by how some western and UK feminists reacted in discussions with women from various Central and Eastern European countries. At times such interactions seemed like mini-battles with everything to gain by 'persuading' these women into 'realising' what 'western feminism', or brands of it, had to offer them. A marked lack of seeing things from (other) women's perspectives seemed apparent.

An outsider in Hungary

Many distinctions came into play on my first few visits to Hungary between 1984–6. While my 'status' as a western academic gained me some entrées, the 'strangeness' of my topic – the situation of women – led to some hilarity on the part of men. Women with whom I discussed my research commented on how strange it was for them that I was interested in their lives, and we often smiled at the unusual privileges we created as 'women together' because that was what the visiting researcher was working on. Thus, sometimes a husband or partner would agree to mind the children while we talked in the kitchen for an hour or two, so that we could gain 'quality' time together as the women were 'helping with research'. More often than not, though, we spent time with children, cooking or tidying and talking, talking.

Hungarian male perceptions of 'western feminists' was something difficult to deal with at first. Being introduced as 'a feminist' was alternatively viewed by them to be scathing, funny, and/or ridiculous, and it seemed aimed to reduce any perceived 'status' that could be allowed to a foreign academic from Oxford. This 'balancing act' was understandable in part, but it often became embroiled within an internal power struggle between the women with whom I was working and their male counterparts. Sometimes the women I socialised with had English language skills and their male partners did not and such situations occasionally turned into power struggles in which the men seemed to have something to prove. By dismissing 'feminism' and any interest in women's situations, they ridiculed the whole idea of privileging women's experiences, testimonies and viewpoints as a 'foreign' notion not worthy of 'real' Hungarian women's attention.

Methodological issues loomed large in the process of carrying out my research work in Hungary. Sometimes the women with whom I was speaking viewed this in terms of violence against women, enforced abortions or politicians' abuse of power – 'the power'.[1] This complex view of 'the power' initiated many discussions about how power abuse within Hungarian society affected both women and men and that private/public distinctions were culturally specific precisely because the state's abuses of power meant that families became viewed as safe havens for individuals. This raised many questions for me in terms of feminist theorising around public/private distinctions. These had never quite 'fitted' complex situations in the West, yet as analytical tools they had been useful in part – certainly in viewing 'politics'. Questions of gender and culture were being centrally raised in my understanding of how we live and how change impacts in multi-faceted ways.

Yet more borders

Around 1987–8, I became increasingly disturbed by media impressions and certain academic notions regarding the political situation in Hungary. The western media viewed Hungary as having gone through some sort of 'economic miracle' and being on the way to a 'new political accommodation' with the Soviet Union. This was not the reality I experienced. During this period my experiences and the knowledge gained of historical developments in Hungarian politics and social life came together and by 1989 made me feel very much more of an 'insider' within Hungary and some neighbouring countries such as Czechoslovakia and Romania, certainly in comparison with many of the western academics who became interested in 'East–Central Europe' following the dramatic developments of 1989.

In terms of feminist analyses of women's changing lives in East–Central European countries, I realise now that from 1989 to 1991 I became immobilised as a writer/researcher and was able 'only' to absorb, to assimilate and reflect on what was happening to friends, colleagues and associates in Hungary and some neighbouring countries. I became intensely aware of the dangers of 'reacting in writing' and indeed in over-hasty reactions from some western colleagues.

Some initial reactions included suppositions that 'Eastern' women did not realise what gains they were losing in terms of 'socialism' nor indeed what benefits could accrue for them from 'feminism'. I and many other women attended some harrowing conferences at which women from Central and Eastern European countries were reduced to tears of humiliation and frustration at the lack of understanding of the realities of their situations. At the Women's Conference on Security and Cooperation in Europe (CSCE) in Berlin in November 1990, a network was formed of women from Central and Eastern Europe. Tales were told afterwards of how shocked women were when their 'western' sisters chose to speak 'for' them. The text of the declaration says a good deal about these women's perseverance to network towards change:

> Women from East–Central and East European countries present at the first Women's CSCE came to the conclusion that it is of vital importance to create a network of East–Central and East European women in order to coordinate activities of women's organizations in their countries and share information about the actual situation of women on the broad international level. Such a network is necessary especially as the newly emerging democracies have proved to be conservative and authoritarian regarding women. They perpetuate and promote male dominance in these societies. The best examples to prove this statement can be found in the tendencies to raise the percentage of unemployed women beyond that of men and to curb or even ban the right of abortion.
>
> It is necessary to develop close relations with women from all other parts of Europe and the world because we share the same problems, even if the manifestations are different – in East Europe increasing nationalism and ethnic conflicts, and in the West racism and xenophobia have similar roots in the patriarchy and have the same disastrous impact on all women . . . . (Corrin, 1992: 251–2)

At the same time, some women from so-called 'socialist' parties in East–Central Europe were being invited westwards. Women who had fought with the democratic parties to overturn dictatorships were often not considered 'socialist'. Questions of respect arose – respecting other women's realities and ways of articulating their knowledge. Certain aspects of feminist ethics, learning from experience and not enforcing any so-called 'right' ways of thinking, did not seem to be recognised or respected.

The experiences of women living through 'actually existing socialism' were very different from certain western myths of what 'socialism' could be. Yet, this seemed to be almost 'politically unacceptable' to some feminist academics assuming a classic 'false consciousness' mode. There were lots of women genuinely wanting to 'know' and to learn, yet in meetings the realities were too complex to be reduced to this or that viewpoint/explanation. Some women from Western European countries were blinkered by their own assumptions and unable or not prepared to be sensitive about how they expressed their suppositions about 'other' women's realities. For me, this meant long discussions with friends from East–Central European countries and stepping very far back from academic discourses that seemed partial, patronising and in many ways ignorant.

Thesis or antithesis?

Writing up my thesis in 1986–7 became problematic because of the institutional environment: it became a hoop to jump through for a D.Phil. I was warned not to have 'too many unsupported quotes from women', yet this had been a major aim of my research, to give the subjects of this research a voice. I was aware of how to 'write' in order to translate my work into a form which would gain me a qualification, yet I did not know how to translate it into something useful for the women with whom I had been working. From 1987, when I had finished the thesis, it became a weight on my mind. It could have been published as a scholarly monograph at that time, but this was not what I had wanted. I waited, knowing that the situations of which I had written seemed often limiting for the women involved, and their analyses were in many cases dispirited and pessimistic about the possibilities for positive change within Hungarian society. I thought perhaps in a year or two I would be able to rework the thesis if some aspects of Hungarian society changed. Of course rapid changes did happen throughout most of the East–Central and Eastern European countries. Yet such sweeping developments, and the varied and complex consequences for many women's lives, made the task of trying to encompass such complexities overwhelming.

Soon after the 'celebrations' of 1990, the realisation of how slow cultural change tends to be, coupled with a recognition of the barriers to cooperation, became apparent in discussions with friends and colleagues in Hungary. 'Reform' in whatever form is not gender neutral and women's lives were being affected in so many different ways. Some developments were quickly apparent, such as the declining services in health care and the reduction in state support for child care. Much of the economic change has had far-reaching and unintended consequences. Many women have even less involvement in some of the new political structures. Poverty and insecurity around employment for women are increasing within a context of declining social policy support. The differentiation between individuals and groups of women is ever increasing. Some women entrepreneurs and professionals have welcomed the changes, while many groups, especially older women and women from 'minority' communities, are suffering greatly.

By 1990, I realised that I had become intellectually isolated. Work of mine written in 1987 had been published, but my detachment from it was marked. My concentration from 1990 on, in networking and publishing booklets on women's reproductive health or issues of violence against women (Helsinki Citizens Assembly, 1991a, b), further distanced me from 'academic' writing and collaboration. I had taken up a permanent position as a Lecturer in Politics in 1990, yet I did not feel involved in the academic world. I thought of myself as a teacher and an activist but not an academic and thus as an outsider in academia.

One project that seemed to bring together both teaching and collaboration with women across Europe was a book I edited (Corrin, 1992) entitled *Superwomen and the Double Burden*. This was conceived as a good opportunity to link Eastern European women's work in their own societies with teaching in the UK and elsewhere. With no funding available for translation, this learning resource was available predominantly for western students, yet it has also been read and reviewed by feminists in East–Central Europe.

Of course I now realise many of the mistakes I have made along the way in developing my ideas about change in women's lives in East–Central Europe, not least in some of the work I have written about 'western' comparisons. Sometimes I learn fast and at other times very slowly. In my academic career, I have felt the lack of feminist colleagues to talk with. There seemed very few people to read the work I wrote and no apparent network of feminist academics interested in East–Central European women's experiences. Publication of an earlier paper (Corrin, 1990) did have the positive effect of at least gaining some critical feedback for me, several years later. Nora Jung's (1994) 'Eastern European Women with Western Eyes' rightly pointed out that in this I was in danger of 'averaging' women's experiences. Despite having talked at length in Hungary about how older women on fixed incomes in the UK were often at great risk, when it came to writing about Hungarian women's situations I did not clarify such differentiations and instead compared mythical 'averages'. I am still not sure why I became reduced to this level of non-analysis, except that at the time I wrote it the thesis was becoming an academic weight around my neck.

Throughout this period I knew few other western feminists who had lived and worked with women in East–Central Europe. I was only very slowly finding such rapport with colleagues in the UK. I learnt a good deal from my brief collaborative work with Oxfam in 'action-oriented' research concerned with women's changing needs in Albania and how resources could be chanelled into supporting women's access to opportunities to help support themselves and their families. Colleagues within the Oxfam Gender and

Development Unit (GADU) had a rich understanding of the complexities of women's experiences of change, yet my contact with them at that time was limited in terms of my 'brief' and other commitments. I appreciated such contacts and certainly now in the late 1990s there seems more of a sense of sharing ideas and exchanging experiences in less defensive or pressured ways.

Yet in 1992 to meet many strong women in Albania who were barely surviving in terrible material conditions taught me a great deal about where my priorities lay. I realised that I was good at political organising and fundraising for women's projects. Did this mean that I was a 'failed' academic? I knew I was a good teacher. It seemed that the borders between these various modes of action were more connected to time and resources than failure or success. I choose to give my time to teaching in the UK and to political activism in the UK and elsewhere, but I am still unsure whether or not writing is something I want to prioritise.

Perhaps the role of writing is to understand the processes of change. Further analysis of women's activities towards change across 'Europe' (however defined) during the first five years of the 1990s would, I believe, be very worthwhile in terms of exploring the various borders, perceived and otherwise, that have been crossed and are perhaps still to be acknowledged in terms of feminist understanding of women's changing experiences. From 1990–3 onwards, my working with women active in attempting to change their own situations seemed vital in breaking down borders – between countries and borders across which women did not otherwise have opportunities to meet; between those of us who promoted women-only space for developing our thinking and those who were wary of this; and between perceived 'academics' (writing and/or teaching within higher educational institutions) and 'activists' (some of whom were also academics). These meetings were very important in terms of developing all of our thinking across the sometimes falsely created borders of how women can collectively create change.

One example has involved discussions of violence against women. Women from the former Yugoslavia and from the Transcaucasus talked about their different war-time situations and the varying impact of such inhuman conditions on women's lives. In this instance feminists from Serbia, Croatia, Bosnia and Macedonia discussed their similar analyses of why male abuse of power was increasing within their societies during war-time. Participants from the Transcaucasus, on the other hand, felt that issues such as domestic violence were less worthy of analysis when their countries were at war. A lot was learnt about how different theoretical positions affect how we view developments within our societies. Certainly feminist perspectives cut across many of the borderlines that divided us in other ways.

Becoming a teacher – and another kind of outsider

It would have been good to have felt part of a similar 'feminist community' within the UK. It seems that for many southern-based academics, Scotland is too far to travel for meetings. Perhaps I have created another border for myself around being 'academic', in the sense of not giving my energies to producing written work. As I noted earlier, a fundamental issue for me concerned 'translating' the lives and experiences of women expressed on so many different levels into 'academic writing'. I constantly think 'who am I?' to presume to write of this. Yet, it is expected that I 'produce' written work as part of my paid employment. I do this by choosing to write about political change at the level of 'civil society' (Corrin, 1993a) or about defining aspects of women's politics (Corrin, 1994b) or by writing on some aspects of lesbians' experiences within UK higher education (Corrin, 1994c). My thesis book, *Magyar Women*, was eventually published as a scholarly monograph with some minimal 'updating' (Corrin, 1994a). It will not be widely read.

I keep returning to the crossroads in making choices of what to say 'no' to. I have turned down many invitations to speak about 'women in Eastern Europe' because of the difficulties of how to articulate the complexities involved in any discussion of 'women' or 'Eastern Europe'. Maybe I have created false borders around 'activism'. I recognise feminist writing as a form of activism. For me, though, the small English-speaking and relatively well-off audiences that have access to academic texts from the UK raises questions about where and how to be active in the world. This is the crossroads to which I am constantly returning.

Thinking of crossroads here reminds me that many of my apparent choices in terms of academic involvement have been actually random and unplanned. Having drifted into academic life, firstly as a mature student who could 'earn' more by studying full-time, and then as a research student, my progression to becoming a full-time teacher seemed fraught with indecision. I left Oxford to take up a six-month research assistant post which did not work out well and I again felt 'at the crossroads' in terms of whether I wanted to become an 'academic'. The opportunity to leave the UK to teach for a year in Malaysia in 1988 deferred a decision about this. Returning to a one-year contract in a UK university, I decided to 'have a go' at entering academia more permanently. When I moved to Glasgow in September 1990, I had chosen to accept a permanent academic position. I wanted to develop teaching courses and I was glad to be moving to Scotland. Yet I do not 'fit in' particularly well in either the department or the university. By this I mean both specifically in terms of my teaching methods and ideas on pedagogy, and more generally in terms of my lifestyle as a feminist lesbian activist. In terms of teaching, there is an apparently accepted border or division within the department between 'theory' and 'institutions' – one is expected to be either/or. I am neither or both. I teach two courses which I have written on 'State and Society in the New Europe' and 'Feminist Thought and Political Theory'. The former is placed within 'institutions' and the latter within 'theory'. It seems to me unthinkable that anyone could teach anything about institutional arrangements in societies from anything other than an informed theoretical base. In turn, to theorise about human ethics and interactions without cognisance of the subjects of such theories seems equally odd.

In terms of gender relations, the department has fifteen permanent staff, of whom I am the only woman. This has many disadvantages and I experience a good deal of exclusion in terms both of judgements about my subject areas – viewed as 'soft' options, more like sociology – and in terms of 'not being one of the boys' in any sphere. The jokes about my 'being a feminist' range from school-boy humour to contempt for a set of faddish notions that do not have a place within 'real' academic thinking. In this vein, when one of my women students put forward a dissertation topic to a male colleague he criticised it openly as not being 'objective' enough – it was something that Chris Corrin would be interested in as she was 'more like a sociologist'. I roared with laughter when this was repeated to me. I have never been willing to submit to others' boundaries, and the academic boundaries constituted by disciplines have never made sense to me. In writing about politics we are writing about people. For me it is that simple, or that complex. Over time the success of students on the 'Feminist Thought' course has raised eyebrows amongst colleagues, yet only very few give the subject serious consideration. Aspects of gender politics are taught on other 'mainstream' courses only when I teach them. I hope this may change over time, but I cannot keep extending my teaching to develop this. The old jibe about feminists not having a sense of humour often springs to mind. I will not allow misogynists to invalidate my sense of humour and in chosen company such incidents can form very amusing anecdotes. Such chosen company for me are close women friends, many of whom work within equally patriarchal situations.

Recently when I was asked about my current research for one of the endless reports now required in universities, I noted my work on feminist resistance to violence against women. My head of department questioned whether violence against women is 'really politics'. I am no longer shocked but still find it wearing; I worry too about becoming accustomed to this hostile environment and thereby losing my critical edge and my talent for asking uncomfortable questions.

Being lesbian is an added complication for my colleagues, yet a liberating factor in my life. I have written elsewhere of the contradictions that can arise for lesbians in higher education. In the context of borders I believe my physicality is a border across which few of my male colleagues choose to cross. My appearance bespeaks my lesbianism. As I am 'out' at work, my colleagues know that I am lesbian and I choose to cross such boundaries at will. I have frequently been astonished at the 'threat' that I seem to pose to them by doing so. It feels strange to have such defensive postures taken against me when I seldom feel 'powerful' in any material sense. Various gendered 'jokes' or insults come my way regularly. Colleagues choose to redefine my politics in terms of my being 'over committed' to feminist analysis and thus not able to teach in a 'neutral manner'. I consciously choose not to let the barbed words or open prejudices of colleagues affect me too much.

In writing about lesbians working in education in Scotland (Marchbank et al., 1993; Corrin, 1994c), I have discussed the pressures and the pleasures of working as lesbians and feminists, inside and outside of the academy in

Scotland. It is certainly true to say that our personal/political connections have sustained us by creating spaces of well-being in often overtly hostile situations. There are specific difficulties faced by lesbians in higher education. Yet as the years go by I no longer need to 'come out' to students because the grapevine works well. I have experienced good times with students doing human rights work on lesbians and gay men in our European politics classes and in exploring various aspects of our lives within the 'Feminist Thought' and 'Political Theory' courses. Generally two or three lesbians 'come out' to me each year and I can support them in various ways, even in some contexts as a form of 'role model'. In these situations I do feel part of a learning community, even if for only short periods of time.

Feminist thinking and practices have brought many progressive changes into the academy, both in terms of what we choose to learn about and how we learn it. However, some of the most disturbing trends within university education at the moment are around the encouragement of instrumental attitudes towards teaching and to learning. The educational culture in many institutions, including the one in which I am involved, is becoming more 'market-oriented', which in reality means teaching more students in bigger groups with less resources. 'Research' seems to be more about bulk publishing quickly any rapid results that can be gained, rather than creating new ways of understanding complex and shifting patterns of human interaction. Some colleagues are now 'buying themselves out' of teaching for as long as possible and some even take sabbaticals to be interviewed for their professorships.

I feel I am in a small minority within my current institution of those who have certain, perhaps idealistic, notions of what learning and educational development can be about. I have always recognised that passing a 'degree' of whatever sort is about jumping through particular hoops, yet there was so much to be gained along the way that the hoops were not too important. Now students have to prioritise the hoops; and, without even basic funding and inadequate welfare support, many potential students may have to choose not to enter higher education.

Still learning, still on the borders

There have been costs for me in crossing borders. I have long felt and still feel under constant pressure of lack of time – how to live, to enjoy my life in all its aspects. I often feel that I'm being pulled or pushing myself in too many different directions and constantly needing to keep assimilating my experiences and attempting to learn from them. Trying to weave together the threads of my involvements into some seamless whole would be challenging, yet I do wish to feel the wholeness of my life. Unfortunately, outside of my teaching, the academic part of my existence seems largely sterile and full of borders that I cross at my expense. Challenging such borders, living in the margins, does not now give me any satisfaction, if it ever did. I deal with this by looking outwards to my community networks and involvements to be able to give and receive some of the joy of living as a feminist and as a lesbian who wants to keep working towards positive changes in our lives.

But at the same time there *are* areas of my life, at least in the past, in which I have gained tremendously from crossing borders. To collaborate in the energetic commitment many feminists in East–Central and Eastern Europe have given to creating change for themselves and other women has been a privilege for me. The ongoing learning involved in breaking down borders to our realisation of negotiated and shared goals has created richer understandings of ourselves, each other and how we can collectively create social change. Also I am now beginning to feel part of a number of international academic feminist communities. The development of women's studies courses and centres and feminist research projects across Central and Eastern Europe provides opportunities for involvements and cooperation between feminists from all areas of Europe and elsewhere. Even as slaughter continues in the Balkans, many feminists from the region came together with women from other countries at the United Nations Women's Conference in Beijing, crossing many more borders with courage and determination. Although I am still at a crossroads, the signposts seem to me clearer and less confusing.

Notes

My thanks to Clara Connolly for helpful comments on an early draft and to Liz Stanley for her generous and thoughtful editing.

    1. The term 'the power' was generally used as a cover-all phrase noting the power of the state structures and political forces in an 'us' and 'them' context.

References

Corrin, Chris (1990) 'The situation of women in Hungarian society', in Bob Deacon and Júlia Szalai (eds), *Social Policy in the New Eastern Europe*. Avebury: Gower. pp. 179–91. (originally a paper for the Social Policy and Socialism Conference, Leeds, April 1988)

Corrin, Chris (ed.) (1992) *Superwomen and the Double Burden: Women's Experience of Change in Central and Eastern Europe and the Former Soviet Union*. London: Scarlet Press.

Corrin, Chris (1993a) 'People and politics', in Stephen White, Judy Batt and Paul Lewis (eds), *Developments in East European Politics*. Basingstoke: Macmillan. pp. 186–204.

Corrin, Chris (1993b) 'Is liberalisation damaging Albanian women's health?', in *Focus on Gender: Perspectives on Women and Development* (35–37). Oxford: Oxfam Publications 1: 3.

Corrin, Chris (1994a) *Magyar Women: Hungarian Women's Lives 1960s–1990s*. Basingstoke: Macmillan.

Corrin, Chris (1994b) 'Women's politics in "Europe" in the 1990s', *Women's International Studies Forum* Special Issue 'Images from Women in a Changing Europe'. 17 (2/3). pp. 289–97.

Corrin, Chris (1994c) 'Fighting back or biting back? Lesbians in higher education', in Sue Davies, Cathy Lubelska and Jocey Quinn (eds), *Changing the Subject: Women in Higher Education*. London: Taylor and Francis. pp. 58–74.

Helsinki Citizens Assembly (1991a) *Reproductive Rights in East and Central Europe*. Prague: HCA Publications Series 3.

Helsinki Citizens Assembly (1991b) *Violence Against Women in Eastern and Central Europe*. Prague: HCA Publication Series 8.

Jung, Nora (1994) 'Eastern European women with western eyes', in Gabriele Griffin, Marianne Hester, Shirin Rai and Sasha Roseneil (eds), *Stirring It: Challenges for Feminism*. London: Taylor and Francis. pp. 195–210.

Konrád, György and Szelényi, Iván (1979) *The Intellectuals on the Road to Class Power*. New York: Harcourt, Brace, Jovanovich.

Marchbank, Jennifer, Corrin, Chris and Brodie, Sheila (1993) 'Inside and "out" or outside academia: Lesbians working in Scotland', in Mary Kennedy, Cathy Lubelska and Val Walsh (eds), *Making Connections: Women's Studies, Women's Movements, Women's Lives*. London: Taylor & Francis. pp. 155–66.

8

Still Seeking Transformation: Feminist Challenges to Psychology

Sue Wilkinson

Psychology as oppressor

Feminists have always criticised psychology and have worked for change in its theories, institutions and practices – but the discipline remains resolutely misogynist (Ussher, 1991), heterosexist (Kitzinger, 1990) and racist (Sayal-Bennett, 1991). Unlike sociology, where the feminist project has been said to have 'come of age' (Roseneil, 1995), feminism within psychology is still desperately struggling for autonomy and influence. Why is the development of feminism in, and against, psychology apparently so much slower? What has impeded us in our struggles to transform the discipline?

Psychology is highly institutionalised, relative to other disciplines. Its professional bodies – the British Psychological Society (BPS) in the UK, and the American Psychological Association (APA) in the USA – regulate the content and practice of the discipline. These bodies validate undergraduate and postgraduate courses, gatekeep the most prestigious academic journals, operate a professional registration scheme for psychologists ('chartering' in the UK), and determine the criteria for judgements of mental health and 'illness' (APA's *Diagnostic and Statistical Manual*). Feminist psychologists' challenges to and attempts to transform psychology are inevitably determined by, and constructed in opposition to, these institutional structures of the discipline.

Throughout the (relatively short) history of psychology, feminists working within and beyond the discipline have criticised its treatment of women, exposing both the prejudices cloaked by the mantle of 'science' and the damages perpetrated in the name of 'therapy'. Early twentieth-century feminists such as Helen Thompson Wooley (1910: 340) – a psychologist herself – commented on research purporting to demonstrate women's mental inferiorities that: 'There is perhaps no field aspiring to be scientific where flagrant personal bias, logic martyred in the cause of supporting a prejudice, unfounded assertions, and even sentimental rot and drivel, have run riot to such an extent as here.' More than half a century later, as second-wave feminism gathered momentum, feminist activist and psychologist Naomi Weisstein (1968: 197) asserted that: 'Psychology has nothing to say about what women are really like, what they need and what they want . . . because psychology does not know.' Other feminist psychologists characterised the discipline as 'a psychology against women' (Nancy Henley, 1974: 20) which has 'distorted facts, omitted problems, and perpetuated pseudoscientific data relevant to women' (Mary Parlee, 1975: 124). The whole patriarchal mental health system was indicted by feminist psychologist Phyllis Chesler (1972) in her classic book *Women and Madness*; in 1970 Chesler had taken the platform at the annual APA conference, not to deliver the expected academic paper but to demand that the APA provide 'one million dollars "in reparations" for those women who had never been helped by the mental health professions but who had, instead, been further abused by them' (Chesler, 1989: xvii).

Feminists, especially lesbian feminists, have always been – and still are – located in the contested borderlands of the discipline. We occupy a marginal space in which definitions and practices are *not* simply taken for granted, but subjected to constant interrogation and (sometimes) reformulation. Our very existence challenges psychology's hegemonic accounts of behaviours and identities appropriate to our sex: we are not 'proper' women. Our work transgresses the discipline's authoritative statements of scientific orthodoxy: we are not 'proper' scientists. Our exposés of psychological theory as 'rot and drivel' and of mental health practice as 'abuse' threaten seriously to bring the discipline into disrepute: we are bad, mad, and very dangerous to know. So, psychology's response to such criticisms from the borderlands has not been to apologise, to pay out the million dollars, or to put its house in order. Rather, it has resorted to various forms of exclusion: in particular, physical exclusion accompanied by hostility; exclusion by definition; and exclusion based on liberal rhetorics. Together, these constitute a formidable array of armaments in establishment psychology's battery of responses to feminist challenges. And, of course, in addition to the external obstacles which have been put in our way, feminists in psychology (as in the women's liberation movement more generally) have had to confront the difficulties inherent in working together across our differences and in spite of the things that divide us.

Feminist challenges

Historically, psychology's central assertion is that women are inferior to men. Feminist challenges are lodged within five distinctive theoretical traditions: (i) psychology is poor science – it has mismeasured women; (ii) the problem is oppression, not women; (iii) women are indeed different from men – but superior; (iv) mental health is unrelated to sex/gender; and (v) psychology is asking the wrong questions. Feminists have institutionalised these challenges via intellectual and political alliances: the USA Association for Women in Psychology (AWP), founded in the late 1960s; and the UK Women in Psychology (WIP, recently relaunched as the Alliance of Women in Psychology) and the Lesbians in Psychology Sisterhood (LIPS). These informal organisations later functioned as pressure groups for the formal representation of feminist work within the professional bodies. AWP was key to the establishment of Division 35 ('Psychology of Women') within the APA in 1973; WIP successfully campaigned for a BPS 'Psychology of Women' Section in late 1987; and LIPS, having failed to get a BPS 'Psychology of Lesbianism' Section, is now leading the struggle for a 'Lesbian and Gay Psychology' Section.

The mismeasure of women

This tradition of feminist research refutes mainstream psychology's statement that women are inferior by arguing that mainstream researchers have consistently omitted women from their samples, or mismeasured us – it says that psychology as presently conducted is lousy science. Many of psychology's classic theories (e.g. Kohlberg's theory of moral reasoning, Erikson's theory of lifespan development) have been derived from all-male samples; and its empirical studies are riddled with technical flaws (e.g. experimental biases, inadequate sampling techniques, lack of control groups, insufficiently sensitive measures), which function to reinforce the ideological biases from which it suffers (e.g. sexism, heterosexism, racism, classism). Naomi Weisstein (1968: 197), castigating sex differences research as 'theory without evidence', indicts the practice of sexist researchers: '[They] simply refuse to look at the evidence against their theory and practice. And they support their theory and practice with stuff so transparently biased as to have no standing as empirical evidence.'

Feminist activism has also provided a spectacularly successful institutional challenge to the whole mental health system in the USA. Two particularly misogynistic diagnostic categories – 'Self-Defeating Personality Disorder' (masochism) and 'Late Luteal Phase Dysphoric Disorder' (premenstrual syndrome) – have now been removed from the DSM, following their exposure by feminists as 'without any adequate scientific basis' (Franklin, 1987) and as 'deeply flawed and dangerous' (Caplan et al., 1992).

The problem is oppression

This feminist tradition *accepts* psychology's assertion of women's inferiority – but contends that such 'inferiority' is simply an index of our oppression, arguing that women's shortcomings arise from gender-related motives, fears or concepts which lead us to act against our own best interests. Matina Horner's (1972) concept of 'fear of success' provided a classic – and very popular – explanation for women's failure to advance in professional life. Other explanations have included lack of assertiveness, low self-esteem, poor self-confidence, under-estimation and under-valuation of achievement, and failure to develop an autonomous self (Tavris, 1993).

Innovative (in psychology) in its focus on women *per se* (rather than in relation to, or comparison with, men), this framework remains the dominant one in contemporary feminist psychology. It underpins both the therapy industry (which is seen as offering 'compensatory socialization': Marecek and Hare-Mustin, 1987, cited in Crawford and Marecek, 1989) and the growth in pop-psych, self-help manuals (e.g. *The Cinderella Complex* – Dowling, 1981; *The Doormat Syndrome* – Namka, 1989). It seems to be popular because, if women's failings can be placed at the door of oppression, we do not have to blame ourselves, and because it suggests ways in which individual change wrought by therapy can improve women's lives. This tradition has been institutionalised by the growing range of feminist counselling and psychotherapy services, such as The Women's Therapy Centre, in London and New York (individual and group therapies, plus therapist training), and The Pink Practice in London (counselling and psychotherapy for lesbians and gay men).

Women are different – and superior

The third approach of feminist psychologists is to agree that women *are* different from men – but to argue that women's characteristics are superior, rather than inferior, to men's. These researchers *maximise* – and celebrate – sex differences. Broadly akin to what is sometimes labelled 'cultural feminism', and largely in response to androcentric theories in psychology, classic work in this tradition has identified women's distinctive 'ways of knowing' (Belenky et al., 1986) and women's 'different (moral) voice' (Gilligan, 1982; Brown and Gilligan, 1992). Helen Haste (1994), seeking to document and explain the huge influence of Carol Gilligan's (1982) book *In a Different Voice*, suggests:

> Gilligan's work touched a nerve . . . For all the criticisms of the book's limitations in the academic community, the message was novel and it was important . . . women were being denied a voice; and philosophically, it meant there *was* an alternative voice in the culture – that there is more than one way of looking at the world. (pp. 399–400)

This kind of approach has been enthusiastically embraced in a range of applied areas, particularly youth work and secondary education. It has been institutionalised in, for example, research on young women's experiences in schools, commissioned by the American Association of University Women (1991); the development of feminist pedagogy and curriculum materials – including 'retreats' for teachers to consider 'what it means to be a woman teaching girls in this culture at this time' (Brown and Gilligan, 1992: 241–2); and the launch of a glossy magazine called *New Moon*, which celebrates young women's growth, development and 'self-affirmation' throughout their teenage years.

Mental health is unrelated to gender

The fourth theoretical tradition of feminist psychology argues that women are neither inferior nor superior to men – in fact, these researchers refuse to compare the sexes. They *minimise* – indeed, undermine – the importance of sex differences, arguing that being male or female is not a central determinant of psychological functioning. Rather, there are elements of masculinity and femininity in everyone, and a key aspect of mental health and wellbeing is the ability to deploy these flexibly according to the situation (so we are able to be relatively confident and assertive in a job interview, say, while being relatively self-effacing and sympathetic to a friend in distress). Back in 1974, Sandra Bem first proposed such 'psychological androgyny' as 'a new standard of mental health, one that removes the burden of stereotype and allows people to feel free to express the best traits of men and women' (Bem, 1974: 125).

Perhaps because it removes the critical spotlight *both* from psychology *and* from women, and also offers a reframing of the familiar concept of 'sex roles' in the positive context of improving mental health, this work has had surprising success in penetrating mainstream psychological theory. Detached from its feminist intent, it sits comfortably with the discipline's liberal rhetorics – and also offers the bonus of an associated measuring scale: the Bem Sex Role Inventory (BSRI). This was widely used in the 1970s and 1980s to correlate androgyny with many different indices of mental functioning, and it is still one of the most popular scales in use in (mainstream and feminist) social psychology today.

These are the wrong questions

Finally – and most recently – feminist psychologists working within the framework of social constructionism (e.g. Hare-Mustin and Marecek, 1994; Hollway, 1994) have argued that sex/gender should no longer be theorised as 'difference', but reconceptualised as a principle of social organisation, structuring power relations between the sexes. In this tradition of feminist psychology, as within postmodern varieties of feminism more generally, sex/gender is seen as a relatively flexible – albeit politically-driven – process, rather than as a relatively fixed set of attributes; it is also acknowledged to be highly historically, culturally and socially contingent (Bohan, 1992).

This tradition of work has gained almost no institutional toe-hold in psychology: indeed, to most psychologists it is unrecognisable as psychology. Its institutional challenge is provided by its transdisciplinary nature – and the opportunities it affords for alliances with feminists (and other critical theorists) outside psychology: both in other social science disciplines and in a transdisciplinary women's studies context. Particularly challenging work is being done where feminist psychologists are entering into dialogue with historians and sociologists of science to develop transdisciplinary analyses of psychology's particular oppressive practices (e.g. Bhavnani and Haraway, 1994; Morawski, 1994); and where feminist psychologists are orchestrating and contributing to key debates in contemporary feminist theory (e.g. 'heterosexuality': Wilkinson and Kitzinger, 1993; 'representing the Other': Wilkinson and Kitzinger, 1996).

These five competing feminist traditions offer different, and often incompatible, theoretical and/or political tools for challenging and transforming psychology. All five can also (in different ways) be dismissed, ridiculed or assimilated by the mainstream of the discipline. In the final section of this chapter, I will look at the ways in which psychology actively and systematically excludes feminist theoretical challenges – and the theorists who provide such challenges.

Psychology's exclusions

Feminist incursions from the borderlands, as exemplified by the theoretical challenges outlined above, are comprehensively and systematically excluded from psychology's institutions and practices. Three kinds of exclusion are commonplace: (i) physical exclusion and hostility: (ii) exclusion by definition; and (iii) exclusion by means of liberal rhetorics.

Physical exclusion and hostility: Are you normal?

The most effective means of excluding particular kinds of theory is to exclude the theorists. Historically, the exclusion of women from all higher education was justified with reference to psychology, which provided the 'evidence' that women were mentally and physically unsuited to such exertions (Ehrenreich and English, 1979). Within psychology itself, there is a contemporary gender imbalance in the higher reaches: in (British) academic psychology, although women constitute nearly 80% of undergraduate population, they constitute only about 20% of university teaching staff. In clinical psychology, while almost all trainee places are filled by women, they hold less than 25% of Top Grade posts.

Such imbalance is underpinned by a whole range of academic and professional practices which ensure that women remain marginalised within psychology. These include: the portrayal of women in negative and gender-biased ways in introductory psychology textbooks (Peterson and Kroner, 1992); minimal coverage of 'psychology of women' (let alone feminist psychology) in most British undergraduate psychology degrees; limited representation of women on the major committees and in the senior membership grades of professional bodies such as the BPS (Wilkinson, 1990); citation practices which ensure feminist psychologists cite mainstream work but that the practice does not happen in reverse (Lykes and Stewart, 1986); and a rated status of 'psychology of women' as lower than almost any other area of the discipline – excepting lesbian and gay psychology (Harari and Peters, 1987).

Organisational struggles within British psychology provide some vivid examples of the overt hostility which often accompanies such physical exclusion. In 1985, the proposers of the BPS 'Psychology of Women' Section were told: 'we would not expect to have a psychology of animals section' (BPS, October 1985: letter to section proposers, circulated to supporters). In April 1995, *The Psychologist* (the house journal of the British Psychological Society, circulated monthly to some 24,000 psychologists nationally and internationally) published the following letters under the heading 'Are you normal?':

... I object to the misleading use in a publication of a scientific society of the inno-cent-sounding word 'gay' when referring to what is the abnormal practice of anal intercourse between males. Secondly, I object to attempts to mislead readers about the epidemiological incidence and prevalence of male and female homosexuality which in statistical-mathematical terms is fortunately still tiny. (Hamilton, 1995: 151)

... at work, as elsewhere, there is, indeed, a normality of life for the vast major-ity of people ... It is certainly not a matter of heterosexuality being flaunted – it is simply the ordinariness of life from which homosexuals and lesbians, however much they may wish it were different, are perforce excluded. (Davis, 1995: 151–2)

Horrific as these statements may sound to non-psychologists, for those of us working within the discipline they are entirely unsurprising. They are simply the most recent manifestations of psychology's anti-feminism. The let-ters are responses to a review article on lesbian and gay relationships (Kitzinger and Coyle, 1995), published alongside the lesbian feminist-led ini-tiative to establish a BPS 'Psychology of Lesbianism Section'/'Lesbian and Gay Psychology Section'. Such appeals to 'normality' (elsewhere 'the natural order of things': Davis, 1995), buttressed by the 'scientific' tools of 'epidemi-ology', 'statistics' and 'mathematics', are an all-too-familiar armament in establishment psychology's battery of responses to institutional challenges.

Exclusion by definition: politics not science

Guillaumin (1995: 156) notes that the first texts of minority groups are always discounted as *theory*, and presented as '*political*' products. The exclusion is particularly easy to achieve in mainstream psychology, which defines 'science' and 'politics' as polar opposites, and legitimates psychological theory as a product of 'science' alone. '[W]hen I write as a feminist,' observes Celia Kitzinger (1990: 124), 'I am defined out of the category of "psychologist". When I speak of social structure, of power and politics, when I use language rooted in my understanding of oppression, I am told what I say does not qualify as "psychology"'.

Exclusion of feminist work on the grounds that it is 'politics, not science' is a constant refrain. In commenting on the initial 'Psychology of Women' Section proposal, the BPS (July, 1985) suggested that it was 'loaded politi-cally', and that a clear distinction must be made between 'the scientific duty [sic] of the psychology of womanhood' and 'a feminist pressure group'. A recent letter to *The Psychologist* (Martin, 1995) deemed the proposal for a 'Lesbian and Gay Psychology' Section 'more like a self-interested political initiative than one inspired by scientific curiosity'.

Exclusion by liberal rhetorics – we don't discriminate

As in other highly bureaucratic, patriarchal institutions, the BPS makes heavy use of conventional liberal rhetorics – 'meritocracy', 'equal opportunities', 'inclusivity', 'non-discrimination' – to justify its actions (see Wilkinson, 1990 for examples). Such liberal rhetorics are used, first, as a way of defusing political challenges to the organisation, and, second, as a way of assimilating dissidents and neutralising their disruptive influences. This is apparent in early arguments against the formation of a BPS 'Psychology of Women' Section: 'In a nutshell, the argument was put forward that to single out the psychology of women in this way could be regarded as patronising to women, or, at best, an admission of failure' (BPS, October 1985, letter to 'Psychology of Women' Section proposers). A related argument favoured a 'more inclusive' grouping called 'Psychology of Gender'. A variant of the 'non-discrimination' rhetoric appears in opposition to the proposed 'Lesbian and Gay Psychology' Section (along with assertions that 'Psychology of Sexuality' would be 'more inclusive'):

> the creation of a Gay and Lesbian Section in the Society would itself [sic] be the ultimate in homophobic actions, damaging the very cause it seeks to promote. . . . To create such a grouping is surely to stereotype homosexual people and to exaggerate differences between them and heterosexual people beyond the sexual domain. (Seager, 1995)

This kind of 'more liberal than thou' assertion has been a powerful strategy in mainstream psychology's dismissal of feminist theories which *maximise* sex differences (such as Gilligan's 'different voice') – and it may also account for the relative success within the mainstream of feminist theories which *minimise* sex differences (such as Bem's 'psychological androgyny'). 'Reversal' strategies, such as the accusation that feminists are seeking to substitute matriarchy for patriarchy, or ignoring the oppression of men, are used to mock, trivialise, and dismiss feminist challenges. They are, of course, self-protective and self-interested ploys used by those who stand to gain by not having to engage with theoretical and institutional challenges to their power base.

Feminist psychology's internal problems

A key strength of feminist psychology is the vigour and variety of debate within and between its various theoretical traditions. The greatest internal threat to feminist psychology is not debate and disagreement between different theoretical positions or empirical approaches but problems of envy and competition between women. In common with many feminist organisations, the early history of the BPS 'Psychology of Women' Section was beset by power struggles between individuals, and later, there was a split over the proposed formation of a 'Psychology of Lesbianism' Section (c.f. Comely et al., 1992). A second threat to the efficacy of feminist psychology is excessive preoccupation with internal affairs. Thus, internal BPS paperwork dominates the committee meetings of the 'Psychology of Women' Section; and meetings are spent wallowing in the minutiae of memos from the secretariat and endlessly redrafting documents which outsiders will never read. Feminists have made little or no impact on BPS initiatives of key importance externally, such as on its recent Working Party on Recovered Memories, which addressed crucial issues around child sexual abuse and 'false memory syndrome'. The BPS has not contributed to key parliamentary debates on single mothers or commented on crucial legislation such as the Child Support Act. The 'Psychology of Women' Section has done virtually nothing to prompt the BPS into appropriate action on such issues. Collective activism is needed to avoid the organisation being co-opted (or exhausted) by the demands of the system. The challenge for feminist psychologists in the future is to regain a sense of unity and political purpose, and to work effectively together on an agenda which reflects our own political priorities.

Toward transformation

Despite the wealth and diversity of feminist theorising within psychology, the formidable exclusionary practices of the discipline and its institutions, some of which I have discussed here, are a substantial barrier to change and transformation. Nonetheless, there have been large and small successes both within and beyond the institutional framework imposed by professional bodies like the BPS. Within the BPS, the 'Psychology of Women' Section *has* been successful in a variety of ways: as a forum for debate and development within the field of feminist psychology; as a crucial life-line for many individual women within a deeply hostile discipline; as a catalyst for raising the general awareness of women's issues and creating change within British psychology. It remains to be seen whether it can sustain and develop these roles; and what might be achieved, in theoretical and institutional terms, were the initiative for a BPS 'Lesbian and Gay Psychology' Section to succeed.

Outside the BPS, and sometimes in direct opposition to it, the reconstituted pressure group, now called the Alliance of Women in Psychology, has a membership which explicitly includes users and survivors of psychology. Also independent of the BPS, the international journal *Feminism & Psychology*, now in its sixth volume, has a subscription base of around 1000 and still rising. Both the Alliance and the journal 'put feminism first' as a political priority, and, by virtue of being outside the BPS, are less vulnerable to assimilation by the mainstream than is the 'Psychology of Women' Section. Both also benefit from alliances with other feminist organisations, and explicit dialogue and debate within transdisciplinary contexts.

Feminist psychologists are still in the borderlands of our discipline. We do not have the luxury of deciding deliberately to 'confine ourselves to the margins of the academy' (Roseneil, 1995: 196) – we are resolutely positioned there by the psychological centre. Our struggles are not yet against incorporation, but still against exclusion. There are, of course, benefits as well as disadvantages of being so positioned. Our exclusions as feminists, and as lesbians, from the mainstream of British psychology have provided the impetus to struggle for change – and arguably have provoked more radical initiatives (sometimes followed by more radical transformations) than would have been likely in a more liberal context. For example, if the BPS 'Psychology of Women' Section had offered regular and explicit platforms for its lesbian members, it is unlikely that the proposal for a 'Psychology of Lesbianism'

Section would have been initiated; and had POWS supported this initiative from the outset, it is unlikely that it would be continuing, albeit in a different form, or that it would have had such an impact both within and beyond the BPS. Similarly, the context of exclusion has informed several recent analyses of hegemonic identities: e.g. masculinity (Griffin and Wetherell, 1992), heterosexuality (Wilkinson and Kitzinger, 1993) and whiteness (Wong, 1994).

Further, the paradoxical location of feminist psychologists – simultaneously within and against an academic discipline – offers us both 'insider' and 'outsider' viewpoints to inform critique and political action. From our enforced vantage-point on the margins of psychology, we are well-placed to analyse the discipline's oppressive practices and seek their transformation. As Jill Morawski writes:

> many of us have spoken and written about how our inquiry pushes against the dominant narrative of scientific change, a story whose plot is overdetermined by the myths of positivism, progress and democracy and by a politics of memory that over and over again forget the gender arrangements of science. (1994: 69)

As we have seen, feminist psychologists are making a distinctive contribution to the development of feminist theory and practice in transdisciplinary arenas: perhaps in another twenty years we will have 'come of age' *within* our own discipline. In psychology, we are still seeking transformation.

Acknowledgement

Thanks to Celia Kitzinger for helpful comments on earlier drafts.

References

American Association of University Women (1991) *Shortchanging Girls, Shortchanging America.* Washington, DC: AAUW.

Belenky, Mary, Clinchy, Blythe, Goldberger, Nancy and Tarule, Jill (1986) *Women's Ways of Knowing.* New York: Basic Books.

Bem, Sandra L. (1974) 'The measurement of psychological androgyny', *Journal of Consulting and Clinical Psychology*, 42: 155–62.

Bhavnani, Kum-Kum and Haraway, Donna (1994) 'Shifting the subject: A conversation between Kum-Kum Bhavnani and Donna Haraway', *Feminism & Psychology: An International Journal*, 4(1): 19–39.

Bohan, Janis S. (ed.) (1992) *Seldom Seen, Rarely Heard: Women's Place in Psychology.* Boulder, CO: Westview Press.

Brown, Lyn Mikel and Gilligan, Carol (1992) *Meeting at the Crossroads: Women's Psychology and Girls' Development.* Cambridge, MA: Harvard University Press.

Caplan, Paula, J., McCurdy-Myers, Joan and Gans, Maureen (1992) 'Should "Premenstrual Syndrome" be called a psychiatric abnormality?', *Feminism & Psychology: An International Journal*, 2(1): 27–44.

Chesler, Phyllis (1972) *Women and Madness.* Garden City, NY: Doubleday.

Chesler, Phyllis (1989) Preface to 2nd edn of *Women and Madness.* San Diego, CA: Harcourt Brace Jovanovich.

Comely, Louise, Kitzinger, Celia, Perkins, Rachel and Wilkinson, Sue (1992) 'Lesbian psychology in Britain: Back into the closet?', *Feminism & Psychology: An International Journal*, 2(2): 265–8.

Crawford, Mary and Marecek, Jeanne (1989) 'Psychology reconstructs the female 1968–1988', *Psychology of Women Quarterly*, 13: 147–65.

Davis, Michael (1995) 'Are you normal?' (Letter), *The Psychologist*, 8(4): 151–2.

Dowling, Colette (1981) *The Cinderella Complex: Women's Hidden Fear of Independence*. London: Fontana.

Ehrenreich, Barbara and English, Deidre (1979) *For Her Own Good: 150 Years of the Experts' Advice to Women*. London: Pluto.

Franklin, Deborah (1987) 'The politics of masochism', *Psychology Today*, January: 57–9.

Gilligan, Carol (1982) *In a Different Voice: Psychological Theory and Women's Development*. Cambridge, MA: Harvard University Press.

Griffin, Christine and Wetherell, Margaret (eds) (1992) 'Open Forum: Feminist psychology and the study of men and masculinity', *Feminism & Psychology: An International Journal*, 2(2): 133–68.

Guillaumin, Colette (1995) *Racism, Sexism, Power and Ideology*. London: Routledge.

Hamilton, Vernon (1995) 'Are you normal?' (Letter), *The Psychologist*, 8(4): 151.

Harari, H. and Peters, J. (1987) 'The fragmentation of psychology: Are APA divisions symptomatic?', *American Psychologist*, 42: 822–4.

Hare-Mustin, Rachel T. and Marecek, Jeanne (1994) 'Asking the right questions: Feminist psychology and sex differences', *Feminism & Psychology: An International Journal*. 4(4): 531–7.

Haste, Helen (1994) '"You've come a long way, babe": A catalyst of feminist conflicts', *Feminism & Psychology: An International Journal*, 4(3): 399–403.

Henley, Nancy (1974) 'Resources for the study of psychology and women. *R.T.: Journal of Radical Therapy*, 4: 20–1.

Hollway, Wendy (1994) 'Beyond sex differences: A project for feminist psychology', *Feminism & Psychology: An International Journal*, 4(4): 538–46.

Horner, Matina S. (1972) 'Toward an understanding of achievement-related conflicts in women', *Journal of Social Issues*, 28: 157–76.

Kitzinger, Celia (1990) 'Heterosexism in psychology', *The Psychologist*, 3(9): 391–2.

Kitzinger, Celia and Coyle, Adrian (1995) 'Lesbian and gay couples: Speaking of difference', *The Psychologist*, 8(2): 64–9.

Lykes, M. Brinton and Stewart, Abigail (1986) 'Evaluating the feminist challenge to research in personality and social psychology: 1963–1983', *Psychology of Women Quarterly*, 10: 393–412.

Martin, Brian H. (1995) 'Sectional misapprehensions' (Letter), *The Psychologist*, 8(9): 392.

Miner, Valerie and Longino, Helen E. (1987) *Competition: A Feminist Taboo?* New York: The Feminist Press.

Morawski, Jill G. (1994) *Practicing Feminisms, Reconstructing Psychology: Notes on a Liminal Science*. Ann Arbor, MI: University of Michigan Press.

Namka, Lynn (1989) *The Doormat Syndrome*. Deerfield Beach, FL: Health Communications Inc.

Parlee, Mary Brown (1975) 'Review essay: Psychology', *Signs*, 1: 119–38.

Peterson, Sharyl Bender and Kroner, Traci (1992) 'Gender biases in textbooks for introductory psychology and human development', *Psychology of Women Quarterly*, 16: 17–36.

Roseneil, Sasha (1995) 'The coming of age of feminist sociology: Some issues of practice and theory for the next twenty years', *British Journal of Sociology*, 46(2): 191–205.

Sayal-Bennett, Anuradha (1991) 'Equal opportunities – Empty rhetoric?', *Feminism & Psychology: An International Journal*, 1(1): 74–7.

Seager, Martin (1995) 'Sectioned off?' (Letter), *The Psychologist*, 8(7): 295.

Tavris, Carol (1993) 'The mismeasure of woman', *Feminism & Psychology: An International Journal*, 3(2): 149–68.

Ussher, Jane M. (1991) *Women's Madness: Misogyny or Mental Illness?* Hemel Hempstead: Harvester Wheatsheaf.

Weisstein, Naomi (1968, reprinted 1993) 'Psychology constructs the female; or, the fantasy life of the male psychologist (with some attention to the fantasies of his friends, the male biologist and the male anthropologist)', *Feminism & Psychology: An International Journal*, 3(2): 195–210.

Wilkinson, Sue (1990) 'Women's organisations in psychology: Institutional constraints on disciplinary change', *Australian Psychologist*, 25(3): 256–69.

Wilkinson, Sue and Kitzinger, Celia (eds) (1993) *Heterosexuality: A 'Feminism & Psychology' Reader*. London: Sage.

Wilkinson, Sue and Kitzinger, Celia (eds) (1996) *Representing the Other: A 'Feminism & Psychology' Reader*. London: Sage.

Wong, L. Mun (1994) 'Di(s)-secting and dis(s)-closing "whiteness": Two tales about psychology', *Feminism & Psychology: An International Journal*, 4(1): 133–53.

Wooley, Helen Thompson (1910) 'Psychological literature: A review of the recent literature on the psychology of sex', *Psychological Bulletin*, 7: 335–42.

9

Feminist Theology: Myth, Mystery or Monster?

Elaine Graham

Exodus or ingress? Locating feminist studies of religion

Twenty-five years ago, on 14 November 1971, the Roman Catholic theologian and philosopher Mary Daly was invited to preach in Harvard Memorial Church, USA, the first woman to do so. Daly was rapidly gaining notoriety as a trenchant critic of women's oppression at the hands of the Christian Church; three years earlier, she had published *The Church and the Second Sex* (1968), its title consciously echoing that of Simone de Beauvoir's feminist classic. Upon reaching the pulpit, Daly announced her conviction that the irrevocable misogyny of the Christian religion obliged her to abandon the Church, and she urged all those who agreed with her to accompany her on a symbolic 'Exodus' to signify their refusal to remain within such a damaging institution. She then led a procession of hundreds of women and men out of the chapel (King, 1993: 170; Daly, 1993: 137ff).

Nearly a quarter of a century later, in April 1994, a group of women in an English cathedral were involved in a kind of reversal of Daly's exodus, as they became the first women to be ordained priests in the Church of England. As with Daly's action, the event carried a deal of symbolic significance: these were not the first women to be admitted to ordained ministry, but their induction into the Established Church carried sociological as well as ecclesiastical significance. The occasion was notable for the intensity of the media coverage, for an uncharacteristically Anglican exuberance at such a formal event – and for a blanket avoidance of the 'F-Word':

> 'Is it a great day for feminism?' I asked a visiting Anglican priest from Washington, DC, expectantly. 'It's a great day for the church,' she beamed in return. (Baxter, 1994: 12)

The twin poles of Daly's exodus and the ingress of women priests reflect far more than the mere passage of time. They reveal many of the perennial tensions – or dissonances, depending on one's viewpoint – between feminism and religion; and these contrasts help us to locate the issues which preoccupy those who are committed to working in academic studies of religion from a feminist standpoint. In this chapter, I want first to identify some of these 'fault-lines' which serve to demarcate the territory upon which feminist studies of religion are located – the 'borderlands' of contested debates, methods and objectives; and secondly to use some contemporary work in feminist Christian theology which illustrates some substantive areas of discussion, in the form of the three categories of 'myth', 'mystery' and 'monster'.

The two vignettes quoted earlier illustrate many of the tensions and contradictions concerning women and religion. Feminist studies of religion necessarily transcend the boundaries between the academy and the various faith-communities. Daly's protest arose not only from her own personal journey in relation to institutional religion, but from a struggle to establish the intellectual credibility of feminist theology in Church and academy. Similarly, the decision of the Church of England to ordain women followed fifteen years of scholarly debate over the *theological* foundations of ecclesiastical change: the tools of academic theology (especially of Church history and Biblical exegesis) were harnessed to the decision-making processes of a confessional community of faith.

A further tension is discernible in attitudes of women of religious faith towards the theory and practice of feminism itself. Feminist analysis – in all its diverse forms – has informed and affected contemporary studies of women and religion to varying degrees. Inevitably, opinion is divided between those who advocate an explicitly feminist analysis of the effects of religion on the lives of women, and those who eschew such a perspective. The new women priests were part of a campaign for the ordination of women which often felt uneasy about associating with a movement regarded by many within the Church as extreme, divisive and inimical to religion.[1]

Daly's rejection of patriarchal institutional religion is in stark contrast to other women's active struggle for the right to claim a priestly vocation and a place within the ministerial and symbolic life of the Church. However, the anatomy of feminist-inspired activity within religion most accurately spans a diversity of commitments. Many women actually occupy ambivalent, temporary or shifting vantage-points, neither absolutely or unequivocally 'out' or 'in'. Total rejection of religious institutions and world-views is but one end of a confessional and strategic continuum, along which also lie alternatives of resistance, reform and assimilation.

Yet the question for religious feminists – should I stay or should I go? – appears irrelevant and incomprehensible to many 'secular' feminists who wonder why their sisters should torture themselves so unnecessarily. This exposes an additional 'fault-line': that of the fundamental in/compatibility of a feminist standpoint with a religious conviction. Daly's excoriation of patriarchal religion serves as the supreme challenge to those who seek to combine religious faith with feminist integrity; but Daly's repudiation of such a possibility remains the only valid option for many.

However, Daly's anger at patriarchal religion is not only a refusal but also an acknowledgement of its power over women. It may rage against the abuses committed in the name of the Father (Daly, 1984) but it cannot deny the significance of religion in shaping the historical and contemporary structures, symbols and norms of patriarchy. Arguably, therefore, feminist analysis of women's subordination and contemporary gender relations fails to be adequately comprehensive if it neglects the role of religion.

Moreover, such a marginalisation of religion in the lives of women reflects some peculiarly modern and western presuppositions: the products of an intellectual tradition which is historically and culturally contingent. Secular feminism here reveals its roots in post-Enlightenment humanism which regards religion as a dimension of a pre-modern world of superstition and unreason; the eclipse of religious faith is seen as an inevitable consequence of the triumph of progress, science and rationality. Feminism is therefore assumed to be ineluctably atheistic; but this was not always so. Many of the so-called 'first-wave' feminist social reformers – such as Elizabeth Cady Stanton and Josephine Butler – were informed by religious faith. Their project was to liberate women from patriarchal culture and ideology; and a necessary part of that struggle was to rescue androcentric interpretations of sacred texts and teachings in order to restore what they regarded as religion's essentially egalitarian spirit (King, 1993).

Similarly, the preoccupations of black feminist thought often contrasts with the atheist and secular assumptions of white western feminism, in integrating references to spirituality and religion (Thistlethwaite, 1990). While these are by no means synonymous with church institutions or formal belief in a deity, they still transgress the boundaries of sacred/secular which most white academic feminism regard as axiomatic. And yet, under the pressures of global difference and post-modernity, the dichotomies of belief/unbelief, religious/secular, theistic/ humanist are beginning to collapse. As a consequence, it may be time to re-evaluate the marginalisation of feminist studies of religion. Religion may actually constitute a crucially contested territory as western society itself reconceives the boundaries of sacred and secular; and it is significant that this is proving another borderland for contemporary feminist philosophy and theology: a new and vital 'space' for much innovative feminist thinking on spirituality and subjectivity (Berry, 1992; Jantzen, 1995).

Feminist theology and its contexts

There is a growing awareness of questions of gender and feminism throughout the world's religions. Feminist studies of religion are beginning to emerge, and there is now a well-established academic literature on the role of religion – including the New Age and New Religious Movements – in defining and reinforcing the roles and symbolic representations of women (Ahmed, 1992; Cooey et al., 1991; Gross, 1993; Holm, 1994; King, 1995; Knott, 1994; Plaskow, 1990). However, I intend to concentrate on feminist Judeo-Christian theology and its derivatives in order to illustrate some of the contested areas I have already identified. Where are established knowledges and conventions being transgressed, and what new territories are being charted?

Christian theology

It is important to emphasise the diversity of feminist theological studies. Firstly, there is 'feminist theology', debating the fundamentals of Christian thought and practice. Its political focus is often one of seeking greater participation and recognition for women within the mainstream churches; although, as I have already remarked, not all those who campaigned so hard and long for the ordination of women, for example, would necessarily identify with feminist principles.

Global and cultural diversity

Women in the world churches are also gaining greater prominence in feminist studies of religion and in theology. The World Council of Churches declared 1988–98 the Decade of Solidarity with Women, which has served to highlight the global nature of feminist theology, and its transposition into a variety of cultural and ecclesial forms. Thus, it is important to consider 'womanist' (Black, Afro-American or African) feminist theologies; Latin American or Hispanic-American 'mujerista' theology; and also Asian feminist theology. All these genres reflect the roots of Christian cultural forms but have also merged with indigenous religious traditions – frequently practised and handed on by women in defiance of the 'Christianising' influences of patriarchal religion – to generate syncretic theologies (Chung, 1991; Grant, 1989; King, 1994; Tamez, 1989).

Woman-centred spirituality

A range of practices and philosophies span the spiritual quests of those who have chosen to pursue conventional Christian commitment outside the established institutions, to those who embrace forms of neo-paganism, such as varieties of ancient goddess religions, or 'wicca' rituals and communities that draw upon witchcraft and woman-centred spirituality (Plaskow and Christ, 1989). In attempting to depart from patriarchal imagery of the monotheistic, transcendent God, adherents may evoke feminine symbolism for the god/dess or even maintain a 'non-realist' understanding of divinity. For this reason, it has become conventional to use the term 'thealogy' for this strand of feminist spirituality.

Despite their diversity, all these theo/alogies share a critical awareness of the gendered nature of religious experience and doctrinal teaching. Feminist theo/alogy is constantly having to refute the misogyny of traditions that regard men as normative and fully human, and women as monstrous and misbegotten. The recognition that patriarchal perspectives and interests have silenced and subordinated women is the starting-point of all feminist critiques of theological tradition and discourse (Ruether, 1992).

One of the important tasks has been to challenge the inevitability of this exclusion, and to regard it instead as one of the ways in which patriarchal religion has marginalised and demonised women's identity and concerns. But equally, the reconstructive project of women's own naming of reality is deemed important; and so the second task of feminist theo/alogy is to articulate the grounds on which a renewed spiritual and political sensibility is to be claimed. Crucially, this frequently presents itself as an issue of whether the inherited tradition – teachings, texts, established practices – can be redeemed to provide sufficient and adequate resources for women's religious integrity, or whether women must consciously abandon the heritage as irrevocably patriarchal and misogynist. In practical terms, therefore, feminist theo/alogians' relationship to the established historical and textual tradition illustrates the shifting boundaries of *orthodoxy* and *heterodoxy*: on whose authority are certain sources and interpretations accepted as authentic and legitimate; and who determines in what direction revisionist understandings might move?

Feminist theo/alogy straddles many different boundaries, spanning the 'fault-lines' of theory/practice, public/confessional, academic/popular, outsider/insider, reform/rejection. However, there is a further conflict of loyalties often ignored by feminist theo/alogians, but of critical importance to the self-understanding of the discipline. It concerns the position of feminist theo/alogy within the broader community of feminist theory and academic practice, and the contested space around the boundaries between belief and unbelief. Can feminist theology justify its position as a legitimate field of study which offers both critical *and* reconstructive perspectives on the role and status of women?

Feminist theology: myth, mystery or monster?

To those without a formal religious background or commitment, the juxtaposition of the terms 'feminist' and 'theo/alogy' may seem ridiculous. By its nature, a discipline of 'feminist theo/alogy' will seem 'mythical, mysterious and monstrous'.[2] Mythical, understood as a world-view long since rendered anomalous and redundant, the relic of a pre-modern, pre-scientific age; mysterious in the sense of religious conviction in the modern world as incomprehensible and quaint at the least, dangerous and incoherent at worst; monstrous as fearful hybrid, the misbegotten ideological offspring of patriarchal religion. However, it may be possible to chart another course through this trinity of categories, in a way that not only illuminates the substance of feminist theological scholarship, but also underlines its diversity and draws out its potential for wider feminist endeavours in the academy.

Myth

One of the most important preoccupations of feminist theo/alogy is the critical interrogation of the major scriptures, stories and symbols of the Judeo-Christian tradition. The quintessential task is to expose the androcentric nature of most textual and historical sources. The assembled canon of myths, law and narratives has been deployed to foster and uphold patriarchal authority; but feminist theo/alogians claim an equal and opposite power, one of women's retelling and reclaiming of such resources. This establishes the priority for feminist theo/alogy of the twin tasks of *critique* and *reconstruction*.

In challenging the authority of androcentric interpretation, and replacing it with what they would regard as a more authentic witness, feminist theo/alogians seek to construct a theology of liberation from patriarchy that will recast the norms of conventional tradition by appealing to an alternative perspective rooted in the collective experience of women (Ruether, 1992). Some feminist theologians would argue that while the dominant traditions and their sources are patriarchal, alternative perspectives within the canon of scripture and tradition as it stands can support a more positive view. They argue that the tradition is in fact pluriform, and contains strands both of misogyny and affirmation. The latter Ruether calls 'usable tradition' (1992: 21) and serves for her to fuel a critical theology of liberation. This perspective would argue that the original teachings of Jesus and the earliest Christians were those of iconoclasm and prophetic witness, and that this constitutes the normative centre of the Christian message, the underlying 'critical principle' or hermeneutic against which all historical evidence should be judged (Ruether, 1992; Young, 1990).

Other perspectives go beyond a simple retrieval of the past, arguing that however the tradition is constituted, it still bears the marks of androcentric and ideological distortion. Elizabeth Schussler Fiorenza adopts what she calls 'a hermeneutics of suspicion' towards the tradition, acknowledging that texts are never neutral records of historical events but ideological documents, designed as works of apologetics (Fiorenza, 1983). The intention of the text is never clear; we have to reconstruct the social and ecclesial context which gave rise to the authoritative stories and myths of tradition, to read through them, to a world beyond and behind the text. The texts bear witness to a community of faith which articulated and contested its vision via the myths, rituals and texts which survive today. However, such scriptures assume no final authority. In Fiorenza's words, they are not 'archetypes' or blueprints for eternal truths, but must serve merely as 'prototypes': witnessing, albeit imperfectly and provisionally, to a vision that can ultimately only be authenticated via the inclusive practices of today's '*ekklesia* of equals'.

Mystery

Feminist theology has long emphasised the contribution of exceptional and visionary women to the critical and redemptive project. The collective re-membering of women – well-known and forgotten – from Christian history has been a key element of the reconstruction of the tradition according to women; and, in particular, the prominence of women in prophetic and millenarian movements has served as an example of the significance of women's radical vision at times of upheaval and renewal. Such exemplary figures – women deacons and missionaries in the earliest Christian communities, women mystics throughout the medieval and reformation periods, women prophetesses and preachers in the sixteenth and seventeenth centuries – suggest that women's appropriation of charismatic gifts has often been a powerful means of sub-verting patriarchal dominance and winning the space within which social and ecclesial change can be realised (Jantzen, 1984).

Parallels with the outbreak of religious fervour as an expression of frus-trated political ambition, and the 'hysterical' eruption of repressed psycho-sexual instincts, have frequently been drawn. Whether such religious protest is a channel for, or diversion from, effective social change is open to debate. However, it is intriguing to see how the transgressive potential of women mystics and prophetesses is currently a favourite theme of contem-porary Francophone feminists, especially Luce Irigaray and Julia Kristeva (Berry, 1992). They equate the realm of 'madness, holiness and poetry' as a unique channel for the feminised unconscious, or 'imaginary' which serves as a repository of uniquely woman-centred knowledge and experience. But this is not to be necessarily equated with conventional theism. In this sphere of feminist spirituality, 'the Goddess' has been supplanted by 'the Divine': a theo/alogical and philosophical term which speaks of divinity and transcen-dence in analogical and discursive, rather than referential, terms (Kim et al., 1993).

Women's recourse to mysticism is no surprise to such feminists, who see its transgressive potential to speak from a space not colonised by patriarchy and available to women for the articulation of an alternative discourse. As a result, many feminist theo/alogians are exploring how the arena of ritual, spirituality and liturgy may provide a 'space' – be that political, epistemo-logical or psychological – within which such transformative sensibilities may be forged (Berry, 1992; Graham, 1995a; Jantzen, 1995). Feminist liturgies are becoming particularly evocative and creative forms of feminist *praxis*. They re-enact the central events of the tradition, deploying word and symbol, frequently organising themselves around specific rites of passage, thereby connecting with the rhythms of everyday life (St. Hilda Community, 1991; Ruether, 1985).

Monster

Feminist theologians can assemble a gruesome rogues' gallery of arch-misog-ynists, beginning with the Church Fathers [sic]. Church tradition has offered the legacy of woman as either the mystical source of all sin, in the person of Eve, or as the embodiment of sexlessness, in the contradictory figure of the Virgin Mary, who effortlessly combines the twin vocations of women under patriarchy: those of virgin *and* mother!

So how are feminists reading these images? Mary Daly has exposed much of the 'monstrous' legacy of gynophobia in Church and society, and has sought to name new words and strategies that harness the power and anger of women in a 'cosmic covenant' to overthrow patriarchy and its religious hand-maidens. The death of God the Father is an essential part of that, thereby releasing women to articulate a distinctive spiritual and ethical reality – a new way of 'Be-ing' uninhibited by men's hatred of women. In Daly's more recent work, the weaving/spinning of a new language – new ways of speaking and naming – constitutes a harnessing of the transgressive and monstrous power of women, and a celebration of their autonomous and aw(e)ful potential (Daly, 1987).

The role of religion within the Third World stands in many respects in complete contradiction to the story of 'secular' western contexts: religion as a primary source for revolutionary movements, serving as the metaphor for resistance to the globalising tendencies of industrial modernity. Christian women in the Third World represent a dynamic force in contemporary feminist theo/alogy. They serve to remind Liberation Theology that its struggle against colonialism, militarism and economic exploitation must also contain an analysis of the endemic sexism in those systems; but they also challenge First-World feminists to recognise the significance of class and 'race' (as well as gender) for a vision of global justice (King, 1994).

Thus, the vitality of womanist and mujerista perspectives, not to mention their leadership and ministry, provides a glimpse of religion as a powerful social force which, when allied to a feminist social analysis, offers new ways of 'being church' for many women. They arise from a socio-political context in which the articulation of women's experience is also the naming of the evil monsters of racism, poverty and dispossession that frame and underpin the lives of women in the Third World. Here, the resources of faith are integral to the struggle for justice and empowerment; but there is often a contradiction at the heart of such a theological vision. It provides the vocabulary and underpins the networks by which women find a voice and engage in social transformation; but these are frequently very conventional articulations. For example, the figure of the Virgin Mary serves both as a symbol of conservative prescriptions of submissive womanhood, and also as a populist icon of the 'preferential option for the poor' at the heart of the Church's social theology (Chung, 1991; Tamez, 1989). This is indicative of another 'fault-line' in the process of critique and reconstruction: that between feminine imagery as the reinforcement of patriarchal norms and the authentic expression of woman-centred culture.

A reclamation of women's sexuality is another example of the way feminist theo/alogians are not only challenging the given norms of the tradition, but reconceiving new ways to express and articulate women's spiritual and political aspirations: from women's sexuality as monstrous and taboo, to erotic power as redemptive. Some of this work speaks from a lesbian-feminist standpoint as the articulation of the transgressive passion of women, be it friendship (Stuart, 1995) or erotic love (Hunt, 1991). In self-giving, unconditional love that dares to break the taboos and cross the boundaries of convention, woman-identified women are the bearers of a Christlike witness. Carter Heyward (1989) sees sexual desire as a elemental force, tamed by heterosexism and convention, but now freed by lesbian passion to achieve a new personal and political vision.

From theory to praxis

My own interests in feminist theo/alogy are, broadly, orientated more towards the realm of Christian practice than Christian thought. My earliest research was an enquiry into women's virtual absence from theological literature about ministry and pastoral care. Pastoral Theology, as conventionally conceived, affords little attention to the pastoral needs of women; it is a discipline almost entirely devoid of any 'client-centred' perspective, so women are practically invisible as the recipients of care. Yet their historical exclusion from the accredited or ordained leadership of the churches means they rarely feature as the agents and ministers of care, either. This set me thinking about the possibilities of subverting these dominant paradigms of 'clericalism' and 'sexism' via the recovery of marginal traditions of woman-centred support and care, the recognition of formerly occluded areas of women's pastoral needs throughout the life-cycle, and the forging of new models of pastoral practice within a feminist framework (Graham and Halsey, 1993).

Essentially, therefore, I am concerned to trace whether communities of religious faith actually practise what they preach; and whether forms of feminist *praxis* in liturgy and ritual, in new forms of giving and receiving care and support, new ways of envisioning and building communities of faith and action, may actually serve as transformative practices which point towards a redemptive vision of the Ruether's 'full humanity of women'.

In other work, I've been concerned to go beyond the rather superficial references to gender difference which characterise much of the debate on the ordination of women and to explore how religion both reflects and constructs gender identity, relations and representations. In this respect, I find myself at the 'border' of feminist theory (most particularly, theories of gender) and feminist theology: interrogating and interpreting one to the other, hoping to develop and consolidate strands of dialogue between the two (Graham, 1995a, 1995b).

Feminist theo/alogy seeks to move from misogyny and injustice to self-affirmation and empowerment. In the process, it transcends many boundaries, and necessarily inhabits the contested territory of critique and reconstruction. Feminist theo/alogians increasingly identify their allegiances as transcending the divisions between the academic, the civic and the ecclesial; they argue that purposeful community underpins feminist responsibility and construct models of 'Women-Church' or basic communities of women which intentionally span the demarcations of intellectual and symbolic, theoretical and practical. The realm of feminist *praxis* – which many feminist theo/alogians would claim as the heart of their endeavours – signals a commitment to value-informed and value-directed action which cannot be satisfied with the abstractions of traditional academia.

Similarly, in deploying the aspirations of sexual passion and social justice, feminist theo/alogians depart from many of the acceptable academic criteria of objectivity and decorum: the personal as the political (and theo/alogical). In this respect, feminist theo/alogy shares the concerns of other feminist disciplines in challenging the primacy of rationality and abstraction over other forms of knowing and acting. Yet feminist theo/alogians are also daring to recover some of the repressed categories of western modernity: the categories of the sacred, ritual, and the divine, are re-emerging as ambivalent but powerful dimensions of feminist discourse and subjectivity. Is this the final taboo: the ultimate borderland for feminism?

Notes

1. Baxter's account of the ordination of the first women priests in the Church of England confirms other evidence which suggests a division amongst the campaigners for the ordination in this respect. As with many other areas of political strategy and intellectual endeavour, therefore, not all women are feminists – but equally, not all feminists are women. For a more detailed account of the politics of the campaigns for the ordination of women, see Dowell and Williams (1994) and Armstrong (1993)

2. These categories were originally inspired by Marina Warner's study of the 'myths and monsters' of masculinity (Warner, 1994).

References

Ahmed, Leila (1992) *Women and Gender in Islam*. New Haven: Yale University Press.

Armstrong, Karen (1993) *The End of Silence: Women and Priesthood*. London: Fourth Estate.

Baxter, Sally (1994) 'I'm not a feminist but . . .', *New Statesman and Society*. 18 March: 12–13.

Berry, Philippa (1992) 'Woman and space according to Kristeva and Irigaray', in P. Berry and A. Wernick (eds), *Shadow of Spirit: Postmodernism and Religion*. London: Routledge. pp. 250–64.

Chung, Hyun-kyung (1991) *Struggle to be the Sun Again*. New York: Orbis.

Cooey, Pamela M., Eakin, William and McDaniel, Jay (eds) (1991) *After Patriarchy: Feminist Transformations of the World Religions*. New York: Orbis.

Daly, Mary (1968) *The Church and the Second Sex*. New York: Harper & Row.

Daly, Mary (1984) *Gyn/Ecology: The Metaethics of Radical Feminism*. Boston: Beacon Press.

Daly, Mary (1986) *Beyond God the Father*. London: Women's Press.

Daly, Mary (1987) *Websters' First New Intergalactic Wickedary of the English Language*. Boston: Beacon Press.

Daly, Mary (1993) *Outercourse: the Be-Dazzling Voyage*. London: Women's Press.

Dowell, S. and Williams, J. (1994) *Bread, Wine and Women: The Ordination Debate in the Church of England*. London: Virago.

Fiorenza, Elizabeth Schüssler (1983) *In Memory of Her: A Feminist Theological Reconstruction of Christian Origins*. London: SCM.

Fiorenza, Elizabeth Schüssler (1994) *Searching the Scriptures (2 Vols)*. London: SCM.

Graham, Elaine L. (1995a) 'From space to woman-space', *Feminist Theology*, No. 9: 11–34.

Graham, Elaine L. (1995b) *Making the Difference: Gender, Personhood and Theology*. London: Mowbray.

Graham, Elaine L. and Halsey, Margaret (eds) (1993) *Life-Cycles: Women and Pastoral Care*. London: SPCK.

Grant, Jacquelyn (1989) *White Women's Christ and Black Women's Jesus*. Atlanta: Scholars' Press.

Gross, Rita M. (1993) *Buddhism after Patriarchy: A Feminist History, Analysis and Reconstruction of Buddhism*. Albany: State University of New York Press.

Heyward, Carter (1989) 'Sexuality, love, and justice', in Judith Plaskow and Carol Christ (eds), *Weaving the Visions*. San Francisco: Harper & Row. pp. 293–301.

Holm, Jean (ed.) (1994) *Women and Religion*. London: Pinter.

Hunt, Mary (1991) *Fierce Tenderness: A Feminist Theology of Friendship*. New York: Crossroad.

Jantzen, Grace M. (1984) *Julian of Norwich*. London: SPCK.

Jantzen, Grace M. (1995) *Power and Gender in Christian Mysticism*. Cambridge: Cambridge University Press.

Kim, C.W. Maggie, St. Ville, Susan M. and Simonaitis, Susan M. (eds) (1993) *Transformations: Theology and the French Feminists*. Minneapolis: Fortress.

King, Ursula (1993) *Women and Spirituality*, 2nd edn. London: Macmillan.

King, Ursula (ed.) (1994) *Feminist Theology from the Third World: a Reader*. London: SPCK.

King, Ursula (ed.) (1995) *Religion and Gender*. Oxford: Blackwell.

Knott, Kim (1994) 'Women and religion in post-war Britain', in Gerald Parsons (ed.), *The Growth of Religious Diversity: Britain from 1945. Volume II: Issues*. London: Routledge. pp. 199–230.

Loades, Ann (ed.) (1990) *Feminist Theology: A Reader*. London: SPCK.

Plaskow, Judith (1990) *Standing Again at Sinai: Judaism from a Feminist Perspective*. San Francisco: Harper & Row.

Plaskow, Judith and Christ, Carol (eds) (1989) *Weaving the Visions: New Patterns in Feminist Spirituality*. San Francisco: Harper Collins.

Ruether, Rosemary Radford (1985) *Women-Church: Theology and Practice of Feminist Liturgical Communities*. San Francisco: Harper & Row.

Ruether, Rosemary Radford (1991) 'Renewal or new creation? Feminist spirituality and historical religion', in Sneja Gunew (ed.), *A Reader in Feminist Knowledge*. London: Routledge. pp. 277–89.

Ruether, Rosemary Radford (1992) *Sexism and God-Talk*, 2nd edn. London: SCM Press.

St. Hilda Community (1991) *Women Included: A Book of Services and Prayers*. London: SPCK.

Stuart, Elizabeth (1995) *Just Good Friends: Towards a Lesbian and Gay Theology of Relationships*. London: Mowbray.

Tamez, Elsa (ed.) (1989) *Through Her Eyes: Women's Theology in Latin America*. New York: Orbis.

Thistlethwaite, Susan Brooks (1990) *Sex, Race and God*. London: Geoffrey Chapman.

Warner, Marina (1994) *Managing Monsters*. London: Vintage.

Young, Pamela Dickey (1990) *Feminist Theology/Christian Theology: In Search of Method*. Minneapolis: Fortress.

Young, Serenity (ed.) (1992) *An Anthology of Sacred Texts By and About Women*. London: Harper Collins/Pandora.

10

What are Feminist Academics For?

Sue Wise

Disjunctures: neither fish nor fowl

The purpose of this chapter is to explore 'what feminist academics are for' through an examination of my own experiences as a worker in higher education. It is possible that most people go through life feeling that they don't 'fit', recognising that the way they live, or the things they feel and think, or the way they look, is somehow at odds with the way that it's *supposed* to be. I know I have. Most of my life I have felt like an in-betweenie, never quite belonging in the milieu in which I found myself: a working-class girl in a middle-class grammar school, an out lesbian in a homophobic world, a feminist woman in the last bastion of male privilege – higher education. However one deals with these contradictions, with being an in-betweenie, it seems clear that they offer an interesting way of understanding one's position in the social world and of how ontology relates to epistemology. Like others who share such an ontological position, I am constantly required to account for what I am doing here, what it *means* for me to be here. In what follows I explore how I 'fit' in relation to my job of work as an academic, a site where the identities of working class, lesbian, feminist and woman form an alien territory.

The starting point to explore the way in which my place in higher education is framed is not initially related to identity, but rather to the physical reality of distance, separation and travel. Each week I embark on the 56.4 mile, one and a half hour journey that separates my home from my work, my home self from my professional self. The disjuncture that I feel between my self and my self in academe therefore starts with a physical and practical manifestation. I travel through a borderland: the journey home from work is a physical territory, a kind of corridor through which I travel, sometimes on a daily basis. But this is a geographical space that is also a symbolic space, one in which I try to make sense of the way that I live and the work that I do. My 'work' self sleeps in a different bed, drinks different water, engages with different people, from my 'home' self. In this parallel universe I 'become' a different person because everything and everyone that I interact with, and define myself by, changes.

Work and home

I have been doing this journeying for six years now, and I know I am not alone in this situation: many colleagues and friends with partners (usually those with partners also working in higher education) are leading such bifurcated existences, the Jekylls and Hydes of academia. We have to go where the work is, and in higher education the openings are few and the location rarely convenient. The living patterns available seem to be either one partner having a part-time home life and a career in a totally separate place, or else both partners working in the same university or, sometimes, the same department. I can't think which is the worse arrangement. Certainly I suffer from the dislocation of living in two places when I long for home, while others deal with it better than I. It is no doubt a serious personal failing, but I am a Capricorn after all – home-loving, steady, unadventurous (boring!). But could I cope with the other extreme of working in the same department as my partner?

If I were a husband or a wife perhaps I wouldn't have this problem, since tradition and expectation might offer a solution. It seems to be the case often that wives still follow husbands' careers, or, if they don't, it is they who have put their foot down and said 'I am not uprooting myself to follow you, if you want a home base, you will have to commute!' Never have I heard a male academic say that he is moving in order to be with his female partner. The difficulties of having a professional career as an academic, while simultaneously conducting a relationship with another academic, is a continuous puzzle to me and one that is rarely overtly discussed. I'm sure I can't be the only one who finds this problematic, but perhaps I am one of the few where the solution is not arrived at through traditional means.

The realms of work and home are confused for most of us who work in higher education. It is extremely difficult to place boundaries around what is work and what is home. If we have a study at home, if we bring work home because we can't get it done in the 'office hours' of the institution, if we choose to spend our 'research days' at home in order to avoid the same interruptions – then the border between what is home and what is work is blurred at best, and non-existent at worst. If we add to that a partner who is similarly engaged in work activity that is often best performed on home turf, then we have a situation where the borders between work and home-life become, not so much negotiable, but a constant potential source of friction.

If boundaries within the home are a problem, then how on earth would I deal with them in the workplace too? It seems very easy for work to 'take over' when it comes into the home in a way that cannot happen the other way around: a couple in a department are still only a small minority after all. 'Work' is more frequently, and necessarily, something that happens 'at home', so that all of one's life becomes highly pressurised work, but at least I can try and ensure that my 'home' does not come to work. All things considered, perhaps the trauma of separation of workplace from home is an easier option all round.

I am by trade a social work academic.[1] In order to become a social work academic, I have previously practised as a professional social worker and my qualifications are a mixture of academic degrees and professional training and experience. In addition to these, I did a Sociology PhD before becoming a lecturer,[2] all together thirteen years of studying and practising to be qualified for this job. The transition from professional practitioner to academic was not an easy one and involved a major occupational culture shock in two ways.

Firstly, the shift from the professional world of social work to that of higher education was a massive culture shock in work ethics. I came from a profession which is (numerically) female dominated and necessarily involves co-operative working, to a higher education sector which is male dominated and intensely competitive. The male domination and competition aren't necessarily connected, since many women academics are as intensely competitive as men, although I wonder if this would still be the case if the proportion of women working in higher education was more equal. Clearly, the male domination of social work academically is highly problematic, given the tiny proportion of men who actually inhabit the profession as a whole (SSI, 1991), although this is little discussed or commented upon, even by the Central Council for Education and Training in Social Work (CCETSW) which prides itself on its equal opportunities stance.

Secondly, alongside the huge shift in occupational culture, I moved from being a well-established, successful and respected professional in one sphere, to being a novice, a total incompetent who needed to learn a new trade, that of teaching, researching, administrating and generally how to operate, within a new and very different kind of organisation. This was a very deskilling experience and one that was exacerbated by the current emphasis on demonstrating performance through various means of inspection. Even in local government, I have never worked in an environment that is so thoroughly inspected at every turn: in the few years that I have been in higher education I have been personally appraised (twice), considered by committees for promotion (twice), and my department has been internally reviewed, externally reviewed (twice), externally assessed for teaching quality (twice) and externally assessed for research output. And in between these inspections, as a new academic I have had to learn to teach, write and be an administrator in a new system, virtually overnight. Those with pre-Teaching Quality Assessment and Research Assessment Exercise experience tell me that at least it was possible in the 'old days' to get teaching experience under your belt before it could be reasonably expected that you would start publishing. These days, you must do it all, simultaneously. If you can't hit the ground running, even though the playing field isn't level (to mix metaphors wildly), then you don't stand a chance. I have heard, on more than one occasion, (female) senior academics use the willingness to work both evenings and weekends as a measure of how 'far' someone is going to go: working excessive hours, it seems, has crept up slowly to become the 'norm' for those who want success, or, increasingly, who just want to do the job properly. Clearly, those with responsibilities at home, and those who simply (and reasonably?) want a life outside work, are destined not to 'go far'.

This bland description of how I got here disguises the actual lengthy and convoluted manner of my arrival within the academy. A former student said to me recently, 'You know, the first thing you say to new groups of students is, "I'm working class, I'm a lesbian, and when I left school I went to work in Walls' Sausage Factory."' Good grief, I thought, do I really? I know I frequently joke about getting into higher education by the backdoor after leaving school at sixteen and later studying 'O' levels and 'A' levels at college and nightschool. Wheelchair-using students usually enjoy the irony of this – they're still using the backdoor, even after they got here! I think the ex-student was overstating it somewhat, but there is a sense in which she was probably right – I do want my students to be clear about how I identify myself. But is this because I want to position myself within and against the institution, or because I want to position myself alongside them? There are important differences between the two.

Being 'in' but not 'of' the academy

It is no longer fashionable to speak of identity politics in order to understand the multi-faceted nature of the lives of individuals. Multiple identities can be seen as shifting and changing and equally important and their 'meaning' for an individual can be seen as crucial, although this approach has now come under attack as supposedly 'essentialist'. My own list of how I identify myself includes 'woman', lesbian, feminist, working class, amongst others, but the forms of my own 'identities' in the context of my academic professional self are not equally relevant; instead they are context-specific, and depend upon: which 'bit' of the academy I am engaged with, which 'constituency' I am interacting with (students, colleagues, institutions, disciplines), and how I am, in turn, seen by these 'others'.

While most academic feminist women seem to experience mainstream academe as an assault on their identity as women, this is not always my own experience. Certainly I am very aware that at times I am the only woman in a room full of grey suits and I see all around me the ways in which the boys' club that is higher education gatekeeps women's participation and privileges only boys who 'play the game' and kiss the right backsides. Although I remember from time to time to be truly shocked that this state of affairs can persist in a profession purported to contain such great minds and liberal values, I really am not surprised. In this sense, being a woman in higher education is like being a woman everywhere else: male privilege abounds and is fairly intransigent.

In this setting, my identity as a person with a 'working class' background predominates, and deeply affects the way that I feel about the work that I do. This is because it is the only place left that I 'feel' working class, where I am surrounded by people (other academics and many students, women as well as men) who are decidedly posher than me, who have had a 'better' education, gone to the 'right' school, speak differently and, for all I know, think differently.

Outside of my place of work, and paradoxically because I have used a similar education institution to effect my own social mobility, and because I now work in this institution, I am to all intents and purposes a member of the educated middle class. That is, people (neighbours, family) see me as middle class because they compare me with themselves, whereas colleagues who might compare me with others in our institution, see me – how? In a way, how they see me isn't important, because what matters and is consequential is how I see myself, in particular how I see, understand and experience what it is to be 'my self'. This has epistemological as well as ontological ramifications: it affects what I think I 'know', what I feel some certainty about knowing, and it also affects what I feel about this and how I behave, accordingly.

The way that I feel at work is that although I am in. I am not of, the place and I have, therefore, a critical response to the institution which is embedded in those autobiographical structures and meanings referred to by the short-hand of 'identity'. Similarly, while I occupy the margins of the academy, along with feminist colleagues, my place on the margin is also fractured along the identity lines of sexuality and class. In other words, I don't quite 'fit' anywhere: in the margins my identities of sexuality and class marginalise me yet further, while in the mainstream my identity as a woman and a feminist woman overlay these. The notion of working class identity implies a fixity and unity that aren't actually there when I think about it in a more measured and analytical way. That is, emotionally I have recourse to ideas about class and background, while analytically I know that I always felt an outsider even before I got an education and now I have it there's no going back – I am not of that background and class anymore, and in a sense I never was. Most of my undergraduate students are women who have come into the university via access[3] routes and so, on one level, I identify with them and I can let them know that I have struggled in the same way and that, if I can do it, so can they (oh God! I think I'm a role model!). For all that I have points in common with students, these are points in common with a past that I can never return to, and nor would I want to. I am helping them to escape from an identity that I escaped from myself in an institutional setting where my current experience gives the lie to that possibility ever being completely successful. There are other issues that this positioning of myself around ideas about identity raises, which I shall come to later, but first I must say something about positioning myself in relation to theory and practice.

As feminists we have made much of the relationship between the personal and the political and between theory and practice. In academic social work, those connections are absolutely central, which leads both to exciting possibilities and to enormous dilemmas. As a social work academic, the fragmentations of my work are great. I do not have the option of an ivory tower existence, since my work has a grounded instrumentality. My concerns are with how to teach well and publish widely, but also I must work effectively with professional social workers who are part of the training process, design my curriculum and teaching methods to be acceptable to both the vocational validating body and to the university, as well as always remembering that what I do with students has serious consequences, not only for them, but also for the clients that they will soon be let loose on.

It is very difficult to have so many constituents to please, so many and often contradictory expectations to meet, pushing and pulling my professional self in different directions. I toyed with the idea of looking for a job within a clearly defined 'pure' discipline (i.e. sociology, the focus of my PhD) rather than in the applied field from which I had come (i.e. social work) and even declined a temporary post in a sociology department. If I had that choice again, in retrospect I wonder what I would do. At the time, I hadn't fully realised the huge differences between working in a 'pure' field and an 'applied' field. For, if the shift between competent professional and academic ingenue wasn't deskilling enough, I very quickly became aware of the negative status accorded to those who teach 'vocational' subjects in 'applied' disciplines vis-à-vis those who teach 'pure' subjects in 'real' disciplines. As a consequence, and despite the extremely lengthy time necessary to become qualified for the job of teaching social work in a university setting, it is hard to feel that the social work academic is taken seriously by the wider academic community, which includes those feminist academics who value 'theory' above all else.

'Life-long learning', and the necessary connections between education and training, are increasingly promoted by government and senior academic commentators alike. Yet there are still many in higher education who do not share this enthusiasm. The divide between 'vocational' and 'academic' teaching (or training vs. education) has become the new binary divide within higher education, with the former occupying the same status as the old polytechnics. In other words, second class. There are a number of reasons for this, including the elevation of abstract theorising as the zenith of intellectual achievement, and a valid concern about the outside 'interference' in teaching of validating bodies whose concerns are at odds with the aims of the university. In my experience of teaching a vocational course within a university setting, neither of these concerns can be lightly dismissed as élitism.

In 'pure' social science areas one would hope that the main emphasis is on thinking critically – everything is open to question, everything is open to challenge, there are no 'correct' answers. 'Pure' disciplines have the luxury of independence; they need 'only' concern themselves with their academic community, potential funders and student numbers. Teaching can be innovative, experimental even, the curriculum can shift and change according to new developments in the field, and the changing interests of the developing and changing academic. Students can be exhorted to take risks, to study abstract and obscure areas, the more abstract and obscure the better. For students and for staff, the only limitation on what is possible is the imagination of each, coupled with the practicality of wanting to get a good degree result. In a 'pure' discipline, then, one needs only to have cognisance of the discipline, the funding context and the needs of the students.

In an 'applied' discipline such as social work, there are many other constituencies to be considered, including CCETSW, which is the professional validating body of the British social work qualification; members of the profession, who both use the social work knowledge produced in the academy and take part in the educational process; and finally the clients who are at the receiving end of both student and qualified social worker attention. In 'applied' areas such as this, students need to have some solid ground to build upon, rather than to critique and deconstruct and, indeed, if one questions the received wisdom, this creates enormous anxiety amongst students. Challenging here is experienced as pulling out the rug from under the students and it also goes against the grain of the training regulators of CCETSW, who have a clearly laid out syllabus and clearly preferred means of teaching and assessment, based explicitly on a 'competence'[4] model.

The level of intellectual and pedagogical independence, then, for vocational courses is a serious problem for those academics in higher education who teach and research in these areas. At worst it means that students are encouraged to learn an entirely instrumental set of 'facts' by rote in order that they should know how to cope with this or that social work problem. In a sense they may learn 'what' to think, not 'how' to think. Yet problems with a totally abstract theorising should not be overlooked. There should be as much to concern us in an academic approach that is totally divorced from life, where the elegance of a theoretical turn of phrase matters more than the relevance that it might have to everyday living. There is a tension for me between being excited about ideas and theorising in precisely this way, and wanting there also to be an impact of ideas on the real world. I suffer from a kind of academic Protestant ethic, perhaps a legacy from my social work background, in that I want what I do to make a difference in the world.

Some days I hate my job and sometimes I get excited by the fact that it is an applied one, that it can offer access to higher education to women who will be doing good work with disadvantaged people. There is pleasure to be taken in skilfully guiding students towards the integration of practice with theory and vice versa. Perhaps this is where I occupy yet another 'in-betweenie' identity, in between the pure theory and the instrumental application. This results from having been a practitioner in the field about which I teach. As a practitioner, I used to bemoan the fact that social work texts had little to tell me about the work that I did. They were detached and separate and the connection between theory and practice rarely seemed to be made successfully. I wonder if I have become that kind of academic, and I wonder if it is inevitable. After all, it is a long time since I was a social worker and things have changed dramatically. Both the changes and distance in time between 'me academic now' and 'me social worker then' create a detachment, the kind of detachment that I used to critique so mercilessly in others, and this forms yet one more of my fragmented identities.

Being 'alongside' students

As a woman from my kind of background, there are many areas of commonality between myself and my students, which can create for me confusing and frustrating relations with students. Typically I experience students as having simultaneously high expectations of me and little respect for me. Students expect, not just *a* thing, but *every*thing, from me. I must be an expert in whatever field the student needs to write an essay on, and I must be able to deal with the fragmentary and contradictory demands that students impose, which includes not only totally up to the minute knowledge of the academic literature and debates on a very wide range of subjects, but also an overview of the current state of (all) social work practice. And I must be able to give cutting-edge opinions on those areas of social work about which I have published and have a national reputation. But I can't meet these demands: I can't be simultaneously the perfect academic and the perfect practitioner, and also the perfect feminist critic of each and of the institution in which I work (something which is also 'required' by some of these constituents). Despite the requirements and demands of students' charter, I cannot meet all of these demands.

At the same time that they turn to me as an 'authority', the students simultaneously deny that authority by virtue of the fact that I am too much 'like them'. I am too 'nice' to be taken seriously as an academic. If I have no airs and graces and don't 'fancy myself' enough, then I can't be a 'proper' academic. Perhaps most important of all, if I don't dress things up in mystificatory language and am able to explain complex phenomena in everyday, accessible language, then I do not pass the 'real academic' test. A bit like Groucho Marx, who never wanted to belong to a club that would have him because that proved that it was unworthy, so working-class students of working-class teachers seem to feel cheated that they have not got the 'real' thing too. Élitism, here, is something that students have striven for, and to arrive at university only to find that your 'own kind' are there before you in positions of authority is an extreme disappointment. How much more gratifying to find a world that *is* different and élitist, but one that you too can now join. None of this should be surprising. I wanted to 'escape' my working-class roots, and why should present day students feel any differently?

My status as an academic seems to be 'tainted' by vocational teaching and with my inability to put on academic airs and graces. One might think that social work students and colleagues would appreciate me for exactly those reasons. In practice it seems to be the case that most social work students despise social work academics and many social work practitioners also resent us. I well remember this from my own days as a student on a social work course. The contempt comes from being seen as a 'failed' social work practitioner, and I have even been told – with a straight face – 'those who can, do, and those who can't, teach'. Students typically think that I have nothing to teach them because I have not recently been in practice. Social work practitioners often share the same views, not least because they do have a genuine grievance that their experiences are very little reflected in what passes for social work 'knowledge'. On top of that they have other resentments, because they think that social work academics have higher status, better pay and conditions and, oh yes, what about all those lengthy holidays?

This is one of the features of my job that I find particularly deskilling, since it simultaneously denies my former skills as a practitioner at the same time as questioning my present skills as an academic. I find myself, almost in spite of myself (and note these warring selves), wondering if I really am here under false pretences. Do I have any useful role or function at all? This is a particularly disempowering aspect of my working life because of the fact that I spend a lot of time with these people: contact with students and with social workers constitutes one of the main parameters of my working life and it is therefore not surprising that it affects how I think of myself and the job that I do.

While I think that students from a similar background have all kinds of ambivalent feelings about me, I certainly have ambivalent feelings about them. I do not want to be their friend, nor their confidante, and given that I receive such little support for my position as an academic, I do want a measure of respect and acknowledgement that I have earned the position that I hold. Contrary to much of the received wisdom in feminist pedagogy (reviewed in Luke and Gore, 1992), I do not want to be 'alongside' my students, but instead I want there to be very clear, explicit and agreed boundaries between us. A key connecting theme for me between being a feminist academic and being a social work academic is that of the perceived illegitimacy of using authority in both roles. In both spheres it seems to me that the 'problem' of authority is dealt with most unsatisfactorily, apparently by 'giving it away' through talk of 'empowerment' (Ward and Mullender, 1991).

Clearly social workers and their clients, and academics and their students, are in artificially-created, structurally unequal, instrumentally specific and, usually, time-limited relationships. All unequal relationships carry the potential for exploitation or abuse, and to acknowledge this means to acknowledge the necessity to guard against such an outcome. There are a number of ways of approaching this and the solutions offered in social work bear close resemblance to those proffered by writers on feminist pedagogy. In social work, it is argued, both female social workers and their (usually) female clients share positions of structured subordination in patriarchal society; therefore the worker should do all she can to establish an equal working relationship, working alongside the client in order to 'empower' her through consciousness raising. The flaws with this proposal are immediately obvious when one considers the frequent legitimate control and gatekeeping functions that social workers perform. Perhaps the flaws are less obvious in the academic-student context.

Feminist academics frequently feel guilty about the fact that they are in a superior position to their students, that they have control over an important part of their lives (that is, what degree marks they get) and that they can be a very influential figure in a student's development. Some try to deal with that guilt by simple denial: they deny the power that they hold, by making friends of their students and by devising means of not having to assess and evaluate their work, sometimes going so far as to eschew evaluation altogether. This is all well and good on courses where marks do not matter, but it is totally inadequate for the vast majority of students in higher education. What they need, and what I need, are clear boundaries. I am in a position of power and authority in relation to their lives and the only guard against exploitation of that role is for it to be clearly and unambiguously owned and stated. While they have to jump through hoops and I am the one holding the hoop, it is disingenuous of me to handle my authority through denial of its very existence. Similarly, some students place their feminist lecturers on an unreal pedestal and fall 'in love' with them, either intellectually or romantically, hanging on their every word, taking all their courses, turning up with one 'problem' after another that needs lengthy, tearful discussion. I have long since ceased to be flattered by such attention and, instead, have recognised the very vulnerable position that such a student places herself in. For her sake, as well as mine, this is one of the clearest examples available where clear boundaries are absolutely essential, and where woolly notions of 'sisterhood' are totally inappropriate.

Reprise: what are feminist academics for?

The role of 'the academic' in the late twentieth century is a topic that concerns many, and has been theorised in terms of the rejection of the age of science and reason by intellectuals who have lost their role and are searching for a post-modern substitute (Bauman, 1988). Feminist academics have these lofty concerns to deal with, but they also have a more grounded agenda with which to grapple. Given that feminist scholarship is avowedly partisan and is seen by many to be an integral, if not leading, part of the feminist struggle for social transformation, we must examine whether it is possible, or desirable, to see feminist academics in this way. In other words, is the role of the feminist academic (and see here Morley and Walsh, 1995) that of the urban sophisticate revolutionary, or is it 'just a job' in the public sector, like being a nurse or a civil servant?

If we see it as just another public sector job, something which many writers on feminist pedagogy are loath to do, then we can see that feminist academics are located squarely within an overall political framework that determines what is possible through financial and policy controls creating national as well as local constraints on what can be done. The broader context that I have sketched out above includes the constant evaluation and assessment of teaching staff and institutions, lack of funding and poor working conditions, overcrowded classrooms, and ambiguous relationships with vocational partners and validators, amongst many other negative elements. In a climate where the UK government is hostile to the higher education sector in general, and to anything vaguely 'pinko' or subversive in particular, it seems clear that the role of 'academic freedom' becomes crucial and precious here and something that feminist academics need to be clearly defending. What is less clear, however, is how many of us are willing to make use of our academic freedom if we want to 'get on', or when, as is increasingly possible, we are threatened with possible redundancy or 'early retirement'. It is in this practical world of cuts and threats to livelihood that the realities of principles versus pragmatism are being played out: as I discovered long ago, if I am reliant upon my job to pay my mortgage, then I am only rarely going to take the risk of being unable to pay my mortgage.

The atmosphere and constraints created by external forces impinge massively upon students, whose day-to-day lives affect how they are able to 'consume' what is on offer to them at university. The assumption seems to be, in some of the more romanticised discussions of feminist pedagogy and the feminist presence in the academy more widely, that these things are almost an irrelevancy, that some kinds of students, women's studies students specifically, are different, and that 'feminist revolution' *can* take place in these classrooms. But this belies the realities of huge funding shifts, dramatic changes in the composition and scale of higher education, large student numbers, students with debts and three jobs who are barely awake, anxious students demanding instrumental learning in order to equip them for the jobs market. In the same way that feminist academics may be doing 'just a job', so now many students are doing courses 'just' to get the qualification.

If this sounds pessimistic, it really isn't meant to be. There are no doubt still some students, female and male, who will have life-changing and positive experiences of higher education, who will be challenged and excited by ideas, and whose histories, and perhaps those of others, will be changed by the experience. In my experience, the biggest difference in students' 'before and after' stories is in mature women returners, for whom exposure to ideas, sometimes feminist ideas, coupled with a taste of freedom from the constraints of who they have been, often produces the kind of radical life changes which some feminist pedagogues would like to promote. But what I am arguing is that if this happens, then it happens regardless of, or in spite of, the constraining features of higher education. Such students are motivated by a great need and hunger; they are self-starters and, whatever obstacles are placed in their way, they will overcome them. This student usually is a single parent with four children and is *still* the only one to get all her assignments in on time. Just as students aren't completely determined by external circumstances, so the particular attributes of an individual teacher do not determine her impact as a teacher.

If all of us who are feminist academics could agree upon our role and purpose, and set out to pursue a common feminist end, then we would still end up with very different results. This isn't because some are better at being feminist academic revolutionaries than others, but simply that we each bring our own biographies into the academy and, like externally imposed constraints, these identities influence what we can and cannot achieve. The kinds of identities that I explored above in relation to myself (working class, woman, lesbian) not only structure how I feel about myself in my role as academic, but they influence how others see me and respond to me. The 'others' who respond to my presentation of self are students, colleagues, including especially importantly feminist colleagues, and the wider academic community. In an interactionist sense, how these 'others' define one makes up a large part of who one is or is allowed to be. In this sense, I am suggesting no essentialist view of 'the feminist academic'; instead, her own perception of her role is mediated by the social relations in which she operates – they both constrain and enable her to perform the social role of 'feminist academic'.

Notes

The title of this chapter borrows from the tale, no doubt apocryphal, of a personal appearance by the movie star Tallulah Bankhead. In her one-woman show, and during a quiet moment, a small child in the front of the audience was heard to exclaim, 'What is that lady *for*, Mummy?'

1. In fact I no longer call myself a lecturer in social work, but a lecturer in applied social science, which more accurately reflects the range of the teaching and research that I do: social policy, social work and women's studies.

2. The basic level of social work teaching, the Diploma in Social Work (DipSW), is at second year undergraduate level and it is unlikely that lecturers will be required to have a PhD. In those universities that offer DipSW coupled with BAs and MAs, and where departments are research active, it is increasingly necessary to have a PhD.

3. This term refers to non-standard qualification routes to university entrance, usually specialist preparatory courses taken by mature students.

4. A model which relies explicitly on the practical skills of the student, rather than on abstract academic criteria.

References

Bauman, Zygmunt (1988) 'Is there a postmodern sociology?', *Theory, Culture & Society*, 5, 2–3: 217–38.

Luke, Carmen and Gore, Jennifer (eds) (1992) *Feminisms and Critical Pedagogy*, New York: Routledge.

Morley, Louise and Walsh, Val (eds) (1995) *Feminist Academics: Creative Agents for Change*. London: Taylor & Francis.

Social Services Inspectorate (SSI) (1991) *Women in Social Services: a Neglected Resource*. London: HMSO.

Ward, Dave and Mullender, Audrey (1991) 'Empowerment and oppression: an indissoluble pairing for contemporary social work', *Critical Social Policy*, 32: 21–30.

11
Dancing Between Hemispheres: Negotiating Routes for the Dancer-Academic

Carol Brown

Feminist choreographies: dancing through the academy

Throughout my dance career I have moved inside and outside academic contexts in various attempts to negotiate routes for the fulfilment of my choreographic and feminist objectives. Most recently I have completed a doctorate in feminist choreographies, research for which involved the combining of practical and theoretical investigations, through the Department of Dance Studies at the University of Surrey.[1] The outcomes of this research involved both the production of a written thesis and a number of public performances of original choreography which were part of 'the thesis', although not its specifically *written* aspect.[2] The interdisciplinary and interdiscursive nature of this work as embodied theory was driven by a passionate commitment to both feminism and dancing, and as such it inevitably involved the cross-fertilisation of ideas and practices in the intertwining of roles as dancer *and* academic, theoretician *and* practitioner.

Dancing, for the most part of my early experience of university life, was, however, something that happened only outside an academic context in private dance studios, for dance is a good example of the exclusions engendered by androcentric constructions of 'proper' intellectual activity. Specifically, dance is commonly regarded as a spurious activity within intellectual life for the following reasons:

1. Dancing is an embodied activity and embodiment has not ranked highly within traditions of Western scholarship which value transcendent reason.
2. Western theatre dance remains associated with femininity and is numerically dominated by women. Activities which are perceived to be of interest to women have not been accredited the same value as 'malestream' areas of interest within academic life.
3. Dancing, in which bodily movement is the primary mode of signification, is commonly perceived as being beyond or before language and therefore

'by nature' untheorisable. That is, dancing is commonly regarded as something that one *does,* and does not talk or write or theorise about.

4. Dancing is entertaining and is not a significant cultural product capable of producing intellectual meaning in the world. The notion of dance as being a cultural 'lightweight' is reinforced by the above points which conflate in popular stereotypes of dancers as docile and dumb, ethereally feminine.

Given this legacy, it is not surprising that dance has only relatively recently achieved university subject status in the UK (in the mid 1970s); while in New Zealand, from where I write, it has yet to achieve this recognition.[3] Indeed the incredulity which currently greets my admission to holding a PhD in dance is a constant reminder of the suspicion that any sustained attention to the body is awarded, as something a priori positioned outside the realm of serious intellectual endeavour.

'Dancer' – I recoil from the term. Call me 'performer/thinker', 'choreographer/scholar', legitimy my practice with intellectual respectability. Marry her body to reason, logic and coherence. Give her body status according to the markers of phallocentric success. I spent years alternating between academic study and professional dance practice, crossing from one mode of corporeality to another, through different cultural spaces, each of which operated according to its own codes and significatory practices. Navigating routes through these diverse fields meant constant negotiations, as conflicting demands were made between different modes of activity and achievement. Dancing happened in studios and theatres amongst communities of women who took pleasure and power in their bodies and the articulations of these in space. Whereas academic work, with its emphasis on speech and writing, was a largely desk-bound activity, contained within lecture theatres, libraries and studies: spaces which numbed my dancing self. The polarising of these spheres of activity frequently engendered a sense of being all-body or no-body at all.

Despite the potential for points of confluence between studies in women's history and a dance training which emphasised the embodied knowledge of women as agents of cultural production, dance was largely ignored within the emerging field of women's studies in the early 1980s. Demands for 'women's voices' to be heard were central to feminist incursions within academic life in this period. However, this too operated its own politics of exclusion. Sustained attention to the search for a 'woman's voice' discouraged and excluded, not only women who, because of their skin colour, class membership and ethnic identity, experienced middle-class Anglo feminist theory as totalising and colour blinkered, but also those for whom the exploration of women's lives became inhibited within a literate tradition in which speech and writing were privileged over all other forms of discourse (Lugones and Spelman, 1992).

Given the proliferation of diverse work by feminist artists of different kinds and critical discourses relating to this within the academy in the 1990s, it has crucially become necessary to re-assess the forms that feminist theory takes. Embodied theory, as feminist figurations in space and time, alters the character of knowledge through its refusal to distance thinking from moving, knowing from being, thought from the material specificity of bodies.[4] Such a perspective demands that theorising operate on multi-discursive registers of subjectivity and recognises non-hegemonic modes of discourse as valid representations of women's agency. Alice Walker is one artist who recognises the limitations for women who have unequal access to language and to speech in proclaiming their difference, and she sees dance, craft and story-telling as fruitful sites for 'womanist' culture. If one speaks as a woman, might not one therefore also consider moving, painting and humming as a woman?

The anatomy of reason

> *I have all these bits and pieces: a left side and a right side*
> *an upper body, a middle body, and a lower body, a front and a back, a top and*
> *a bottom, an inside and an outside. And when I was very young, I*
> *imagined that all of these bits (and pieces) could fold in on themselves*
> *and that I could make myself into a work of origami. And then I*
> *would imagine that I had a join through the middle, running from*
> *the top of my head to the base of my pubic bone, and that I could fold*
> *in half like a suitcase.[5]*

The image of a body divided into parts capable of multiple enfoldings recalls the experience of pliability I had as a young girl studying dance and gymnastics. These 'bits and pieces' can also, however, be seen to operate metaphorically as the tensions, contradictions and fragmentations which arise through the assuming of different roles and identities as female-feminine-feminist, as dancer/choreographer, as dancer/scholar, and as New Zealand/European. In this sense, the image of the suitcase as a precondition of travel and mobility references the re-locations, physical and intellectual, inspired by the fulfilment of these roles in the interaction of diverse fields of endeavour in different contexts.

Part of the attraction for me in pursuing an academic career through feminism has been the syncretic possibilities attached to its potential for transdisciplinarity. Feminist re-visions and re-makings of culture and knowledge expose the connections and continuities between 'different' cultural practices and domains of social existence. Within feminist cultural production, the traditionally discrete zones of the practitioner and the theorist, the performer and the critic, break down. Transdisciplinarity can in this way be regarded as 'intergrative and syncretic' (Walsh, 1995: 56). Spurred on and inspired by the feminist poetics of artist-theorists such as Audre Lorde, Maya Angelou, bell hooks, Toni Morrison, Alice Walker and Trinh Minh-Ha, with their multiple identities as poets, activists, film-makers and theorists, I am encouraged to follow my interior compass and allow eclecticism to splinter singularity, to open new horizons in my body by refusing to accept the dictum that dancing and theorising do not go together. Feminist methodologies offer dance research a range of possible approaches for the interdisciplinary study of dance and for the reformulation of knowledge from the subject position of the dancer/choreographer. To position my own dancing body within the frame of academic research is to collapse the subject/object divide which subtends rationalist discourse. It positions the dancer as knower, as well as that which is known.

One month after completing my PhD I am interviewed for my first academic post. I confront the gatekeepers of academic life, representatives from a variety of academic departments entrusted with ensuring standards of scholarship and teaching within the university in the appointment of new members of staff. Questioning is brisk and thorough. I position myself as a feminist choreographer. Situating my knowledge base in this way, however, leads to suspicion, as expressed in the following question addressed to me as part of the interview process: 'But how do you manage to stay in shape as a dancer and maintain your academic work?'

Western scholarship is assumed to be a sedentary activity, and thinking and moving are frequently regarded as incompatible, entirely separate activities. Feminists have exposed how the 'ideophilia' of classical rationalism has constructed disembodied reason as the primary mode of intellectual production and how this has averted the scholar's gaze from *his* own material specificity, thereby turning objective scholarship into a long-distance view, separating mind from body, subject from object, self from other.[6] The body in this context becomes immobilised through its emphasis on head-bound thought. Dancing bodies, through their mutability, non-reproducibility and materiality, disturb the symbolic limits of the academic frame, disrupting the ideophilia of 'body as object' with 'body as subject' and 'in here', not just 'out there'.

The spaces of academia provide a framework through which certain modes of knowledge production become privileged. The body in academia comes to have meaning within these culturally constructed notions of space, and it must therefore either submit to authority within organised space, or else carve out particular spaces of resistance – heterotopias – through strategies of trespass and transgression. Bringing the dancing body into the academy means creating spaces which enable movement and which can accommodate the messy materiality of bodies. It means situating knowledge in the mobile body with its multi-sensory capacities and inherent instabilities. It means refusing the division between thought and action.

'Exercise is to the body what thinking is to the mind', said Arveyda, gasping. She, who never exercised but was always in motion on errands for her mother, ran easily. Breathing and running and never thinking of them as separate events. (Walker, 1989: 19–20)

My research happens in a variety of locations – studios, libraries and studies as well as on the train, in nightclubs, on beaches, in parks and theatres – through multifarious activities, including writing, dancing, walking, running and reclining. As a choreographer, I am responsive to the store of sensations – tactile, visual, aural and kinaesthetic – that accrue through the felt experience of daily life. These are stored in the feeling-memory and recycled through the organisation and manipulation of drives, flows and intensities in the choreographic process. To be a choreographer in this sense is to be a person who works through the felt experience of the body, and who organises, manipulates and invents the traces and markings of these experiences on individual subjects into dances. As a feminist, this process is, for me, worked through the critical frame of feminist theory.

Choreographing theory and theorising choreography means constant interruptions; one type of activity substitutes another as I move from one kind of space to another through different registers of corporeality. Dancing upstages theory and theorising stills dancing. Inscribing theory through practice means exploring the materiality of ideas through the intermeshing of discourses. Dancing across the borders of diverse fields of knowledge and cultural spaces involves surprise and the unexpected. Navigating these unexpected occurrences ruptures my own expectations, splintering the homogeneity of a singular point of view through new couplings between texts and movements, bodies and theories. Making a spectacle of theory in this way mutates disciplines, creating new hybrid forms which displace distinctions between critic and performer, theorist and practitioner, body and knowledge. But for the post-colonial nomad, the absence of foundational supports makes for volatile conditions. An unstable footing seems inevitable. I struggle to hold my centre, to hold my course.

To keep re-balancing the shifting mass of my body through these mobile supports, I have to keep changing gear. Exhaustion and confusion take hold of me, threatening to still these corporeographies. I fear not being a 'good-enough dancer', a 'good-enough academic'. But my dancing feet are swift, they can move at speed in any direction, responding to the volatile conditions before thought congeals action and gestures become paralysed. They can carry me elsewhere.

> *alternation proliferation signification improvisation*
> *falling-into-becomings*
> *with glimpses of past narrations*
> *my body is theatre and writing instrument*
> *pulse blood rush weave*
> *reflexes activate memory*
> *breath threads through spasms making imprints*
> *on musculature and bone*
>
> *tendons articulate the 'Ileye'*
> *and spinning, tripping, spilling*
> *move to an-other place*
>
> *eyes everywhere*
> *speaking with the whole body*

The writing of this chapter coincides with a number of shifts in focus and location: from student to professional; from a university context to that of professional theatre and studio; from the UK to Aotearoa (New Zealand).

Air miles accumulate, I experience the friction of distance. 'I have all this critical baggage'.[7] I am held over in airports, spaces of liminality, neither here nor there, suspended in space-time enfoldings. Yesterday is tomorrow. A spatiality of perception turned inside-out, upside down, in moving from Summer to Winter, North to South, and back again.

Transmigration

I return to New Zealand after an absence of more than three years to perform my solo, '*The Mechanics of Fluids*'. Although this work came into being through University-based choreographic research, it now takes on a new life as a public performance event.[8] As a cultural product which can be packaged, marketed, toured and promoted, which can appear in various contexts on different sides of the world, to different constituencies of audience, it changes character and is reinvented with each new performance.

The work is to be performed in four cities in New Zealand as part of a tour supported by the Arts Council of New Zealand, Toi Aotearoa.[9] I arrive in Auckland two weeks before my opening night at the Watershed Theatre as part of the Next Wave Dance Festival. Publicity for the event is being generated through various media. Posters hang in shop windows, are pinned to noticeboards and pasted on billboards; postcards adorn shelves and tables in cafes, shops and galleries; newspaper adverts appear and the radio announcements are made as part of 'what's on' diaries of cultural activities. The machinery of promotion is underway. This is the business of art, of art as marketplace, of getting 'bums on seats'. My work becomes a cultural product, packaged and marketed through glossy postcards, posters and press releases which speak in hyperbolic terms. I play down the 'intellectual baggage' I carry with me fresh from the fields of intellectual endeavour. A prominent critic advises against including the word 'feminist' in my publicity, a deception which years of feminist activism has not prepared me for. I compromise, becoming selective with what I divulge about the work to whom. Self-censoring. This is an-other self-representation. I become 'other' to myself. As the machinery of promotion gathers momentum, a gap opens between the media representation of the event and the experience of it as I prepare for these performances through a tough rehearsal schedule pursued at a local community centre. I lose sight of the dance in my experience of the media hype. But can the dance be said to exist apart from my-self?

Publicity for the work is part of its framing as performance and as such shapes audience perceptions about it. But decisions are made according to different sets of criteria. Appeals to the senses unmediated by feminist consciousness distort my intentions. I experience the contradictions of being a performer, of having to 'sell' what I do, of becoming a public artifact. Through dancing, the body is made highly visible as a site for cultural production, it is exposed and made vulnerable as 'object', but it is also empowered as a site of cultural agency. Like many women who perform, my responses to this are deeply ambivalent. Performing on stage, I can feel enormously empowered and enabled and I can use the vulnerability of objectification strategically. But off-stage, I am aware of how quickly these self-representations of myself which I have carefully constructed can be taken hold of and used/abused in contexts which alter their meanings, can be appropriated in the reproduction of dominant imagery of dancer as body-object.

Images of my body semi-clothed appear on the publicity. Seeing these images on billboards along Karangahape Road adjacent to the sex shops and strip clubs which proliferate in this area, I am forced to consider the possibility that my 'post-modern parodic appropriation' of 'Woman as Body' will be collapsed into the inflated feminine excess of the neighbouring strip club advertising. Across the poster and postcard the words 'Whose body is it anyway?' are written. I wonder.

Images of my performing self proliferate. A newspaper photographer turns up at my rehearsal studio and wishes to 'shoot me' on my plinth, semi-naked. The image is hard and awkward, I spend an hour balancing on the edge of a table top, my body in a grimace.

I network furiously, trying to attract an audience through secure channels. I go to the Women's Studies Department at the University of Auckland. Students flood the office, buying course materials for the Stage 1 paper 'Representing Woman: Images and Words'. Their lecture schedule covers film, literature, popular culture, traditional Maori art practice, but not dance. I leap in and suggest the staff and students come to my show. They are interested and may have me back for a post-performance lecture.

I am interviewed by two women in the women's hour of the BFM radio, an upbeat sassy interview in which topics range from female desire to dance in the 1990s. I feel the message is getting through. Perhaps I will have an audience after all. An interviewer from the *New Zealand Herald* comes by and we talk. I am racing, talking too fast, my language is difficult, obscure – speaking in tongues – yet the dictums of advertising copy require simple, unambiguous statements. The preview comes out a few days later and, yes, I am characterised as a 'brainy' dancer and my work is described as 'heady stuff' (Rae, 1995: 15).

Opening night and, yes, we have managed to attract a respectable audience even though it's a six o'clock showing. The theatre is positioned on the Auckland City harbour waterfront facing out to sea. The hour-long performance is over quickly, and it is memorable for the unexpected occurrences: the doll which is a focal point for much of the work falls over; and rain falls thickly on the roof of the theatre as I roll upstage, drowning out any other accompaniment but in the quiet moments of the work adding a splendid deluge of new possibilities. The work is greeted enthusiastically as the lights go up at the end of the show. I feel I have arrived.

Emerging from the dressing room I am tentative about meeting members of the audience and seek the anonymity of the bar. That is where a number of women from the audience approach me, offering their thoughts and feelings about the work. In the main it is women whom I have never met before. Their responses range from physical embraces to the embrace of superlatives and the considered analytic response of the critic.

If we want feminist theory to make a difference to people's lives, then how should it be presented, what forms should it take? Performing this work outside the university context within which it was constructed involves negotiating the divide between different cultural spaces. It means confronting the traditions involved in being a woman performer within a society which continues to enforce hierarchical distinctions between forms of cultural production and dichotomies of gender. In moving inside and outside the academy, the work I am engaged in addresses a much wider constituency than it would otherwise if confined to conventional methods of academic practice – writing and publishing and lecturing. This is no easy task, however. Moving outside the university context, tellingly, brings the need for clarity and accessibility. Performing for different constituencies means ensuring the work is couched in terms which are not exclusive and forbidding but which at the same time encourage feminist readings. Universities are one place amongst many in which feminist work is carried out. As a site of knowledge production, the university context can provide critical and creative resources which fuel feminist energies for cultural work. Moving outside the academy, I carry these critical baggages with me, but, in travelling, their contents are re-arranged and made to speak differently.

Cultural translation

Negotiating the academic/professional divide means travelling across borders – between disciplines, between cultures, and between nation-states. Movements which involve a kind of fluidity, in travelling back and forth, but which also create tensions and disagreements. Travelling between New Zealand and its former colonial power, Britain, in pursuit of a combined career as performer/choreographer and dance lecturer has meant confronting difference and otherness. It also means occupying the indeterminacy of being recognisably Other, a difference that is almost the same, but not quite, for the terms of engagement between cultures, as mediated through my own dancing body, are shaped by colonial discourse. Aotearoa/New Zealand is still in the processes of decolonisation. I joined the waves of New Zealand graduates who seek opportunities for post-graduate studies via networks of Empire. Britain becomes a 'home away from home'. It is both a space created within the culture of domination (metropolis/colony, centre/periphery) and a radical creative place which affirms and sustains subjectivity and which offers a new location from which to represent a sense of the world (hooks, 1990).

Returning to New Zealand after years of immersion in the complexities of post-modernisms, post-structuralisms and feminisms, I find that the questions of culture and of identity which I have been engaged in theorising do not apply in the same way. The language of biculturalism predominates in a society where the 'settler' population is predominantly English-speaking and of European/Caucasian extract. On the immigration papers required on re-entering New Zealand, I enter my nationality as New Zealand European. This designation of ethnicity creates the curious paradox that though categorised as 'European' in New Zealand, in Europe one is categorised as 'Other'. To be 'New Zealand European' in this sense connotes the status of 'in-between-ness' as *Manuhiri* (visitor) in Aotearoa and expatriate 'Kiwi' in England.

The affirmative policies of bi-culturalism have not yet cancelled out the internal colonialism which continues to foster New Zealand's tutelage to overseas metropolitan powers, especially Britain. The forms and practices of colonialism survive internally in the systems and structures which regulate relations between First Peoples, and the 'settler' and subsequent migrant populations of New Zealand. The challenge is to find a national imaginary responsive to and responsible for the transmission of relations of 'indigeneity' as well as to relinquish the hold of European metropolitan power (in particular British) over New Zealand's cultural, economic and political forms and relations (Bennett and Blundell, 1995).

Given this, it is not surprising to find that the cultural struggles of the indigenous population of New Zealand (First Peoples) have resisted assimilation by the politics of plurality and interculturalism, for the issues at stake in the politics of 'indigeneity' are different in kind from those which characterise the pluralising of diverse diasporic relations and identities. Questions of place are more important than those of space, as the politics of 'territorial ground-edness' takes precedence over notions of 'diasporic dispersion' (Bennett and Blundell, 1995: 2). For the indigenous population of New Zealand, issues of culture and of identity are inextricably caught up with issues of land and self-determination.

The indeterminacy which I embrace as part of a nomadic consciousness is radically different from the imperative felt by many in New Zealand to mark the boundaries of their culture according to rights of land ownership.[10] Though the Maori are *tangata whenua* (of the land), the *Pakeha* as *Manuhiri* (visitor) is not. This means that, unlike the indigenous Maori people of New Zealand, the *Pakeha* belongs, in a foundational sense, neither here nor there.

Re-locations bring disjuncture and dis-location and the need for cultural translation. Dance is not a universal language but a culturally specific mode of artistic production. Re-locating my work across the globe involves cultural translation. I worry that my work is so context-specific that it may not travel well. *The Mechanics of Fluids* was informed by Anglo feminist theory as well as by the context of professional dance theatre practices in Europe. At the same time, it came into being through the mediation of these theories and practices through my own dancing body with its inheritances from previous cultural habitations. The body as marked marker. Years of practice as a dancer in Europe, on the other side of the world, means that my body becomes configured within European stylisations of movement. I recognise this difference when I return to New Zealand. I am (an)other to myself, perceived to be English; it's a case of mistaken identity.[11]

Dancing across borders constructs spaces of 'in-between-ness' and liminality, in the gaps between, in the margins and the interstices. Symbolically these spaces have become privileged sites of enunciation within the post-humanist frame. For the feminist, however, these spaces are contested zones, for, while they enable the re-negotiation and recomposition of identities, they also risk dissolving feminist horizons. As I move between hemispheres I experience shifts in the spatiality of perception. Mapping the globe through air travel, these nomadic shifts create new areas of contemplation and sites of signification but they can also impose limits on the dance. Refusing the fixity of any one place, and any one essential way of being, means confronting a certain restlessness. An inability to put down roots brings the confusion of facings and orientations and the problematics of centring one's weight, in refusing to allow the body to settle around the breathing. The politics of indeterminacy replaces the politics of location, but if we wish to transform society then the complex nettle of spatial and temporal conceptions and practices requires addressing both depths and surfaces, form and matter, passion and reason, across both left and right, north and south hemispheres.

Shifting horizons inside and outside the body. Uneven patches of motion, incomplete gestures, corporeal shifts and contiguities, marking time and marking steps. Repetitions, inversions and splicings, substituting one code with another and flashbacks – re-memberings, hesitations, interruptions, stillnesses and silences.

A certain kind of body-writing of body-speak in which thoughts come together, collecting around a posture, a movement, a phrase, making images in the mind's eye – body-stories – narrations which resist closure. Exploding fictions and then separating, going in all directions, splintering standpoints.

From motion to stillness, stillness to writing and back to moving again. Hesitations, backtracks and then springing off again. Questioning what if? And questing.

Interrupting oneself for no apparent reason. Continuing later on, further on, in someplace else. Differently but similarly. A choreography of displacement. Making it up as I go along – improvising.

The inevitability of the organisation of limbs, levers, tendons. Traces of past habitations. No ready-mades, no grids to squeeze into. She flies off, springing in all directions. A rising to the skin-sense of selves she never knew.

The ceaseless clustering of thought-waves and the clinging to words within figurations and the will to cast them off – to avoid becoming fixed, immobilised.

Her corporeal plurality, her polymorphous sexuality. When she wanders too far she stops, and begins again from elsewhere.

Conclusion

Feminist theory has exposed how certain ideas and concepts within western phallocentrism cut across multiple sites of domination. Dualistic thinking, as a central organising concept in western social existence, has led to the categorisation and separation of spheres of activity according to hierarchies of power and influence which are gendered. Given this legacy, individual subjects become categorised according to existing oppositional labels. In the context of this discussion, these can be seen to contain the individual within unitary conceptions as either thinker or mover, performer or critic, colonised or coloniser. The gatekeepers of academic life, professional practice and nation-states demand identity papers which offer unambiguous explanations as either/or, not both/and. The feminist academic, in advocating the indefiniteness and indeterminacy of the latter, risks exclusion and inevitably encounters conflict and tension. However, the openendedness of such a position, on the margins and in the interstices, can also be said to incite multiple possibilities for mobility and movement.

Within the context of feminism in the 1990s, issues of mobility have become crucial. As Rosi Braidotti (1994) explains, throughout the history of western thought and culture women have been represented as passive and immobile. Women who take the opportunity to get up and to go someplace else, in a physical, metaphysical *and* emotional sense, have a stake in the reconfiguration of meaning and matter which is a major challenge for feminists in the present context.

Issues of corporeality, while central to the feminist dance scholar's practice, are also crucially important to other women within the academy. It is women's bodies' markings as 'Other' which have been the focus for their marginalisation and exclusion throughout the history of western culture. To move is to draw attention to one's own corporeal specificity; it is to refuse the presumption of neutrality which has dogged rationalist humanist explanations. To keep moving is to go beyond the imposed limits and constraints of bounded discourses, to loosen the hold of certainties and truths, to animate boundaries in the reconceiving and resignification of identities and disciplines 'in' here and 'out' there as well as 'over' there.

Notes

1. *Inscribing the Body: Feminist Choreographic Practices*, PhD Thesis, Department of Dance Studies, University of Surrey, 1994.

2. The dance works which evolved through this process were, *Dancing Through the Wild Zone* (1992), *Bloodsongs* (1993–4) and *The Mechanics of Fluids* (1994–5).

3. The only degree level education in dance in a New Zealand University is the Stage Two paper in Dance Studies offered as part of a Bachelor of Physical Education degree at the University of Otago.

4. Embodied theory emerges within feminist challenges to patriarchal knowledge to counteract both sexually specific theory which parades as objective knowledge and the epistemological fantasies of *becoming* multiplicities within deconstruction. Such a position recognises that knowledge is always situated, partial and provisional and that it has a material as well as an ideational reality. See for example Braidotti (1994).

5. Text performed as part of the solo *The Anatomy of Reason* (1994).

6. See for example Grosz (1993) and Lloyd (1989).

7. Text spoken in performance for *The Mechanics of Fluids* (1995).

8. *The Mechanics of Fluids* was premiered at the University of Surrey, 15 March 1995. It was subsequently performed at the International Dance and Discourse Conference at Surrey in April 1995. Sections of the work were also included in various dance festivals: Resolutions! (February 1995, The Place Theatre, London); Mosaics (December 1994, Lilian Baylis Theatre, London); the Woking Dance Umbrella (April 1995); and the Rhythm Method (May 1995, the Purcell Room, London).

9. Performances in Auckland, Palmerston North, Wellington and Dunedin in the period June–November 1995.

10. See Braidotti (1994) on the possibilities for feminist nomadic subjects in resisting the fixed categories of binary thought.

11. Being of Irish descent (through my maternal grandparents), I carry dual nationality, both New Zealand and Irish.

References

Bennett, Tony and Blundell, Valda (1995) 'First peoples', *Cultural Studies*, 9(1): 1–10.

Braidotti, Rosi (1994) *Nomadic Subjects: Embodiment and Sexual Difference in Contemporary Feminist Thought*. New York: Columbia University.

Brown, Carol (1994) *Inscribing the Body: Feminist Choreographic Practices*. PhD Thesis, Department of Dance Studies, University of Surrey.

Deepwell, Katy (ed.) (1995) *New Feminist Art Criticism*. Manchester: Manchester University Press.

Grosz, Elizabeth (1993) 'Bodies and knowledges: Feminism and the crises of reason', in L. Alcoff and E. Potter (eds), *Feminist Epistemologies*. New York: Routledge. pp. 187–215.

hooks, bell (1990) *Yearning: Race, Gender and Cultural Politics*. Boston: South End Press.

Humm, Maggie (1994) *Contemporary Feminist Literary Criticism*. Hemel Hempstead: Harvester Wheatsheaf.

Lloyd, Genevieve (1989) 'The Man of Reason', in A. Garry and M. Pearsall (eds), *Women, Knowledge and Reality: Explorations in Feminist Philosophy*. Boston: Unwin Hyman. pp. 111–28.

Lugones, Maria and Spelman, Elizabeth (1992) 'Have we got a theory for you! Feminist theory, cultural imperialism and the demand for "The Woman's Voice"', in Janet A. Kourany, James B. Sterba and Rosemarie Tong (eds), *Feminist Philosophies: Problems, Theories and Applications*. Englewood Cliffs, NJ: Prentice Hall. pp. 378–90.

Rae, Bernadette (1995) 'Mechanics of fluid at the Watershed Theatre', *New Zealand Herald*, Friday 30 June, 15.

Walker, Alice (1989) *The Temple of My Familiar*. Harmondsworth: Penguin.

Walsh, Val A. (1995) 'Eyewitness, not spectators/activists, not academics: feminist pedagogy and women's creativity', *Deepwell* (1995): 51–60.

Wolff, Janet (1995) 'The artist, the critic and the academic: feminism's problematic relationship with "Theory"', *Deepwell* (1995): 14–19.

Choreographies

Dancing Through the Wild Zone. Choreographed by Carol Brown for Carol Brown and Company. First performed at the University of Surrey, 10 December 1992.

Bloodsongs. Choreographed by Carol Brown for Carol Brown and Company. First performed at the University of Surrey, 28 January 1994.

The Mechanics of Fluids. Choreographed and performed by Carol Brown. First performed University of Surrey, 15 March 1995.

The Anatomy of Reason. Choreographed and performed by Carol Brown. First performed Lilian Bayliss Theatre, London, 9 December 1994.

12

A Fantasy of Belonging?

Johanna Alberti

Coming home to exile

I have never lost the feeling that I am a stranger. My roots are colonial and contingent. My father was a Protestant Ulsterman, my mother is the daughter and granddaughter of missionaries to the island of Mauritius in the Indian Ocean. They became strangers in the lands of their birth, and for my mother in her old age the only sense of belonging lies in the past, in her childhood. For my father the army became home, but it made him a wanderer and my birthplace was Egypt. My earliest years in wartime were spent in my mother's childhood home in Mauritius and I came to England as a stranger, unable to speak the language.

My mother hated being an army wife and resisted learning the rules of its hierarchy. She was never able – and I think never expected – to settle or belong in one place. My own sense of being a temporary visitor is akin to hers, but my expectations were different. I expected to belong. We settled into the London suburbs and my parents did their best to give my sister and me a place in the middle-class professional world.

At the age of thirteen I was sent away to a school which was founded in the 1870s with the intention of giving girls what their brothers got from school, including 'houses', 'fags' (younger girls who did a variety of 'humble', and humbling, tasks) and games every afternoon: hours and hours of cricket but no white flannels. There were compensations. One was the solitude: the ancient library fostered in me a love for books and a capacity for inwardness. The women who taught us were precisely those single, academic women of the interwar period whom I would later study as a historian. In the 1950s they succeeded in dissuading me from becoming what my mother would have liked and found acceptable, a nurse, and I attempted to turn my love of reading into academic ambition.

At Oxford the joys of close friendship continued, but my love of history was choked by the dust of daunting libraries, superior tutors and a syllabus which gave virtually no purchase for my fascination with human beings and their motivation. I lacked the confidence to choose my own reading, and solitude seemed to be a mark of social failure. To be alone in a corridor of empty rooms on a Saturday evening became my greatest fear. It seemed to presage a life-long loneliness. So I leapt gratefully into the arms of the first attractive man who offered release from this prospect. I decided to teach because it seemed convenient for a married woman and it meant I could stay in Oxford to do a 'Dip. Ed.' I then taught in schools, but I did not look ahead to a career as a teacher. I subsumed my being into that of a man whose profession, medicine, allowed me a vicarious sense of being useful, of my life holding some meaning. The school had intended to give me an identity of my own, but that identity seemed to involve a solitary existence and competing in an academic world which I saw as beyond my abilities – or desires.

This was the beginning of the 1960s, the decade of the dawning of the second women's movement. I married the year after the publication of Betty Friedan's *The Feminine Mystique*, a book which I have never been able to face reading. I became marginally aware of the personal relevance of women's liberation in the early 1970s, by which time I had two small children. A woman with whom I was both at school and at university once identified our position as the in-between generation who felt both that they should have brilliantly white nappies on the line and success outside the home. I don't know what her nappies were like, but she became headmistress in distinguished private schools. I was less focused.

The mixed messages of my past and present pulled me to and fro. I lived in a country cottage, an outsider in country life too. I had lost my faith in private education and joined the Labour Party. I read Germaine Greer's *The Female Eunuch* and listened to women in dungarees getting angry at Labour Party meetings. My husband, driven by his own history as the child of immigrant German Jews, was making a career in academic medicine. Left alone, I was often brought to screaming pitch by the experience of full-time domesticity, but I did not yet consciously analyse my own frustration in feminist terms.

The edge was taken off the frustration when we moved from country to town and I got a job in a sixth-form college. By this time I had a third child and was also politically active. I was an Oxford graduate, a teacher, the wife of a successful professional man and the mother of three sons. But I still felt that I was searching for some place to belong. I did not look upon my job as a career, I resisted being a supportive wife, I failed to value my work as a mother and I knew I did not fit into the Labour Party. I was all these roles on suffrance, feeling fully committed to none of them. Moreover, I filled up my life so that there was no time for analysis, only for survival. Yet on some level I was developing an understanding of what it meant to be an outsider, and that being an outsider did have meaning.

Valuing the outside

My husband's restlessness had not been assuaged either, and I willingly agreed to leave what was both a full life and a rut to move to the North-East.

To start again. Now there was time for thought, and I began a dissertation for an MA on Ellen Wilkinson. Attracted by her politics, I remember also consciously choosing a woman. Although I changed the subject of the MA when I found that Ellen Wilkinson had asked her sister to burn her private letters, I can see now that I was being drawn perceptibly towards feminism. But not immediately towards feminist research in that I allowed the subject of my MA in the end to be chosen for me by my male supervisor.

A crucial turning-point came in the mid-1980s. In the early 1980s I carried a heavier and heavier part-time teaching load at Newcastle Polytechnic. When the job which I was virtually doing was advertised I applied for it. I was interviewed alongside five men by five men. The job went to a man who had risen from the shop floor: class had won over gender. But this meant that I was released to begin to value my own gender and to let go a little of my guilt about class.

I was angry but also relieved to find myself still outside the gates. I dropped my plan to do a PhD and, encouraged by women in a feminist research group, began to write a book. I also started to teach for the Open University and on New Opportunities for Women courses organised by the Worker's Educational Association and the Adult Education Department of Newcastle University. These commitments formed the framework of my life for the next ten years: to a considerable extent, but with different contributions of time and engagement, they still do.

Teaching on a New Opportunities for Women course constituted for me a crash course in feminism as something experienced on a feeling as well as an intellectual level and therefore meaningful to me. The courses aimed to change the lives of the women who attended by shifting their 'dislocated sense of self' so that they developed a 'true, that is inner, autonomy' (Aird, 1985: 7). These were brave words which I find it hard at times to read without a disturbing mixture of irony and nostalgia. At the time I experienced an exhilarating sense of the energy and support which such a feminist community, however temporary, can give to women. I passionately embraced both the ideology of self-discovery and the friendships which grew out of the paired teaching.

My place as teacher is still a contingent one, dependent on the exigencies of student numbers, departmental finances, the choices of men (mostly) with the power to employ part-timers. But now I have an appreciation of the possibilities inherent in outsider status, with its comparative freedom from the playing of institutional politics even if I am still the victim of such manoeuvres.

Sesame and lilies

The structure of the Open University pays more respect to the position of the outsider, the part-time tutor, than any other that I have experienced. As a tutor-counsellor on the Arts Foundation Course, my responsibility for students throughout their degree is recognised in my pay, and respected in the continuity of work I can expect. I also teach a 'third level' history course on which I can expect continuity, although less pay. On both these courses, within constraints, I can teach what I like. The constraints are the givens: essay titles, the basic material of the course and the number of sessions. This framework may sound like a straitjacket, but in practice I have found it supportive, for the constraints also offer a degree of protection to the students from the arbitrary power of the tutor. My relationship to the material and the academic hierarchy of the history department at the Open University is a good case study of its strengths and weaknesses.

The history department of the Open University is staffed largely by pragmatic, British, male historians. My training consisted of a trip to Walton Hall, Milton Keynes, to attend the feedback session from the first year of the running of the course. I walked into a room full of casually dressed middle-class men with glasses in their hands. I was greeted as 'Bill's woman'. Bill is the staff tutor in the region where I worked and who had appointed me. My gender was so unusual among appointments for teachers of the course that it marked me out at once. Since then there has been some improvement in the gender balance, but the course is still largely taught by men and at summer school the male/female tutor ratio varies from 5:1 to 11:1. The student ratio is closer to 1:1.

One of the stated aims of the course – *War, Peace and Social Change: Europe 1900–1955* – is 'to assist Open University students to develop skills in . . . understanding some of the different approaches to historical study', ranging from the highly theoretical (as for example in some forms of Marxism) to the thoroughly empirical (as for example in the approach to history introduced in the Arts Foundation Course), and also quantitative and qualitative approaches (Marwick, 1990a: 10). The introductory section of the first edition of the course units contained a further explanation of this aim, written by Arthur Marwick, who is the course leader and Professor of History at the Open University. After a hostile presentation of 'Critical theory, cultural theory and linguistics', there was a section entitled *Liberal Humanist Approaches*, which continued the attack on 'Marxism, linguistic materialism, and so on . . .'. At the end of this, the students were asked to identify another approach to the study of history which has very much come to the fore during the 1970s and 1980s, and to suggest whether it could be fitted into one or other of the two broad sets already outlined. The significant part of Marwick's answer was:

> Feminism. It is broadly true that feminism in academic work has tended to be associated with Marxism, cultural theory and linguistic approaches, above all in that it has tended to operate within a framework postulating the existence of both capitalism and the new concept of patriarchy (male dominance), and has found the concept of ideology useful in explaining the apparently wide acceptance of masculinist ideas . . . But it is certainly not inevitable that feminist approaches should be incompatible with 'liberal humanism'. The crux is probably whether feminism is regarded as in itself a new kind of history replacing all other kinds, or whether it is seen as offering new perspectives and new insights,

while essentially using the tried and tested methods of 'liberal humanist' history. (1990a: 38)

In itself this paragraph offered the possibility for further discussion with students, while the units and the articles collected in the course reader offered the students a variety of perspectives. But the introduction which I have just quoted from went on to refer to just one text by a feminist historian, an article by Annette Kuhn, which was given as an example of discourse theory. Kuhn's conclusion is quoted: that *Maisie's Marriage*, the film based by Marie Stopes on her own writings, 'became an object of censorship by virtue of its implication, at a particular historical moment, within a certain set of discourses and power relations, which penetrate the text and yet also exceed it' (1986). This conclusion was then 'translated' so that it is presented as saying something different: 'The passage is actually saying that in itself *Maisie's Marriage* is so unshocking as not to have warranted the objections of the censor, that there were factors outside the film' (Marwick, 1990a: 39). I was infuriated both by what I saw as a limited and simplistic approach to discourse theory and the way the one example of feminist history writing was used to attack that approach, and at the summer school in 1992 I took the opportunity to challenge this.

This example drawn from one institution seems to me to illustrate something wider about the way the processes of intellectual and organisational power operate in any institution where relatively junior people tutor and teach within intellectual frameworks and written materials provided by the hierarchically more powerful. And of course in such situations 'the junior' are likely to be women and 'the senior' to be men – and that feminist ideas were at issue here reinforces the 'genderedness' of this example.

In this particular instance it was possible for a tutor to challenge that power. And it was also possible in this case for the wielder of power to allow other voices, even if they were disagreed with, to be heard and read by the students. But this does not vitiate the argument I am making, which is about the interleaving of institutional hierarchies and positions and gender hierarchies, paradoxically perhaps with the result that gender is ignored, not 'seen' as having significance, in the dismissal of feminist ideas.

When I tackled the course leader for his presentation of feminist history in the introduction to the course units, he did not accept my interpretation of the implications of the passages I quoted and did not budge an inch in his views. On the other hand, he did later suggest that an article on feminist/women's history be sent out to future students on the course. This was administratively a complex and relatively expensive process. Nevertheless Jane Rendall's (1991) article 'Uneven developments' was sent to all students with an introduction by the course leader:

> feminist historians have done an enormous service in righting the wrong done to women by traditional historians who, too often, ignore them; but I am suspicious of Marxist-derived theory about dominance, patriarchy, and so on, and also of theorizing about sexual differences as being entirely socially constructed (as distinct from them being ultimately based in biology), and suspicious, above all, of feminist history which simply becomes feminist propaganda.

> However, it has been suggested that . . . I am both neglectful of, and unfair to, feminist history. Since we do genuinely believe in openness and pluralism, and are very happy for students to decide what approaches they wish to follow (provided always argument is rational and supported with evidence), we have added this off-print of an important article by Jane Rendall (Supplementary Reading to A318, Marwick, 1991: 1).

This was followed by my explanation of the problems I had with the presentation of feminist history in the introduction to the course, and with some aspects of the way the history of women is dealt with in the main body of the course units.

In 1994 the introduction to the course was revised, and I was invited to respond to the revision of the section on feminism. This section is now brief, acknowledges that 'there are many types of feminism', and directs the students to read Jane Rendall's article (Marwick, 1994: 37). I also responded – uninvited and to no avail – to the new and much abbreviated section on theory which includes this reassurance to students;

> It is proper to reassure you here that you can work your way through everything in this course without encountering any literary or cultural theory, any faintest whiff of the approaches often labelled post-structuralist or post-modernist. (Marwick, 1994: 35)

Writing this narrative, I swing between thinking I had been unfair to the dominant viewpoint presented by the course leader, and that I had been horribly complacent about the course, and content with too little. What was achieved was an open discussion of difference, and latterly aspects of the same argument, in particular Arthur Marwick's disagreements with 'those who have absorbed the shibboleths of post-structuralism', have reached the illustrious and more public pages of *The Times Higher Educational Supplement* and the *Journal of Contemporary History* (January, April 1995). There his opponent has been Hayden White, whose response identifies the resistances of many practitioners of the writing of history: 'Most historians are not only incapable of analysing the discursive dimensions of their writing: they positively repress the idea that there might be such a dimension' (*The Times Higher Educational Supplement*, 25 November 1994).

Marwick had assumed that Hayden White was trained as a literary critic because he had written of historical writing as discourse. In fact, Hayden White was trained as a medieval historian. It was perhaps this defence of the boundaries of history which fuelled the earlier hostility towards Annette Kuhn's work, exacerbated by a sense that she is not a 'real' historian but is primarily a feminist. Certainly it was feminism which enabled me to escape from some of the constraints of the training in history I had been given, the blinkeredness to theory and reluctance to consider the position of the writer with regard to an understanding of the history she writes.

I want to use two other examples emerging from the same institutional context to highlight the nature of the insecurity and inconsistency of the traditional historian-in-defence-of-his-subject. There is still widespread ambivalence about oral history, which is exhibited in the same course leader's comments on an article by Anna Bravo (1982) on Italian peasant women and the First World War.

> This is a secondary source, a learned article, but almost entirely based on one type of primary material, oral interviews. I have to say that it did strike me as slightly peculiar that a researcher working in the 1970s should be able to interview people about experiences which took place sixty years earlier. I know from my own experience of collecting written testimony from British women who lived through the First World War that they often get things wrong (many actually believed that they were conscripted into the war effort, though in fact, as you know, there was no conscription of women then). (Marwick, 1990b: 118)

This statement seems to me to be quite extraordinary. It is based on the assumption that one at least of the historian's tasks is to judge her sources by some standard of factual accuracy. The richness of oral material lies precisely in the way the witness understands his or her past experience. It is peculiarly extraordinary and wonderful that there are women alive now who can be interviewed about their experiences sixty years ago, experiences which were highly significant for them. No doubt these experiences have been filtered through their lives to form powerful myths. But the writing of history is always a form of myth-making.

My second example concerns what is claimed to be the myth that Victorian women did not enjoy sex. In the first television programme for the Arts Foundation Course an article by Carl Degler (1974) is cited in support of this assertion by the course leader. The Degler article is based on a survey conducted by Dr Clelia Mosner in the University of Wisconsin over a twenty-year period beginning in the early 1890s, while the Arts Foundation course focuses on mid-Victorian England. The genesis of Degler's challenge to the 'myth' of the sexless Victorian woman is not acknowledged, nor is Degler's own appropriately considered conclusion, that the evidence of the survey 'makes clear that historians are ill-advised to rely upon the marital-advice books as descriptions either of sexual behaviour of women or general attitudes towards women's sexuality' (1974: 1489). This example shows how an apparent commitment to the exhaustive and rigorous examination of historical evidence can be significantly departed from because of the way the personal perspective of the historian inescapably moulds his or her views.

There has always been resistance to the challenges to the content and structure of history: 'social' history was for many years seen as something less important and significant than 'political' and 'military' history. Categorisation, especially into hierarchies, can be a mark of that insecurity. The idea that the writing of history might indeed be inescapably a political act is still being resisted. History Workshop has now made that perspective more widely accepted, and has itself now become an institution with its own exclusions and insecurities.

Motherhood and post-structuralism

Hayden White has an interesting passage in the article from which I have quoted above, in which he places the 'notion of history-as-art' against the 'more masculinist idea of history-as-science', and he asserts that the profession has 'cast its lot' with the latter. But he immediately reconstructs the contrast/dichotomy as one between 'not masculinism versus feminism', but 'rather more an issue of critical self-awareness or the lack of it'. He touches on the area of contest about who can claim most credit for the latest bout of self-awareness in intellectual life: feminists or post-structuralists. There is concern in this struggle that feminism could be swallowed up by post-structuralism.

If I want to be dramatic, my entry into that arena suggests the fate of Clytemnestra, murdered by her son. My middle son is doing a postgraduate study in archaeology: his subject area is gender. Feminists have been wary of gender studies, which can be a weapon of defence against the power of feminism, can blunt its political edge. Ben had originally chosen a highly political subject area under the influence of his supervisor. At the last minute he made a very sudden decision to look at gender instead. When he told me of his move he said: 'I hope you do not think I am treading on your toes, Mum.' I was startled, but pleasurably so. I suspect I felt my own choices were somehow validated by his.

As a result of his choice, Ben began to use the ideas of Judith Butler as a theoretical framework for his critique of archaeology. He sent me a copy of Butler's *Gender Trouble*. My contact with post-structuralist ideas had until then been limited to the odd article, and the writings of Joan Scott (1988) and Denise Riley (1988). I had found Scott's ideas immensely stimulating, and her writing on equality and difference had helped me to clarify my thinking on the apparent divisions between New and Old Feminists during the interwar period. I was looking for a way of embracing the deconstruction of gender without losing the politics made possible by 'being a woman'. Judith Butler promised much: 'The deconstruction of identity is not the deconstruction of politics; rather, it establishes as political the very terms through which identity is articulated' (1990: 148). But there was a basic problem with Butler for me, and that was understanding what the hell she is saying. Every now and then I got a whiff, a breath of excitement, but her meanings remain illusive. Butler tracks a path through the psychoanalytical jungle where I can only stumble after her, abandoning my critical faculties because of my own lack of a grounding in that discipline. Could I take Butler's conclusions on trust or was it necessary for me to struggle with the immense oeuvres of Nietzsche and Freud? I felt undermined by the notion that I needed to be familiar with Foucault to get to grips with the history of feminism.

Butler's concept of gender as 'performative' had sent me reeling into space. Nor did I have the intellectual muscle to challenge her. Moreover, my reading of her section on 'Bodily Inscriptions, Performative Subversions' suggested a heavy bias towards a hostile interpretation of mother/child relationships: 'The boundary of the body as well as the distinction between internal and external is established through the ejection and transvaluation of something originally part into a defiling otherness' (1990: 133).

I could accept my own understanding of Butler's contention in her conclusion that 'to be a good mother' is one of multiple injunctions '*to be* a given gender', and that 'the convergence of such discursive injunctions produces the possibility of a complex reconfiguration and redeployment' (1990: 145). But to be a mother of any sort still seems to me to constitute a relationship which has some other dimension than the performative.

Judith Butler's writings have cut me loose from the sense that it was possible to challenge the blinkeredness of the traditional historian from an intellectually intelligible position, while my own sense of being a mother felt undermined by her aim of making possible a 'new configuration of politics' fundamental unnaturalness' (1990: 149). On the other hand, one paragraph at least of *Gender Trouble* has thrown light on my own struggles with 'the inside' and 'the outside' of the academy:

> Regardless of the compelling metaphors of the spatial distinctions of inner and outer, they remain linguistic terms that facilitate and articulate a set of fantasies, feared and desired. 'Inner' and 'outer' make sense only with reference to a mediating boundary that strives for stability. (1990: 134)

To see my desire for belonging, my fear of being always the outsider, as linked to a fantasy of stability can at times be enlightening.

Women of ideas

In the autumn of 1992 I was invited to teach again at the University of Northumbria (as Newcastle Polytechnic had become) for the first time since I had failed to get the job there seven years earlier. I later heard the story behind that invitation. Northumbria has for many years offered a popular part-time MA in the History of Ideas. Five years ago one of the students finally forced them to face up to the total absence of a feminist voice or perspective on that course. In response to her challenge, they cast around for a feminist historian of ideas and thought of me. Since I am pretty sure that the sub-text of my failure to get a full-time job there in the first place was because of their perception of me as a feminist, the irony was pleasing. Thanks to the increasing academic acceptability of feminism, and thanks to an individual feminist, I have achieved a toe-hold in the institution to which I am best suited. Teaching on an MA means teaching 'adults', and it means a sharp intellectual stimulus. Moreover, I find myself serendipitously in a place where there are for me possibilities for belonging: the history of ideas. The eclectic nature of this 'discipline' allows for the breaking down of barriers much as 'women's studies' does. Its commitment to that elusive idea, the rigorous examination of 'texts', satisfies the traditional historian in me. As far as the institution is concerned, the History of Ideas is an outsider, permanently understaffed and under threat of extinction.

Exile can be seen as a place, a position, of choice which is not subject to a dictatorship. Intellectual freedom does still have meaning in the academy in Britain, and one of the consequences of this freedom is the possibility of remaining on the outside without being totally excluded. It is possible to see colonial origins as a metaphor for my experience of never finding a home in the academy. The colonialist has power outside the metropolis but finds it impossible to settle down at home. My inherited lack of belonging was combined with a professional middle-class background which seemed to place me firmly inside a particular milieu. There I could have combined becoming a headmistress in a private school for girls with marriage and motherhood. I struggled with these identities and sought others: historian, feminist, lesbian and writer. I have found a home in none of these and remain an exile, an outsider. But there is perhaps an identity, and certainly there is much pleasure, in embracing wholeheartedly absorption in the temporary, the ephemeral. There is an agency and power in the ability and the willingness to visit.

References

Aird, Eileen (1985) *Breaking Our Silence. From a Different Perspective: Change in Women's Education*. London: W.E.A.

Bravo, Anna (1982) 'Italian peasant women and the First World War', in Paul Thompson and Natasha Burchardt (eds), *Our Common History: The Transformation of Europe*. London: Pluto Press.

Butler, Judith (1990) *Gender Trouble: Feminism and the Subversion of Identity*. London: Routledge.

Degler, Carl (1974) 'Women's sexuality in the nineteenth century', *American Historical Review*: 1477–90.

Kuhn, Annette (1986) 'The "married love" affair', *Screen*, 27(2), March-April: 14–27.

Marwick, Arthur (ed.) (1990a) *War, Peace and Social Change, Book I: Europe on the Eve of War*. Buckingham: Open University Press.

Marwick, Arthur (ed.) (1990b) *War, Peace and Social Change, Book II: World War I and its Consequences*. Buckingham: Open University Press.

Marwick, Arthur (ed.) (1991) *Supplementary Reading to A318*. Buckingham: Open University Press.

Marwick, Arthur (ed.) (1994) *War, Peace and Social Change, Book I: Europe on the Eve of War*, revised edn. Buckingham: Open University Press.

Rendall, Jane (1991) 'Uneven developments', in Karen Offen (ed.), *Writing Women's History: International Perspectives*. Basingstoke: Macmillan.

Riley, Denise (1988) *'Am I That Name?' Feminism and The Category 'Women' In History*. Basingstoke: Macmillan.

Scott, Joan (1988) *Gender and the Politics of History*. New York: Columbia University Press.

13

Identity and Representation: Experiences of Teaching a Neo-Colonial Discipline

Uma Kothari

That woman really gets up my nose. Every time I return home from Dr. Kothari's lectures, I have to rewrite my notes taking out the bias. She has a chip on her shoulder about being a woman and a whole potato on the other about being Indian. (First year British undergraduate)

We feel so proud to see Dr. Kothari here – one of our people in such an important position. (Nepali postgraduate student)

These evaluations indicate the ways in which my identity as a Black woman academic is diversely interpreted and represented by my students. They highlight my 'in-between' academic status, simultaneously included and excluded, belonging and not belonging. The articulation of these different sentiments partly explains the ambivalence I feel in my institutional role. My identity demands a flexibility and self-reflexivity in relating to the institution, students and colleagues, and continual re-evaluation of my work in producing knowledge through teaching and research.

This chapter explores the implications arising out of my experiences as a Black feminist teaching international development studies in a British institute of higher education. The focus is on the construction of the development discourse and the nature of my engagement with, and experiences of, this narrative. The overwhelming feeling I have is one of ambivalence and contradiction.

It is not possible to speak of my experiences as a feminist academic only in terms of unequal gender relations, because, as a Black person, they are also informed by 'race' and racism. However, I do not want to talk about my experiences solely within the context of 'race' as they are more than a response to *racism* (Mirza, 1995). My 'race' and gender are inseparable aspects of my identity and are configured in particular ways which shape the specificities of my relationships with academia.

'Black women academics' experiences, because they draw discursively from meanings constructed within wider social discourse, cannot be analysed only in terms of the unequal relations that prevail within the academy' (Rassool, 1995: 36). Thus, in the first part of this chapter I examine the historical construction of racialised and gendered development discourse. This also provides a basis for understanding my ambivalent relationship to development studies. The second part explores the particularities of my experiences in academia as an articulation of my 'race' and gender. Overall, this chapter challenges dominant development theory and practice and provides a tentative exploration of my experiences within the academy.

Colonial discourse and development studies

> The [development] machine is global in its reach, encompassing departments and bureaucracies in colonial and post-colonial states throughout the world, Western aid agencies, multilateral organisations, the sprawling global network of NGOs [non-governmental organisations], experts and private consultants, private sector organisations such as banks and companies that marshall the rhetoric of development, and the plethora of development studies programmes in institutes of learning worldwide. (Crush, 1995: 6)

I work in this post-World War II machine as an academic, involved in teaching, research and consultancy. Development studies is a relatively new discipline which has its origins in a colonial past, and my experiences as a black feminist in and of this machine can only be understood in this colonial context. A discussion concerning my experiences within academia must be predicated upon an exploration of how colonial power and knowledge have travelled historically and geographically in development discourse and practice. I argue, more specifically, that development studies is a neo-colonial discipline in which particular gendered and racial formations constructed through colonial processes are re-presented and re-articulated. These have implications for the theory, practice and teaching of development studies and make my position in academia complicated and ambivalent.

Colonial roots and heritage

Unlike anthropology and geography, in which crucial forms of knowledge have been 'produced by, indeed born of, colonial rule . . .' (Mohanty, 1991: 31), development studies, while having its origins in colonialism, is better conceived as a post-colonial discipline, in the sense that its emergence as an academic discipline after World War II coincided with the onset of the decline of colonial rule. However, much theory and practice within the discipline and much development discourse suggests that it is also a *neo*-colonial subject since it (re)configures and (re)presents unequal power relations between 'First World' and 'Third World', embodying a continuity of particular relations of power over time (colonial to post-colonial) and space (geographical west and 'Third World') (Mohanty, 1991; see Trinh, 1989). Development discourse assumes power in naming and representing the ways in which people live their lives and articulate their experiences, and in shaping processes of change. Furthermore, development practitioners are primarily white men, who are considered 'experts' in their field. Because knowledge is necessarily situated in our own identity and experience, these men interpret the world from the positions of power constructed out of their race and gender privilege. Certainly, much of their status as development theorists and practitioners derives from their whiteness and maleness.

As a neo-colonial discipline, then, development studies reproduces unequal relations of power. An understanding of this colonial genealogy is essential for identifying problems within contemporary development theory and practice, and the particular authoritative discourse that constructs the 'Other'. In short, in development studies we identify, and in our discourse construct, an entity called the 'Third World' and then present it as an objective reality to its inhabitants 'there' and also to our students 'here'.

This neo-colonial discourse is played out at the level of both theory and practice, as development workers and academics are interpolated by these notions of power. For instance, academics inform practice in influencing which projects should be funded and where aid should be spent and withdrawn. Bluntly, dominant strands within development theory are constructed in the West and implemented in the 'Third World'.

Having identified the (neo) colonial nature of development studies, I now want to focus on how specific ideological formations and persistent normative assumptions and expectations have flowed from a colonial discourse to a development discourse. Mohanty argues that particular relations of rule and forms of knowledge prevalent in colonial times are apparent in contemporary development discourse, and in this chapter I highlight the (re)constitution of gendered and racial distinctions:

> . . . in drawing racial, sexual and class boundaries in terms of social, spatial and symbolic distance, and actually formulating these as integral to the maintenance of colonial rule, the British defined authority and legitimacy through the difference rather than commonality of rulers and 'native'. (Mohanty, 1991:10)

The imperative of colonialism required the construction of the 'Other' to the white, colonial male self. The process whereby colonial rule was legitimised was grounded in a discourse of race and gender which defined colonised people as incapable of self-government (Mohanty, 1991), and inherently predisposed towards wantonness, irresponsibility and childlike characteristics. Colonised men were emasculated yet conceived of as wild and women were eroticised but also imagined as dangerous (Kabbani, 1986).

Pearson suggests that inequalities between colonised men and women were exacerbated during colonial rule.

> . . . there is no doubt that colonial capture and the introduction of exploitative labour regimes led to a marked deterioration in the social and economic status of women relative to that of men. The development of a world economy, and the spread of wage labour in both agricultural and industrial production, assumed very different roles for women and men in the economy, sometimes excluding women from wage employment while relying on their unpaid work on family farms or on low-paid work within the informal sector. (Pearson, 1992: 291)

These boundaries and distinctions, marking the power relations between colonisers and their colonised 'Other', continue to be played out and reinscribed in the teaching of development.

The paradoxes of teaching gender and development

The sub-field of gender and development provides an example of how the power relations identified above are simultaneously challenged and reinforced. Since the mid-1970s, women in development, and now gender and development, have become increasingly important within development theory and practice. In the following section I examine the ways in which the gender and development approach is simultaneously a challenge to dominant (masculinist and racialised) development discourse and reproduces neo-colonial racial and gendered notions and practices. My own ambivalent position in academia is produced out of this paradox.

While development studies does have roots in a colonial past, the discipline is now many headed and politically diverse, with liberal and conservative strands constituting 'conflicting intellectual currents flowing through the contemporary domain of development' (Crush, 1995: 8). Thus, the discipline is itself contradictory, and indeed as a Black woman I am one of the contradictions within it.

Much of the critique of development studies tends to focus on why the poor are still poor after forty-five years of so-called development (Edwards, 1993), rather than on a historical and political critique of the discourse of development. However, it is no longer acceptable to simply accept development discourse without challenging its authority and the manner in which it constructs the world. In part, this is no longer possible because of the 'impact of post-modern, post-colonial and feminist thought which have converged upon the truth claims of modernism and shown how the production of Western knowledge is inseparable from the exercise of Western power' (Crush, 1995: 3).

Teaching gender and development is a mode of intervention into a particular hegemonic narrative (Mohanty, 1991). As such it can pose a challenge to development orthodoxy by demanding the re-examination of the development process with the awareness that it has impacted on men and women differently, with women consistently losing out. A gender perspective is important for men and women to benefit equally from processes of change and for inequalities between men and women to be reduced. This is now widely recognised by large donor agencies, multinational and bilateral organisations and NGOs. Strategies have been adopted to integrate gender into development policies, projects and practices, with varying degrees of commitment and success. However, the fact that gender is now on the development agenda is testament to the progress that has been made in highlighting gender inequalities and analysing gender at all levels of the development process.

The very notion of gender is an assault on the idea that societies are a homogeneous mass of undifferentiated individuals. Talking about gender necessarily posits a heterogeneous society because its basic assumption is that women and men have different experiences. Prior to this in development studies little distinction was overtly made, but with male experiences tacitly assumed as universal.

Although the necessity to challenge dominant development approaches from a gender perspective is unquestionable, the way in which much of the gender and development discourse is formulated is problematic. While committed to the teaching of gender and development, I am uncomfortable with the way 'Third World' people, and women in particular, are represented in much of the literature. Colonial constructions and representations of the 'Third World' in general and of 'Third World' women specifically underpin much of the theoretical debates within development and partly explain the ambivalence I feel as a Black woman academic teaching gender and development in a development studies institute of higher education.

Mohanty examines the representation of 'Third World woman' in development studies, an analysis which is useful in understanding particular aspects of my own experiences. She contends that many gender and development accounts 'discursively colonise the material and historical heterogeneities of the lives of women in the "Third World", thereby producing/re-presenting a composite singular "Third World Woman"' (Mohanty, 1991: 53). In this way, a thread of power and domination emerges in the very discourse it seeks to challenge by being conscripted into the language it disclaims.

The experiences and struggles of 'Third World' women are appropriated and fitted into western conceptual frameworks and interpreted according to western benchmarks. For example, the mere existence of a sexual division of labour is frequently claimed as proof of the oppression of women, although there is little attempt to understand its meaning and value within different cultural contexts, to consider that in a particular local context it may even be empowering for women.

It is difficult to teach students about gender and development when so many representations of 'Third World' women in the development literature present them as 'benighted, overburdened beasts, helplessly entangled in the tentacles of regressive "Third World" patriarchy' (Lanham, 1989). As Crush says, 'this [gendered] imaginary of poverty, powerlessness and vulnerability was readily captured in development discourse' (Crush, 1995: 21). A teacher of gender and development requires vigilance and awareness to challenge these negative representations evoking domination and vulnerability. Innovative teaching methods are necessary to empower students from the so-called 'Third World' when the discourse continually represents them as disempowered and oppressed. I must consider which tools can usefully provide them with the means to participate in the transformation of their world (hooks, 1989: 50). One of the ways in which this can be done is through the use of the individual's personal and work experiences as source material and a basis for discussion. This enables a more participative approach to teaching and allows the exploration of commonalities and differences and highlights the complexities of people's lives. Furthermore, a more extensive use of material from 'Third World' countries enables different perspectives to be presented and discussed. While these remain largely unacknowledged as useful texts, they are now more readily available given the recent challenge to Eurocentric and masculinist discourse from within development studies. Much of this material has emerged from feminist movements in 'Third World' countries and from a recent commitment by some people to 'bottom-up' and 'people-centred' development.

The university academic: female and post-colonial

My academic work involves training students (primarily male and from 'Third World' countries) on development policy and practice, carrying out research into different aspects of development and change, and working as a consultant for governments and NGOs. In these roles my identity as a Black woman is significant in determining the particularities of my experiences and in challenging the expectations of others with whom I work. I am not always the only one who is required to re-assess and negotiate a space, since my very presence can instigate a constant process of negotiation between the reconstruction of stereotypes and their denial.

Part of my ambivalence towards development studies is based on the recognition that development discourse tends to confirm the centrality of western knowledge and power, a legacy that is often reinforced in the 'Third World' through the continued existence of colonial institutions and education systems. I am uncomfortable with the persistent idea that western academia has the answers for the rest of the world and only by gaining an access to education in the West can people from the 'Third World' understand their own histories, societies and economies. In addition, the way in which the 'Third World Other' has been constructed in development discourse and its continuing prevalence is personally and politically problematic. While I am committed to teaching around the exploration of 'race', class and gender, the neo-colonial characteristics of the discipline means it is often bounded by a racialised and masculinist discourse.

One of the problems I have to deal with revolves around the highly charged political issue of who is regarded as the 'expert' with the authoritative voice. Much of the teaching material in development studies assumes authority, revealing its roots in colonialism and the neo-colonial re-formations of gender and race. However, it is rare to find texts which examine issues of Eurocentrism or post-colonial theory on course reading lists in development studies. It seems as though, because so much of our work is apparently trying to solve the problems of people 'out there', and we have been given 'expert' status and the authority to do this, many of us are unable to be self-reflexive. Thus, our assumptions of our 'global humanitarian mission' becomes a means of absolving us of the responsibility of looking at ourselves, and seeing ourselves as implicated.

My relationship with the academy and the discipline, and with my students, highlights further issues of ambivalence and contradiction which cause me to reflect on my identity and position, as I go on to discuss.

The relationship between development studies and the academy

> The discourse of power in the academy has shifted in the past decade from an
> exclusionary practice to one of selective inclusion, which inscribes certain positions
> of desire and success for those 'oppositional' elements who consent, perhaps
> unconsciously, to the position of alterity – a position that is sanctioned only as the
> exception. (Behdad, 1993: 46)

I am aware of this selective or tokenised inclusion, made aware of it through
my experiences in the academy and the daily contradictions of being a Black
woman academic. It would, however, be problematic for me to identify myself
solely on the basis of 'race' and gender, as the 'Other', because, while I am
disempowered in some ways, I am also given an authoritative voice to speak
for specific others. Within academia, my gender and race identity allow me to
speak with more legitimacy for Black people and women.

At the same time, in a discipline which has recently, albeit belatedly,
responded to the critique of Eurocentrism (Crush, 1995; de Groot, 1991;
Said, 1978) and the politics of representation (Duncan, 1993; Katz, 1992;
Kothari, 1995; Spivak, 1987), I become a symbol of transformation, evidence of the commitment to a (post)modern, 'politically correct' development
studies. Being 'a symbol' is neither politically acceptable nor unproblematic
in ontological terms. Indeed, it has implications for who I am and how
I feel.

Moreover, tokenised inclusion does not necessarily signify that radical
changes have shifted the balance of power within academia. In fact, as Behdad
suggests, 'this tokenised inclusion renders the conservative grip more efficient
and powerful, in that voices of resistance are now somewhat contained in the
compartmentalised ghettos of the academy' (Behdad, 1993: 47). While not
agreeing wholly with Behdad's pessimism, since there *are* possibilities for
black people and feminists within academia to challenge, resist and negotiate,
he does raise an important issue for those of us who find ourselves in the
borderlands of inclusion and exclusion, marginality and centrality.

There are many contradictions in these borderlands. In particular here, I
am at the same time marginalised institutionally, yet central in my position as
'expert' in (re)presenting the 'Other'. This ambivalence can be shown through
my relationship with students and my experiences as a consultant.

In the classroom

Most of those studying in the institute in which I teach are from 'Third
World' countries. The majority are men but recently an increasing number of
women are participating in training courses. However, not surprisingly, most
of the students on gender and development programmes are women. My
relationship with the students I teach is mediated by race and gender and
there are inconsistencies in my institutional role and contradictions raised by
my identity as a racialised and gendered person. These constrain and limit
while at the same time they may also provide spaces for negotiation and a
flexibility which is enabling.

hooks suggests that as academics we need first to confront the inequality of the student/teacher relationship and examine how, as teachers, we use this power over others (hooks, 1989). While I certainly agree that there are issues of power in the classroom which need to be challenged, they are not always simply manifest by the teacher's power over the students. Instead, power shifts and is played out in a variety of ways by different actors. My authority in the classroom cannot be taken for granted, for my legitimacy may be, and sometimes is, challenged because of my 'race' and gender identity, rather than on the basis of my knowledge and disposition as an academic. In fact, I often long for affirmation and an immediate recognition of my value as a teacher, despite holding a political standpoint which encourages the challenging of these power relations by students.

When confronted with a Black female teacher, students reassess not only my role as a teacher but also their own positions as students. For many of the students, I do not fulfil their expectations of a teacher in Britain, and therefore my authority and knowledge is questioned. Paradoxically, however, the students may also appropriate me as one of them, as a 'Third World' person, albeit one of the diasporic intellectuals. Simmonds examines the way in which the students relate to her as a Black woman when she writes:

> I am sometimes asked how I cope with teaching nearly all white students. My reply is that I do it, that is my job. However, my students are the ones that have to cope with being taught by a black woman. They have had no experience of that. (Simmonds, 1992: 59)

But few of my students are white. On the contrary, most of them are black and have a great deal of experience of being taught by black teachers, mostly men but sometimes women. However, they come to Britain to gain 'expert knowledge' in their particular field, and almost by definition, many of them perceive expert knowledge as advanced and imparted by white males. Indeed most of the teachers of development studies in British institutions *are* white men; there are very few women and Black people. Thus, I do not fit their preconception of what constitutes the obtaining of a 'good' education in Britain.

I face a similar situation in my role as a consultant. I am often asked to travel overseas and work with local people on particular development issues. However, their expectation of receiving a white, often male, consultant is immediately evident when their faces fall or they look through me when they come to meet the consultant at the airport. The onus is then on me to win them over and to challenge their stereotypes of who possesses knowledge and who is capable, through proving my worth *despite* my 'race' and gender.

Many of the students bring with them presuppositions fashioned on colonial and neo-colonial epistemologies. As Ngugi argues, their minds have become colonised, as is revealed through their engagement with western academic discourse on the 'Third World' (Ngugi, 1992). For many, the only 'true' education can be found in western institutes of higher education where those who possess the significant and privileged knowledge are white men. Furthermore, the persistent power of colonial education systems in 'Third World' countries is manifest by the depth of knowledge concerning British history and geography but the corresponding lack of familiarity with their own history and environments (Guy-Sheftall, 1993). I have to confront this distortion.

As a Black woman in academia, I am not easily placed since my identity and my institutional role appear and indeed are contradictory. The ambivalence in the ways in which I am perceived enables me to shift in and out of different positions in relation to my institutional role and my relations with colleagues and students. This greater flexibility in negotiating and reflecting upon my identity and relationships would not be afforded to those who, by virtue of their 'race' (white) and gender (male), are more readily named and located.

As I shift across the borders of *us* and *them*, at one moment I find allegiances with the experiences of my students and at other times I recognise the power inequalities marked by my position and identity. I often ally myself with my students when we share common experiences, usually in terms of 'race', gender or colonialism. However, while Black and female, I am also an academic located in the West, and recognise the relative power this gives me. In this sense, I do not generally share the same experiences of inequality and powerlessness with my students. This is not to say that all students are in vulnerable and weak positions, but they are represented in this way.

It is not always easy to negotiate this in-betweenness but it is something that I confront and consider daily. A mundane example of this is my deliberations over 'ethnic-cultural' forms of dress in academia. Following Rassool's discussion on this issue, I also have often thought about how I dress and its implications for my inclusionary/exclusionary status. I feel that it would not be in conformity with my academic placing if I dressed 'ethnically', although it may locate me more firmly with my students, as it would too markedly signify ethnic 'otherness' (Rassool, 1995: 31). In this case the 'Other' are the students whom we teach, the people of the 'Third World', who we 'develop'. This does not mean that my conformity in dress locates me as one of 'them', the western 'experts', but it does give me the *appearance* of a distance from the 'Other'. Here, my conformity is in wearing 'western' dress but not necessarily that which identifies me as an 'academic'. Therefore, I do have some flexibility by choosing from a range of (western) dress codes which play a role in (re)constructing my image if not identity.

We are constantly negotiating the positions that we occupy and there is no clear and distinct separation between 'us' and 'them'. Instead, we adopt different strategies in order to manage the contradictions of identity and to move within and across the borderlands of inclusion and exclusion. Thus, as an academic I can simultaneously occupy a position of power *and* powerlessness (Simmonds, 1992). This question of mobile and contingent power is immensely significant if you are to use the university as a useful site for radical political work (hooks, 1989).

While there is potential for empowerment in this dislocation, it can also be used by the institution in various ways which are not so empowering. For example, as a consultant I can legitimise certain forms of institutional power and control. The challenge to Eurocentrism and an awareness of the politics of representation have challenged much development theory and practice. Thus, my identity as a Black woman can be used to articulate a commitment to letting the 'Other' speak. That is, I am the legitimate person to teach gender and development and to go to other countries, as my identity and presence challenges the notion that development is western and Eurocentric. But by doing so I also legitimise notions of 'the West', 'development' and 'western expertise'.

Conclusion: negotiating, challenging and resisting

In exploring some aspects of my identity as a Black feminist teaching development studies in a western academic institution, I have attempted to highlight the feelings of ambivalence created through my simultaneous empowerment/powerlessness and inclusion/exclusion. At certain times in particular spaces you struggle to gain some power and intellectual space which must be constantly (re)negotiated in academia, while at other times, such as in the classroom, it is necessary to be aware of different forms of power relations.

My tokenised inclusion does not necessarily mean radical changes in power within academia (Behdad, 1993). However, as feminists and Black people, we *do* create opportunities to challenge attempts at social and professional marginalisation, through networking, challenging and resisting and thus, however difficult, we do not necessarily collude in our own dispossession (Rassool, 1995). No longer do Eurocentric and male paradigms of knowledge remain unchallenged as 'natural' or impartial in the education system.

In my role as an academic I am involved in the construction of knowledge, through teaching and publishing, and through this position I have the opportunity to challenge masculinist and Eurocentric discourse and offer alternative visions of teaching/learning and development. As Behdad has argued, 'social, cultural and historical diversity (are) a necessity and educational democracy an imperative' (Behdad, 1993: 44). Furthermore, networking with different groups of people within and outside the academy provides a necessary forum for resisting and challenging. It enables the exploration of different ideas in supportive environments and is conducive to intellectual and personal development in the context of what is increasingly becoming a tough and competitive institution in which certain masculinist and Eurocentric forms of knowledge and ways of communicating persist, but no longer remain unchallenged.

On re-reading what I have written, I am rather taken aback by how I have edited out much of my personal feelings and also my failure to furnish the story with anecdotes. On reflection I believe that this represents another facet of my position in the academy; that is, that through the production of ideas I am apt to arm myself with more 'abstract' theory, so that the personal space of emotion and imagination lies unrevealed and thus is not vulnerable to attack by those in more powerful positions in the academy. This does not necessarily mean that by engaging in 'abstract' theory one cannot challenge dominant forms of knowledge and communicating, and there is an argument that this may be necessary to be effective. Instead, we must recognise that there are different ways of posing theoretical questions and issues and some of these are more accessible than others.

References

Behdad, Ali (1993) 'Travelling to teach: postcolonial critics in the western academy', in C. McCarthy and W. Crichlow (eds), *Race Identity and Representation in Education*. New York: Routledge.

Crush, Jonathan (1995) 'The invention of development', in J. Crush (ed.), *Power of Development*. London: Routledge.

de Groot, Joanna (1991) 'Conceptions and misconceptions: the historical and cultural context of discussion on women and development', in H. Afshar (ed.), *Women, Development and Survival in the Third World*. London: Longman.

Duncan, James (1993) 'Sites of representation: place, time and the discourse of the other', in J. Duncan and D. Ley (eds), *Representing Cultural Geography*. London: Routledge.

Edwards, Michael (1993) 'How relevant is development studies?', in F.J. Shuurman (ed.), *Beyond the Impasse: New Directions in Development Theory*. London: Zed.

Guy-Sheftall, Beverly (1993) 'A black feminist perspective on transforming the academy: the case of Spelman College', in S.M. James and A.P.A. Busia (eds), *Theorising Black Feminisms: The Visionary Pragmatism of Black Women*. London: Routledge.

hooks, bell (1989) *Talking Back: Thinking Feminist – Thinking Black*. London: Sheba.

Kabbani, Rana (1986) *Europe's Myths of Orient*. Bloomington: Indiana University Press.

Katz, Cindi (1992) 'All the world is staged: intellectuals and the project of ethnographies', *Environment and Planning D*, 10: 495–510.

Kothari, Uma (1995) 'Reckless eyeballing: the politics of representation in development studies', paper presented at the IBG, Newcastle, January.

Lanham, Jane (1989) *Women and Development in Africa*. Halifax, MD: University Press of America.

McCarthy, Cameron and Crichlow, Warren (eds) (1993) *Race, Identity and Representation in Education*. New York: Routledge.

Mirza, Heidi Safia (1995) 'Black women in higher education: defining a space/finding a place', in L. Morley and V. Walsh (eds), *Feminist Academics: Creative Agents for Change*. London: Taylor & Francis.

Mohanty, Chandra Talpade (1991) 'Under western eyes: feminist scholarship and colonial discourses', in C.T. Mohanty, A. Russo and L. Torres (eds), *Third World Women and the Politics of Feminism*. Bloomington: Indiana University Press.

Ngugi, Wa Thiong'o (1992) *Decolonising the Mind: The Politics of Language in African Literature*. Nairobi: East African Educational.

Pearson, Ruth (1992) 'Gender matters in development', in T. Allen and A. Thomas (eds), *Poverty and Development in the 1990s*. Oxford: Oxford University Press.

Rassool, Naz (1995) 'Black women as the "Other" in the Academy', in L. Morley and V. Walsh (eds), *Feminist Academics: Creative Agents for Change*. London: Taylor & Francis.

Said, Edward (1978) *Orientalism*. New York: Pantheon.

Simmonds, Felly Nkweto (1992) 'Difference, power and knowledge: Black women in academia', in H. Hinds, A. Phoenix and J. Stacey (eds), *Working Out: New Directions for Women's Studies*. London: Falmer.

Spivak, Gayatri Chakravorty (1987) *In Other Worlds: Essays in Cultural Politics*. New York: Methuen.

Trinh, T. Minh-ha (1989) *Women, Native, Other*. Bloomington: Indiana University Press.

14

Borderline Crosstalk

Ailbhe Smyth

I   Borders

are makeshift
always on the make
shifty
not to be depended on
yet unshifting of themselves
shiftless
so how do borders shift
no who shifts the borders?
what difference does a border make
shifting or shifted?

Amazed ashamed I am still full
of the questions I didn't know
I learned the answers first
all the cliches
cartographic fetishes
meridians and parallels
imaginary lines then coloured shapes
why is 'the ussr' red?
no I didn't ask the question then
that came later
too late to shift my mind the order of my mind
the borders of OUR world
neatly ruled, divided and lined
just maps contours of MY world
THE WORLD fifth class tuesday and friday two fifteen
what if the world were shapeless shiftless?

Way out of line
'All disorderly questions will be detoxicated
with instant non-biodegradable answers
and orders'
ours not to question why ours but to learn the lie
of their land

Lines of truths received
more or less willingly thoughtlessly
return to mind
'this large family lives in the desert
they have put up a tent to live in'
'here are two aborigines
they are called nomads as they do not stay for very long
in one place'
Repeating facts
'the border is a fact of Irish history'
In Ireland we knew all about borders
the one that wouldn't shift
bombed out of mind
its ramps and sandbags rude reminders
of stated impotence or incompetence

I took the excursion
one pound on Thursdays up North
over the border . . .
(try that to the tune
of the (London) Derry Air)
A foreign place
where I could buy condoms
and spangles and cheap clothes
with my Belfast cousins
for all the world as foreign as myself

My daughter lives there now way over the line
true
she and her friends insouciant
dance often to the roll of different drums
but otherwise accent apart
the difference can be hard to tell

I still have orderly definitions
'bedouins: tribes that roam the desert'
deserts mountains rivers
cities countries continents
yet not enough always more divisions
packages parcels politics
'Europe the birthplace of civilisation
has spread its culture throughout the world'
Europe was not then shiftless?
'Europeans – tribes that roam the world'
perhaps I don't remember that

'What we are witnessing now
is the disintegration of our civilisation'

devastation degradation
borders in proliferation
the 'Rape of Europa' a master-piece
made violated flesh

Why? I remember
'man began to sail the oceans and explore his world'
which man? big man white man
seeing all before him taking all before him
to draw his lines make his maps
and empires
dividing deserts and whatever else he fancied
for his own use and benefit
not parables or coloured jigsaw puzzles
bodies and hearts and souls separated out
bordered and bounded
white men on the make
Europeans
freeloaders and worse
movers and shifters

'One does not sell the earth upon which the people walk'
Ah, but they did

II Border Crossings

are tricky
'the borders of Europe are opening up'
for whom?
some have rich wine red passports smoothing crossings
through the control zones still in place for others
who cannot buy their way
into the free market free for all for whom?
although they try
for rich wine red passports and the pleasures of plenty
'Affluenza is the plague of the West'
and the European party is exclusive
'the ecstasy of cultural eclecticism'
post-modern European condition of inclusion
for select eclects only

In Albania they had no sugar that's a fact
and no trains in or out freedom of movement
guaranteed
but no way of moving
not only Albania in Greece or Italy or Poland

'poor women go nowhere' she told me
'whatever the colour of their passport'
in Ireland's 'Free State' pregnant women
may be interned

Freedom is not a state only a right
the stateless are humiliated violated liquidated unstated in
every sense
Gypsies everywhere forbidden to halt here
keep on the move
through Serbia the war zone
train carriages are chained tight shut
to keep the travellers in the freedom fighters
out

Strange open Europe fact or lie
it's hard to tell across the fault lines
whose fault? whose facts?
east west south north and across
some have a one-way ticket way in
but no way out and home again
'about 15 million foreigners
are residents of different West European states
almost half of them are women'
foreigners not citizens mark you
migrants not nationals
my foreign-ness the mark of your nationality
in but out separated out
living (*what is living?*)
in separate zones *zonards* controlled
'non-nationals must present their passports'
non-nationals non-people
exiles gypsies nomads
one-way ticket one-way flow
into the European economy
Western Europe in union with itself
united lines of dazzle clean

'A flexible, highly mobile labour force is the basis of
a modern Europe' for whom?
the border-makers who move at will
not migrants moved at the whim
of economic restructurers
(ugly words for ugly facts)
kept on the move
shifting armies 'guests' not conscripts
reluctant border crossers

'brothel owners rotate their personnel
across European borders
to prevent any establishment of longer connections . . .'
sex in the economy
'the free exchange of goods and services'
freely available to the richest bidders
tools instruments bordering on the unseen
obscene exploitation of minds souls bodies
servicing the needs of the market
borderline people

III   Borderlines

are dangerous
complex constructs fervent fabrications
policed realities
'the borders were fixed at Stalin's whim and
by military force'
the markers of our borders can all be shifted
made re-made moved re-moved
but what of gender and ethnicity
which remain intact markers of another kind
for whom do borders shift?
for all the border crossings some differences
remain the same
no shift in power relations

'The peoples of Europe are from a wide variety of cultural
backgrounds'
and foregrounds
some more fore than most
and some have no grounds
some are open territory up for grabs
some are caught borderline cases
'5,000 muslim refugees mostly women and children
fleeing Bosnia's hungry and war-devastated capital'
'the past year of conflict in what was Yugoslavia
has displaced 2.2 million people'
'40,000 women raped at least'
(what more can there be?)
in the name of nations states and freedom
where is the borderline between
nationalism xenophobia racism fascism?
parallels if not synonyms
my nationalism
you feel as hatred death

not pride and glory
gynocide as genocide
your national identity
wipes me out
and off the face of the map
'the forced deportation of people is now being carried out
with military precision'
shifted across back and forth regardless of humanity

States of greed
fortresses buttressed against invaders
and pollutants
nations need territories and territories need borders
and non-people need nothing

IV   Crosstalk

is difficult
I can (not always) imagine
an unbordered world
shapeless shiftless infinite in its freedom

I cannot redraw all the borders of my self
however they divide and separate
I cannot unlearn all the markers of MY WORLD
whatever their origins (or destinations)
there's always residue
what I can't excise
I carry borders and markers wherever I am
local or global here or there
I cannot talk across them all always

Sometimes
I make do with remembering
good times
the sheets we hemmed and bordered
the cross-stitching learned from
my grandmother whose origin was in that foreign place
over the border
'a stitch formed of two stitches crossing each other
thus X'
and imagine infinite intricate cross-stitched
bordertalk

border (n) strip of ground planted with flowers shrubs
herbaceous border

15

Writing the Borders: Episodic and Theoretic Thoughts on Not/Belonging

Liz Stanley

If you go down to the woods today . . .

I am ten, it is 1957, and we are on holiday, camping on the farm where my family had for decades previously gone hop-picking. 'We' is me, my brother, Mum, Dad, cat and guinea-pig; my Aunt Dorrie and Uncle Steve, their three sons, the best friends of two of them and a girlfriend and the girlfriend's younger sister; my Aunt May, her daughter, son-in-law and baby granddaughter; and my granny, Mum to my Mum and Aunts Dorrie and May (and to the absent siblings Ivy and Fred). We all trek off for the day, raggle-taggle over the hills to a small town; shopping, eating crisps in a pub garden and drinking ginger beer shandy. The others play cricket in a field, I reluctantly join in. It rains, and I sneak off to a second-hand bookshop, an unlikely presence here. Returning with my spoils and no holiday pocket money left, I bury myself in Rider Haggard's *She*, one of three books I've bought (I have this one still). I sit reading, reading, dreaming, dreaming. I hear Mum say to Aunt Dorrie there's no point in my cousins tormenting me (they have taken the book twice and I have twice erupted in purple powerless rage), and Dorrie commiserates with 'It's a pity she's always got her head in a book, she's losing out isn't she?' Mum turns her head and winks a puzzled wink at me. I feel a hot shame mixed with love mixed with secret knowledge. They don't know the book is the magic gateway to another world, another time, another place, all times and worlds and places. I am really a princess boarding with these humble but trusty folk the Stanleys until the Arch-Duke collects me; I am a stranger roaming the veldt in search of lost cities and women of fabled wonders. Castles, unending plains, vast mountain ranges, unicorns and changelings, friendship and love, foreign lands, adventures and good times rescued from bad ones all lie through that gateway.

Invitation to sociology

Episodic

As a (slightly) mature external University of London BSc (Econ) student, I 'took' economics and politics for three years between 1967 and 1970. In the case of economics I did so much like taking a pill – hold the nose and down the throat before you taste the damn thing. I certainly did not 'read' economics – who could read micro-economics textbooks when there's an unread telephone directory about? I didn't want to write equations, but to understand the world – and try to change it. My real studies took place in omnivorous reading, political groups and organisations and many earnest conversations with flatmates. In one of these I was invited to sociology, invited to read John Berger's (1963) *Invitation to Sociology*, A Youngish Person's Guide to the Discipline. Revelation was what it seemingly offered: sociology as provider of an explanatory narrative about what's really going on in social life, the truth beneath the surface. How attractive to a working-class rebel (a misfit with attitude). Yes, they *were* wrong, my mum and dad, brother, uncles and aunts and cousins, the neighbours, friends' agitated parents. I was right. I was RIGHT!

Theoretic

Karl Mannheim has written of sociologists as epistemic refugees (often because they were literal ones, as he was from Nazi Germany), people who inhabit 'the interstices' between the social formations that make up the life of insiders to society. Because of their betwixt and between status, such people are in a sense inside, but as epistemic outsiders they can see inside and insiders in a removed and detached way, understand what's really going on. It was this that drew me to sociology. Berger's invitation offered both a practical means of leaving my life so far and also the conceptual means of understanding my criticisms of that life and my perception of not really belonging to it either. Retrospectively, I came to think it provided a pejorative interpretation of what are (were?) for many social scientists the despised knowledges of everyday life, seen as impoverished and attenuated, rather than treating knowledge phenomenologically, as always derived from standpoints, local contexts. The politics of location still constitute the knowledge/power borders between academia and the rest of life: 'we' experts, 'they' life. But in spite of this, what sociology did provide, still provides for many thousands of people, is an invitation to think critically about the world and the way it is. Sociology is an open discipline in which the newly arrived can think aloud, adopt any one of a range of different, indeed competing, conceptual and epistemological perspectives in order to think reflexively and critically about the social world. In the UK at least, it continues to attract students in vast numbers, students who often feel that light-headed excitement that I did on being given a space to think about the social constructionist basis of social life and therefore the fact that it could, and ethically should, be different.

The performing lesbian and the absent woman

Episodic

It is 1973 and at last I set foot in a real university, at Salford as an MSc student on a multi-disciplinary taught Master's programme. I have escaped from being a social researcher in a New Town and a planner in a large corporation. After passing the Master's degree, I get a grant for a PhD and register in the sociology department from 1974 to 1977, the most welcoming and by a long way the most interesting of the departments involved in the Master's programme. During the first year there is a graduate students' research day. My presentation is an analysis of the many hundreds of obscene telephone calls my lover and I had received when our home phone was the contact number for a local lesbian group. There is earnest discussion, but from one or two male graduates only, I note. I am attending a politics class in the department, and a few weeks later we are focusing on the politics of crime and official responses to it; I am the only woman in the class of ten or so. Combing through the official statistics on crime, I notice fascinating sex differences in the crime rates, and then compare this with equally fascinating but converse sex differences in the mental illness statistics. Excitedly I photocopy tables, marshal the evidence of sociology and criminology ignoring or not seeing, in the next class present this as an important sociological topic. There is a silence in the room. The lecturer smokes quickly, lights another, moves us on to a different topic of discussion, the real issues here. I feel I have missed something important but can't work out what it is, only that I have offended in some way.

Theoretic

It must be nearly impossible for younger generations to understand the wall of silence – and silencing – that surrounded women's lives in the early and mid 1970s, the remarkable refusal by most of the social sciences to recognise gender in even its most unthreatening aspect of sex similarities and differences. With the late 1960s renaissance of feminist ideas and women's movements, the absent woman subject became a spectre haunting academic life, entering its portals by clinging to the coat-tails of the motley collection of its women students and minor staff. The actual women present as students and also as staff were tolerated, sometimes even heartily welcomed – so long as we knew our place. It was not our place to invite the absent woman subject to sit by our sides, to be asked questions of, to provoke changing ideas and 'facts' in the disciplines. Those very few of us who were institutionally and publicly 'out' lesbians came through the doors and stepped immediately out of place. We became 'not-women', another kind of spectre but this time in a *danse macabre*: treated as performances, entertainments, neither real women nor serious political subjects, joining the other women perceived as trouble-makers. But this was the fiercest battle raging just before the academic walls were breached. In sociology at least, it wasn't only feminists who achieved this breaching of an erstwhile controlling mainstream. Alongside 'the women' were marshalled the interactionists, the martists, the anti-positivists, the ethnomethodologists and others in search of change. It was the combined weight of our numbers and critiques that achieved it, in spite of the differences within (and even though some of us inhabited all these supposedly separate 'camps'). And equally importantly in relation to sociology in Britain, the sheer size and diversity of the discipline, stretching from pre-sixteen school studies to post-doctoral research, and the reforming stance and women-welcoming presence of the British Sociological Association (the BSA), were crucial in militating against the continuing development of any unitary 'commanding heights' to the discipline. And so sociology became organisationally what it was intellectually from its inception – the first of the post-modern disciplines, an alliance of polyphonous voices and peripheries with no meta-narratives, although some claimants (including those who now proclaim the end of meta-narratives) to provide such.

Where's home, ET?

Episodic

I am staying with my parents in the summer of 1979, during which time passes slower than it ever has before, each minute an hour, each day a month. We talk about the weather, the garden, their cat and my cats, my home and theirs, each of them, me and my partner, the usual domestic round that is also the subject of our twice weekly phone calls. We are in a smoke-filled living room and I fidget, sitting as close to the open window and door as possible. Out of the blue Mum asks what I do about the bigger boys. 'The bigger boys?' Yes she says, what do I do when they misbehave, do I smack them? I think longingly of smacking but reply that they're all eighteen or more, some of them as old or older than I am; I say (lying) that they don't misbehave. She stares at me, puzzled. Saturday afternoon I visit someone who had been my closest friend for several years. Ten years before, we had shared a political analysis and a sense of humour, suffered the Labour Party, caroused and campaigned and had a companionably good time. Her sister shows me in; she is lying on the sofa. Why is your sister here, is it flu, I ask? No, the cancer's recurred, she replies. She tells me I haven't changed at all, that I'm just exactly the same as I was ten years before, just exactly the same. We talk politely, strangers, about a shared past and not a divergent present, behave as though time has not passed; I pass as unchanged, she performs as unchanged.

Theoretic

'Identity' is emergent, subtly shifting and changing with the accumulation of experiences and years. We look back over ten years, twenty years, sixty years, and see versions of 'myself' that are strangers that seem to have few connections with the self we have become. Cross-cutting this, some aspects of identity are seen to be critical, overriding the merely contingent, with sexuality, 'deviant' sexuality especially, the key example here. Homosexuality, 'the literature' confidently asserts, has precisely such a master status (with lesbian women present in brackets here). But the most important way I understand my autobiography is through a prevailing sense of 'not belonging' and which, from the age of around four, was represented by and fought over books: 'in the beginning was the word'. Considerably more fundamental to how 'I am' than anything to do with sexuality or gender, this sense of belonging only in the mind has been a trait, a 'cast of mind', reinforced – and liberated – by becoming an academic. For me, 'an academic' has defining qualities: a unified life of and in the mind perversely achieved through the multiple fragmentations of outer time that 'the job' construed narrowly entails; the requirement of reflexiveness and the pursuit of trains of thought across a mindscape; a concern with ideas for their own sake and a recognition of what can be their life-shattering importance. I became an academic because only within academia are these things ordinary, unremarkable.

Reproduction and the sex of trees

Episodic

Early winter 1981, and I have been a temporary lecturer at the University of Manchester for over three years. I share the 'Women and Society' course we had started in 1978 with two other feminist women teaching in the department. We leave the sociology department for lunch, passing the trees outside. I say something trite about waiting for spring and the delights of new leaves. One of them speaks about the importance of having male and female trees together so that reproduction can take place. I stare at the trees. But they aren't people I say, they are trees I say, they don't have sex, male and female. No no, they say in unison: biology they say, science they say, male and female they say. I can feel a certain reproachfulness, a 'you lesbians would say that wouldn't you', unspoken in the air. I stare at them, look at the trees, think 'you heterosexuals would say that' and start again, invoking the imposition of human categories on the non-human, the intellectual dangers of anthropomorphism. The silence between us grows the more I speak.

Theoretic

For some people, (hetero)sexuality and (hetero)sexual metaphors provide a lens on the world which constitutes the way they see and what they see. From this viewpoint, some of us are seen as standing outside, beyond nature, beyond culture; outside the scheme of things. This is, howsoever expressed, offensive to those of us who are lesbians – the straight mind at work is not a pretty sight nor a mellifluous sound, and it includes all the many casual unthinking exclusions and statements of absolute certainties that are its everyday currency. And, alas, feminists are by no means immune. One contrasting approach is to see feminism as an ethic, a principled rejection of a world-view which claims universalism, an ethic founded on a sense of inequality and injustice to women but linking this to other inequalities and injustices that stem from or are associated with the same false universalism. To proclaim the moral basis of feminism may be anathema to many, but it enables feminism to transcend gender, to insist that all the world is its analytic provenance, and to insist on the symbiosis of politics and ethics.

Un/doing whiteness, or, how much ROM do you need to run a window on 'race'?

Episodic

I am attending a 'gender and development' conference in 1983. Two younger 'movement' women attend, the other twenty or so are academics. The 'movement' types proclaim and insist about the political iniquities of gender as a concept. They are boorish, patronising, and thereby still my own tongue. Others speak of gender issues in talking oh so sympathetically about 'women in the Third World'. I interject about a former student's research in her hometown of Singapore, about local women using factory work for multinationals to effect many small freedoms in their lives. Oh no, they confidently say, the conditions of these women are self-evidently immensely horrible. They sweep on to what 'we', white First World women, should do about 'them'. I feel betwixt and between in the room. The discussion moves on to 'race', black women they say (I think of Pakistani colleagues and Chinese friends and wish they were here), white women they say (I think of myself, my dad, his parents). White, I say, like black, is a complex and socially constructed phenomenon; I am white, but if some people knew what I 'really' am ethnically they might think otherwise, my dad hid his ethnicity I say. There is an awkward silence. The topic changes. Lunch arrives. I wonder when I can decently go home, when one of the organisers arrives to ask me what I meant. You must have meant *something*, she pointedly says. Romany I say, my dad's mum was a settled Irish gypsy, his dad travelling English Rom. She enthuses, asks about rituals and fairs and I feel an inquiry about the price of horses coming on. This information isn't carried in my blood I snap, I was making a point about the complexity of whiteness, of who's in and who's out, not claiming another categorical identity. We finish our sandwiches in silence. The 'movement' women appear and I find myself earnestly defending the political intentions of those who position themselves around gender.

Theoretic

For a lengthy period of time, the analysis of 'race' in western feminism remained impoverished, an automatic genuflection brought about by knee-jerk white guilt in the form of pious statements about racism and adding 'and black women' to sentences. The analysis was misleading as well as patronising: 'they' were completely powerless and 'over there', while 'we' (all white) were 'here' and should help them. The analysis of colonialism, and of the impact of indigenous 'First World' racisms on black women's lives here, is considerably more sophisticated now, because of the challenges, writings and research of women of colour themselves. Still largely absent is a convincing analysis of whiteness, nor is there a convincing analysis of the complex interface between ethnicity and race-as-colour, looking at, for example, the situations of the Irish in Britain and British Romanies and Jews as part of a continuum. With some notable exceptions, whiteness remains a largely single and unseamed category confronting blackness, also confoundingly simple, and thereby excluding all the many who do not quite fit the comforting binaries.

Reproductive technology

Episodic

The 1985 Dublin International Congress on Women has just finished. I stay on to attend a few late meetings of things I want to find out more about. One of these concerns 'new reproductive technologies'. I enter the room and am stared at by many women; nervously, I sit at the back. Someone I know comes to me, asks me outside, tells me I should leave, that I'm an outsider. But I'm interested I say. You should leave she says; she says she can't answer for how others might respond if I stay; she says I'm not welcome. I go, wondering what on earth that was about. Some years later, when a new colleague in the university tells me about her dire experiences at the Delhi International Congress, attacked and criticised in front of hundreds, I realise that the warning off in Dublin could be seen as a friendly and protective gesture rather than a hostile one.

Theoretic

From the 1960s on women's movements across the world have developed their own (changing) mainstream and peripheries, internal challenges for status and power, processes of gatekeeping and exclusion, and means of dealing with competing claims to knowledge/power. There are relatively few feminist analyses of the issues that have arisen when one women's movement group has sought predominance over and against others. Indeed, there have been times and places when to speak of such things has been taken as betrayal, justifying almost any response. Perhaps this has constituted a stage in the evolving organisational life of feminism, and the greater the move away from women's movements towards academic assimilation as women's studies, the more possible it has become to be self-critical without being self-destructive but with a loss of political edge.

A cautionary tale about times changing

Episodic

It is autumn 1989. I am used to being seen as one of the many wild women of British sociology. The editorship of *Sociology*, Britain's main sociology journal, is being advertised (it circulates every three years). I suggest to friend and colleague David Morgan that we apply jointly. Not so many years before, I had thought there was no point in my ever sending anything I'd written to it for consideration; but then I find that some of the male 'names' of the discipline are determinedly critical of both the journal and the BSA, having earlier played a role in founding both, seeing them as captured by 'the feminists' (rather like the Apache perhaps). But times change. Our bid is successful. Later we start, and it's an interesting experience through which I learn a lot. The papers roll in, and I often find myself thinking 'I could have written that' and 'I wish I'd thought of that'. As editors, we accept invitations to speak about the journal and how it works and encourage more people to submit papers. A young woman says to me there is no point in her ever sending to it for consideration anything she'd written; it wouldn't publish things by people like her, with her kind of approach – she is a wild woman of the discipline. She stares and I see I am wearing symbolic twinset and pearls or perhaps one inch of the hem of a purple Goldthorpian mantle. Times change?

Theoretic

Mainstreams are rarely so total as they or their critics proclaim and as they may seem when viewed from the outside; there are always 'submerged alternatives', sometimes not submerged but in the slow ascendant. In British sociology, there was certainly an emergent mainstream in the post-war period, an alliance of empiricism and surveys, class analysis, and the posh Marxism of Oxbridge. But its historical moment was actually brief and even at the time there was a range of burgeoning competitors: the close relationship between sociology and social anthropology in the UK; the highly influential critiques of positivism; the growth of interactionism and its links with phenomenology and hermeneutics; Marxism of a different and 'continental' hue; ethnomethodology and its joining of Durkheimian ideas about structure with Wittgensteinian ideas about ordinary language. And even more threatening to the putative mainstream than these, there were 'the women'. It was the BSA and its conferences and study groups which became the open and highly pluralist forum in which these groupings debated, clashed, influenced, and sometimes settled down to work together. Of course, over time those who worked within the organisational and committee structures of the BSA came to constitute another power centre within the discipline: but one among a number.

Silencing the subaltern, speaking of class

Episodic

I am at an anthropology seminar in autumn 1991, a retrospect on someone's early fieldwork experiences, what led him to anthropology. He speaks of being a subaltern helping 'the men' write better letters to their loved ones, and reading to them the halting efforts of their relatives and partners. Unable to comprehend that a world and a wealth of meaning may be given and recognised and received and returned in 'impoverished' writing and speech, he also describes himself in the lower reaches of the imperial army and so akin to those whose country was occupied, and he thereby manages to make 'the men' vanish entirely. I am mortified by embarrassment and resentment, but fettered by the valedictory atmosphere around this colleague on the edge of retirement. Thus are my uncles and grandfather patronised; thus is the presence of a large subordinate group, a class division within the occupying colonial force, removed from existence. I want to shout down the subaltern, utter inarticulate but forceful protest: shut up! let us other ranks speak! How arrogant these subalterns are, how colossally unaware of the seething resentments they occasion. But I sit silent, eyes castdown.

Theoretic

An uprising of junior officers is a putsch and not a revolution, and it leaves the relations of super- and subordination between the officer class and 'the ranks' untouched, those military relations that inscribe and reproduce class relations. Subaltern studies within post-colonial theory have a curious intellectual flavour when looked at from the viewpoint of class rather than 'race' and colonialism, for the debate here is openly situated in terms of 'the illiterate peasantry, the tribals, the lowest strata of the urban subproletariat' and the move from dominance by a colonial élite to 'an indigenous élite' of intellectuals who will speak for these groups. 'The people' are displaced from a speaking position once more; herein there is also a masked displacement of the women, vanishing into 'the (male) people'. The point at issue seems to be the replacement of a foreign élite with an indigenous one around a fully preserved vanguardist model of the relations of academic life: 'we' speaking for 'them'. There are close parallels here with that other vanguardist model of academic life, the view of academic feminism/women's studies as composed by a professional expert group whose object of knowing is 'women': feminist experts, of women's lives. The rhetoric of radical change used to effect the incorporation of a new élite: a massive contradiction rarely confronted.

The good ol' boys and more reproductive technology

Episodic

Spring 1994 and it is an open day for intending future sociology undergraduates at the university. There is food and drink, present students mill around talking to prospective ones, most of the department's staff are present. I see a new young male colleague smiling and talking and emphasising to the Head of Department. He ducks his head, trying to be less tall than he is. HoD smiles and laughs. YMC smiles and talks and emphasises. HoD beams. YMC has been popping into HoD's room at least once a day, talking of this project and that, this plan and that, this triumph and that, asking this and asking that. I stare, ethnography among the sociological boys. Oh look I say, clutching the sleeve of an equally new young female colleague, oh look, academic men reproducing. YFC does not pop into HoD's room every two minutes but has noticed the YMC does; we both explode into laughter. But it's not funny.

Theoretic

Academic reproduction is in essence a homosocial one in which older men offer patronage to younger men who in return offer the appearance of homage. These are relations of super- and subordination dependent upon those power relations that exist between teachers and taught, initiates and neophytes. Academic reproduction is based on a patronage system, in which gifts and other favours are sought and given: jobs, relief from onerous tasks, privileged access to desirable scarce resources including time, and neophytes being presented favourably to other patriarchs who might offer similar or alternative patronage. Of course this system does not exclusively provide benefit to younger men, nor offer only older men the opportunity for the public demonstration of their power by virtue of control over scarce resources. Younger women can be, but in fact very rarely are, offered such patronage by patriarchs within the disciplines; while older women are only rarely matriarchs who provide gifts and favours and access to other scarce resources such as publication opportunities and invitations to the supposed 'inner councils'. The mythology of this system says it is one of excellence, but in practice it is irrevocably founded upon mediocrity. This is a clone zone in which those who 'make it' either produce work instantly recognisable as more of the same old stuff but in newer theoretical language, and/or operate in ways deemed to be safe by not 'causing trouble'. Generally you need a penis for all of this – but don't worry, not all men have them either.

Dissemination

Episodic

It is June 1995 and I am at home on post-operative sick leave, finally reading the many books which have piled up. I read and read and read. I read a cultural theorist's essays, a chapter on dissemination takes my eye and I look for wry comments on phallic language. But no, there is no comment on the sperm count of this word; there are, however, footnotes on Derrida's *Dissemination* spotted messily about. All research proposals made to the UK's Economic and Social Research Council are encouraged to include proposals for the dissemination of the results; my colleagues speak of dissemination at departmental meetings; faculty meetings resound with the word; feminist colleagues fling it around. I reach for a prophylactic, a Canute on the shore-line whose feet are being lapped by the rising tide of the spermatic economy. Ideas are potent, the thrust is clear, this is seminal work, go forth and disseminate! I wonder if I am on a sticky wicket in protesting? I pick up another book, the backcover of which names feminist theory in terms of feminist philosophy, and grind my teeth at this take-over of a once shared process of theorising, turning it into 'Theory' and the prize possession of only a few. I relax into the book, not so bad . . . I jerk, spilling coffee, a cat flying from my lap. Hell's teeth, she thinks feminist theory is reducible to the analysis of gender; where is power? what of ethics? where are all the others Others? I splutter, mutter, reach for a novel and my knitting.

Theoretic

It is not only academic mainstreams which have gatekeepers, mechanisms for inclusion and exclusion, means of adjudicating knowledge-claims and canons of received ideas and 'significant' literature. In its journey from the outside inward, academic feminism too has developed canonical properties: from theory to Theory, from women thinking and acting to specialist feminist theoreticians. To ask the question, who owns 'theory' and thus knowledge within academic feminism, reveals a singular feature: the extent of the preoccupation with a small theoretical circle, most of the members of which are male and utterly conventional in their style and approach to what constitutes knowledge. The tribal totem 'Marx–Weber–Durkheim' has been replaced by the totem 'Derrida–Foucault–Baudrillard–Barthes–Lyotard–Bourdieu'. Outside of this charmed Parisian circle, with its horde of internationally travelling attendants and neophytes, lies another world, a theoretical world in which gender retains its utility and centrality, but also its limitations. What is surely needed is an analytic engagement with these limitations and a move to something better, comprehensible, retaining a commitment to 'theory as praxis'. Storm the Bastille! Merde!

Being in and out

There are words and phrases that come to mind. The slow thud of ideas marching across the mind to meet and conceptualise what this thinking consciousness contains. Academics never use one or two short simple words where twenty or so long ones will do: liminal, diaspora, fragmentary identities, polyphonous voices, cyborgs, subjugated knowledges, epistemic communities, power/knowledge, gatekeeping. These particular long words express something of it, but what none of them provides is any sense of how it *feels*, of the emotional force and resonance involved. Olive Schreiner expressed this emotion metaphorically as the hulk of a gigantic woman once chained down and only now stirring herself into movement. In her prose we feel the weight of those lost chains, the loss of hope, the agony of moving unaccustomed limbs, the slow perception of power and weight – and we also feel the anticipation of what this colossal woman will do once she is in full movement.

   This is a fine image, as fine in its way as Walter Benjamin's angel (one of those generic beings 'he') caught in the winds of time. Neither, however, have beetling about around the feet and hands of their creatures those human agents who chain the limbs and call up the furious winds. Beneath and behind these powerful metaphors busily move 'the good ol' boys', stroking each other's egos, saving face for themselves and each other, keeping out the troublesome. Being 'in and out' may be a state of mind deeply embedded in some of us, the in-betweenies, but for many more it is an actual interstitial state lying on the boundaries of academia, a transit camp, a shanty town brought into existence through the issuing of passports, the patrolling of borders, the careful regulation of the movement of peoples, the forceful distinction between true citizens and migrant workers and aliens. These issuings and patrollings and regulatings are structures which regulate the relations between states, but they are also social and political processes carried out by actual people, the 'citizens' and 'officials' and 'guards' of academic life.

How comforting it would be to say that all this is the product of men as the gatekeepers of the amazing conservatism and misogyny of academic life, but of course nothing, not even 'the patriarchy', is so simple. Proviso 1: Women do these things too, sometimes even more narrowly marking the borders, more savagely punishing infringements, with the fervour of converts and the anxiety of those admitted under license. Proviso 2: Academia, that strange world within a world, is also still life-changingly welcoming, playfully charmed by ideas and thinking on the wild side, and its borders still relatively open to the stateless and the migrant. The invitation is still there, and, with all its limitations and problems, thank goodness a great many continue to accept it. Defend the Bastille! Hélas!

References

Berger, John (1963) *Invitation to Sociology: A Humanistic Perspective.* Harmondsworth: Penguin.

Frankenburg, Ruth (1993) *White Women, Race Matters: the Social Construction of Whiteness.* London: Routledge.

Heilbrun, Carolyn (1993) 'Afterword' in Gayle Green and Coppelia Kahn (eds), *Changing Subjects: The Making of Feminist Literary Criticism.* London: Routledge. pp. 267–71.

hooks, bell (1984) *Feminist Theory: from Margin to Center.* Boston: South End Press.

Lourde, Audre (1984) *Sister/Outsider.* New York: The Crossing Press.

Mannheim, Karl (1936) *Ideology and Utopia.* London: Routledge.

Mannheim, Karl (1952) *Essays on the Sociology of Knowledge.* London: Routledge.

Mills, Charles Wright (1959) *The Sociological Imagination.* New York: Oxford University Press. (1970 Penguin edition)

Schreiner, Olive (1890) 'Three dreams in a desert' in *Dreams.* London: Chapman & Hall. pp. 55–74.

Walsh, Val and Morley, Louise (eds) (1995) *Academic Feminists: Creative Agents of Change.* London: Taylor & Francis.

Wittig, Monique (1992) *The Straight Mind, and Other Essays.* London: Harvester Wheatsheaf.

Wolff, Janet (1995) *Resident Alien: Feminist Cultural Criticism.* Oxford: Polity Press.

Woolf, Virginia (1937) *Three Guineas.* London: Hogarth Press.

16

What's a Nice Girl Like You Doing in a Place Like This? The Ambivalences of Professional Feminism

Kathy Davis

My career as a feminist academic has followed a trajectory which, at first glance, has all the makings of an American 'rags-to-riches' story. Beginning as an impoverished radical activist in the early 1970s, I turned up my nose at anything that smacked of establishment, including the newly emerging discipline women's studies. When the 1980s arrived, and with them worries about 'doing something with my life' became more tangible, I re-entered the academy – first as a graduate student, and later as an ill-paid, temporary social science researcher. From this position of marginality, I eagerly engaged in the feminist project of criticising masculinist science. I was a woman with a mission – an unwelcome and (therefore) necessary gad-fly in the male-dominated world of the university. Years later, armed with degrees and a list of international publications, I landed my first 'real' (i.e. tenured) position as lecturer – this time as 'token' feminist in a critical, but predominantly male, social science department. While my work was suddenly in some demand ('Could you contribute an article to our book on identity – we need something on "women"?'), I was clearly considered a marginal member of the department – someone who was conveniently forgotten when it came to appointments in powerful committees. During this time, I was able to discuss my situation at length with my women colleagues and feminist friends, who alternately commiserated and offered good advice for how to beat the boys at their own game. At the outset of the 1990s, I landed a hotly coveted full-time position in a women's studies department in the Netherlands – a country where women's studies is more institutionalised than anywhere else in the world. From my perspective, this seemed nothing short of heaven on earth. I had the advantages of being a critic without the disadvantages of marginality. As feminist academic, I had come 'home'. Or so I thought.

After five years in women's studies, I feel like a survivor holed up in a basement in a war-zone, waiting for the next round of shelling. I find myself looking back on my earlier years as a contract researcher or token feminist with unmistakable longing. More and more frequently, I catch myself scrutinising the advertisements for jobs in 'regular' social science departments and, on particularly bad days, imagine what it might be like to work as a secretary in an insurance company or as cashier in the local ice-cream parlour. When the university announces that cutbacks are imminent, I wonder whether I might be eligible for a 'golden handshake' and begin counting the years until I can take early retirement.

Life at the front

> The scene is a meeting in the social sciences faculty. I have just been appointed senior lecturer in women's studies – one of the few in the Netherlands. The chair announces my appointment to the group. I smile proudly. Afterwards, one male colleague comes up and congratulates me. The woman next to him, whom I know slightly, says, 'You're an American, aren't you? I always felt that Americans were such go-getters. It never ceases to amaze me.'
>
> Shortly after I have been appointed in the women's studies department, a staff meeting is held. The professor is called away for a lengthy telephone call and asks me, as next in rank, to take over. One of the staff members who had applied but not got the position I now hold announces that she is not prepared to continue until – as she puts it – 'the boss gets back'.

Just a few examples to set the stage. They are drawn from many similar occurrences which are part of my everyday life as a feminist academic in women's studies. Taken alone, they are not particularly dramatic. The drama is rather in their routine and systematic character. They are personal, but by no means idiosyncratic. Every feminist academic will have her own collection of atrocity tales.

Women's studies is a mine-field. Collective functions – departmental meetings, research groups or informal parties – demand treading with great caution. There may well be an explosive under the seemingly innocuous query or an enemy sniper lurking behind what used to be a familiar face. Old feminist friends and colleagues are unexpectedly distant and surprisingly quick to deliver a barbed remark.

Under the unrelentingly critical gaze of the women's studies community, you soon discover that you do not measure up. The more you do, the more wanting you are made to feel. You have become a workaholic who never puts in quite enough hours. Each weakness looms larger than life, while your strengths seem to have vanished altogether. Thus, the *monologues interieur* begin and you find yourself on a slippery slope: I shouldn't have got the job. It was a mistake. I don't deserve it. I am a failure.

In this paper, I take up the call for an exploration of feminism(s) and the academy. It serves as a welcome opportunity to place my personal experiences as a feminist academic in a broader context – the professionalisation of women's studies – and, ultimately, to understand the troubling and paradoxical problem of why women's studies may be no place for a feminist.

A feminist success story: women's studies in the Netherlands

In contrast to the shaky position of feminist scholarship in most other European – and even North American – countries, Dutch women's studies has become part of the academic mainstream. It belongs to the curriculum of all universities, including the technical and agricultural colleges, and several universities have full-fledged masters programmes in women's studies as well. Fifteen chairs have been specifically earmarked for women's studies and recently a national graduate school for women's studies has been established in the Netherlands – the first of its kind anywhere in the world.

The feminist sociologist Margo Brouns has attributed the unusual success of women's studies in the Netherlands to a felicitous combination of organisational and intellectual developments (Brouns, 1988; Brouns and Harber, 1994: see also Davis and Grünell, 1994). State funding which was provided early on created the material conditions for women's studies. It is typical for Dutch society that institutions and organisations are divided along political and religious lines (pillarization). Not only is each group entitled to have its needs met by the state, but there is a climate of peaceful coexistence. This politics of accommodation paved the way for the institutionalisation of women's studies as just one more academic discipline.

Unlike countries where feminist scholarship has an autonomous existence outside the academy (e.g. Germany, Italy), most feminist academics in the Netherlands have been in favour of integration from the outset. Women's studies was regarded as an intervention in mainstream scientific practice – a discipline with its own theoretical and practical concerns. Practitioners viewed their identity primarily as 'scientists', secondarily as 'feminists' and only rarely as 'women' (Brouns and Harber, 1994: 76).

Intellectually, Dutch women's studies has always been characterised by pluriformity, the willingness to embrace theories from other countries ('import feminism'), and a tendency toward 'talented imitation' (Brouns and Harber, 1994: 74). The well-known Dutch tolerance can be found in women's studies as well as with its preference for 'reasonable radicalness', a profound dislike of 'political correctness', a celebration of different 'positions' and feminism(s), and, last but not least, a marked proficiency in avoiding conflicts.

Thus, the typically Dutch intellectual climate of pluralism and strategic consensus combine with a relatively stable organisational position to make women's studies a 'discipline just like any other' (Brouns and Harber, 1994: 79). A relatively stable institutional position has been a necessary condition for the development of feminist scholarship. However, as academic feminism becomes increasingly professionalised, it becomes clear that the success of women's studies has a shadow side as well.

The gender gap

'The problem with women's studies here,' a visiting friend from Germany remarks, 'is that you have too many chiefs and not enough Indians.'

Women's studies in the Netherlands may be flourishing, but the position of women in the academy couldn't be worse. Although large numbers of women obtained university positions in the 1960s and 1970s, in the 1990s they appear to be dwindling rapidly. In the wake of the current recession, women are the hardest hit by cutbacks. Among the first to open their doors to women, Dutch universities now show an increase in female students, but a decrease in female staff. Moreover, the discrepancy between the sexes becomes greater the higher one ascends in the university hierarchy. Based on an international comparative study, the Dutch educator Greta Noordenbos (1994) argues that the Netherlands – one of the wealthiest countries in the world – also has one of the largest 'gender gaps' in academia: 2.3% of the full professors, 6.1% of the senior lecturers (associate professors), and 15.7% of the lecturers are women (assistant professors). There are fewer women in all university functions than in any major European country, less than in Botswana and just slightly higher than in Iran and Pakistan.[1]

This underrepresentation is attributed to the traditionally low level of women's participation in the labour market and the relatively high standard of living which enables a family to live on one income. Men's reluctance to take on the obligations of parenthood and the lack of day-care facilities leave mothers with the burden of child care, making part-time work the only option for many women. While some universities have affirmative action policies, they tend to shy away from sanctions or quotas. Or, as the well-known American activist Angela Davis remarked during a public lecture on a recent visit to the Netherlands, 'With you Dutch, it seems to be all affirmative and no action.'

Academic feminists in the Netherlands have been wary about having women's studies equated with the overall position of women in the university, arguing – and quite rightly – that women's studies has a different focus. Feminist scholarship is concerned with the analysis of 'gender' rather than with emancipation issues. Moreover, many academic feminists have their hands full carving out a niche for women's studies without having to sit in on hiring committees or tackle the affirmative action policies of their universities. In addition, some feminist scholars are critical of affirmative action for theoretical reasons: it doesn't 'get to the root of the problem' or it 'reifies rather than deconstructs gender dichotomies'.

In practice, the gender gap is just as relevant to women's studies, both in the Netherlands and abroad, as it is to other disciplines. Women's studies programmes are invariably small, understaffed and overburdened by administrative work with little secretarial support. As the Dutch case shows, even the institutionalisation of women's studies into departments replete with professors and tenured staff goes hand in hand with cutbacks in the staff of temporary teachers and researchers who had been doing women's studies since the early 1970s. Feminists who had taught women's studies in their own disciplines were pressured by their departments to abandon their courses with the argument that this should be left to the official women's studies department. Small projects in contract research – a previous source of feminist research – required too much overhead and were discouraged by the university, and grants for PhDs in women's studies remained few and far between.[2]

Although feminist scholars continue to engage with mainstream science, the mainstream seems less eager to engage with feminism. The curriculum for first and second year students rarely contains women's studies courses. With degree programmes becoming more and more regimented, students are increasingly given an 'all or nothing' choice: they either have to take women's studies as their major or forsake it altogether. Predictably, the number of students has begun to taper off, putting women's studies on shaky ground again. When the next round of cutbacks comes around, we may find ourselves having little else to rely on than the administration's willingness to tolerate us as an 'exception to the rule'.

Thus, in the Netherlands, academic women are becoming an endangered species, while women's studies has increasingly taken on a token function for a university more interested in cutting costs than eliminating gender inequities.

Betwixt and between: women and men in the academy

> A talented young feminist has just defended her doctoral dissertation. The committee has adjourned to discuss her performance. The two professors of women's studies, who have supervised the dissertation, are anxious. This is the 'big time' and they want to make sure that their male colleagues realize that women's studies is a force to be reckoned with. Ironically, the five male professors are unanimously positive, praising the dissertation as original and scholarly. The professors in women's studies, on the other hand, quickly point out the 'major flaws' in their supervisee's work, embarking on lengthy displays of their own erudition.

The academy is a 'male world'. Professionality – the 'habitus' of the academic – is competitive, individualistic, and rationalistic. Machiavellian power plays, the bureaucratic fix, and 'old boys' networks' belong to an ethos which is predicated on the exclusion of women as well as the traditionally 'feminine' values of cooperation, communication, egalitarianism, and compassion.

Women in higher academic positions typically find themselves 'betwixt and between'. Although they have ostensibly become regular players, they find themselves having to play the game by different rules. They are, somewhat paradoxically, both marginal to the organisation and highly visible. Femininity is something which requires constant management – or, as Deborah L. Sheppard (1989) notes, a kind of high-wire act. Many women adopt 'blending strategies' which minimise gender and serve to reassure men that despite their female exterior they are in actual fact 'just one of the boys'. This can include anything from wearing tailored suits to distancing oneself from other women, particularly feminists, to laughing at sexist jokes to – as the above example shows – using 'erudition' as a public performance to bolster one's own position at the expense of other women.

For the feminist academic, such strategies are more problematic. She can hardly ignore gender since 'gender' is what her discipline is all about. Nor can she fraternize with the men at the expense of other women or allow herself to be insulted without damaging her credibility as a feminist. While she may engage in some playful attempts to soften her 'otherness' (the feminist professor with lipstick and high heels is a case in point), no one is fooled. In short, she has arrived and yet still doesn't belong.

Impossible dreams: sisterhood revisited

A newly appointed women's studies professor is giving her first public speech. Visibly nervous and somewhat haltingly, she sets out her vision for women's studies in the future. I am sitting next to two members of her department and notice that, at the end of her talk, they do not clap.

A friend who has recently taken on a chair in women's studies asks me to comment on an article she has written. I read it carefully and send her three pages of typed commentary. When the article appears in print, I note that while she has profusely thanked her colleague-professors and the male head of the research school who were responsible for her appointment to women's studies, she has made no mention of me.

To celebrate the publication of my new book, I treat my colleagues at work to coffee and cake. The secretaries, graduate students and researchers congratulate me, exclaiming how beautiful the cover is and how wonderful the book looks. A colleague gingerly picks up the book and leafs through it with a frown on her face. 'Well, I can't say anything until I've read it,' she mutters, placing the book back on the table.

The professionalisation of feminism has dramatic effects on women's relationships with one another. As long as a feminist project is struggling for recognition – whether it is a women's studies department, a therapy centre or a business – women band together in solidarity against the common enemy (the administration, the ministry, the corporate élite). Whatever differences may exist among them, they are temporarily forgotten in the light of a common mission. Ironically, as soon as success is imminent – departmental status, governmental funding, or public recognition – projects suddenly become battlefields (Orbach and Eichenbaum, 1987). Betrayal, anger, envy, distrust and competitiveness abound. Sisters-in-arms turn upon one another with disastrous effects on their organisations or projects.

In recent years, various feminist scholars have explored relationships between women both within and outside feminism (Flax, 1978; Orbach and Eichenbaum, 1987; Brückner, 1995). Drawing upon psychoanalytic insights on gender identity, unconscious conflicts, particularly in the mother-daughter relationship, are cited as the source of the problem: women yearn for connection and have difficulties with individuation. According to Jane Flax (1978), women who enter traditionally male professions are faced with a potentially paralysing conflict between their desire for autonomy and their deep-seated fear of having to relinquish their mothers. If they follow their ambitions, they must abandon all hopes of having their wishes for nurturance fulfilled. If they repress their desire for autonomy, their frustration at having to sacrifice their individuality may well be directed at women who succeed.

Originally, feminism promised a solution to the problem. We could have it all – a supportive community of women *and* recognition for our individual desires for autonomy. The illusion of 'feminism as surrogate mother' was shattered as more and more women demanded recognition for their different perspectives – women of colour, lesbians, disabled or young women. Moreover, women who took up leadership positions within the movement or attained public visibility were subject to distrust and envy by their less successful sisters. As one famous Dutch feminist put it, it's almost as though it's more feminist to try than to succeed (Meulenbelt, 1992).

The feminist academic who rises above her female colleagues – by landing a tenured position or publishing a successful book or pulling in a prestigious research grant – will discover that, rather than being supported, she is viewed with animosity. Her motives are suspicious, her qualifications are inadequate, and her authority is continually undermined. As one newly-appointed professor in women's studies told me, 'I had the feeling that nothing I did was all right.' Whereas it is always 'lonely at the top', feminists who expect backing and recognition from other feminists are in for a rude awakening. The feminist community appears to function by virtue of its members being the same. 'Levelling' is both an automatic reflex and collective response to difference. Weak ego boundaries make it difficult to accept one another's accomplishments as separate from one's own. *Her* success becomes *my* failure and the difference between us must be chipped away until we are just the same.

Other feminist psychoanalysts like Jessica Benjamin (1986) and Janet Sayers (1994) are sceptical about locating envy ('the most feminine emotion') in women's desire for nurturance from other women. Instead, they argue that the culprit is the phallus. In a patriarchal social order, the world of men is idealised. While both sexes yearn for their original love object – the mother – for boys there is a consolation prize. They grow up and follow in their fathers' footsteps, while their sisters remain behind – just 'Daddy's little girl'. The outcome is predictable: idealisation of what they cannot have and a persistent desire for male recognition. Having gained entrance into the idealised world of the academy, the feminist academic finds to her dismay that approving pats on the head are few and far between. The father is just as absent as he ever was.

In short, the price of success is high for the feminist in the academy. The more successful she becomes, the more likely she is to expect recognition and the less likely she is to get it. She finds herself lonely with the girls and invisible to the boys.

Power and feminism

Several years ago, I became involved in a long-term research project in women's studies, together with feminist scholars from several other universities. It was funded by a prestigious research organisation and we all regarded it as quite a plum. In addition to increasing the standing of women's studies in general, the grant actually enabled eight women to engage in innovative feminist research for four years. We could hardly believe our good fortune.

It wasn't long before the disagreements began, however. We found ourselves arguing about what we should be doing, how we should be doing it, and who should be doing what. Our bi-monthly research meetings became contentious, competitive and highly unpleasant.

After the first year, we held a weekend seminar to assess the progress of the project. While no one was happy with the state of affairs, all attempts to alleviate the situation failed abysmally. Some members wanted to talk it through, others wanted to 'stop fooling around and get down to business'. All discussions seemed to degenerate into cut-throat sparring matches which had little connection with the subject at hand. By the end of the second day, some members had gone home, while others were in tears, huddling in the ladies room being comforted by the rest. The professors made feeble attempts to manage the problem, then tried to ignore it, and finally postponed further discussion until the next meeting. We all beat a hasty retreat, relieved that it was over and with all conflicts firmly in place.

The scene is a meeting of the same project. Having reached its last year, the meetings have dwindled in frequency. Three of the members have already been on sick leave, ranging from one month to over a year. The professors are showing signs of panic, worrying about the project's output and their credibility and yet unable or unwilling to intervene. One member of the group is scheduled to present her research today, but, unfortunately, there are only two other women present. Ironically, the person who is supposed to be presenting is not among them.

Research projects are rarely pleasant and co-operative endeavours. It is also far from unusual for funds to be allocated on joint projects which prove less productive than they might have been because the participants are unable to collaborate. Shared theoretical perspectives and research aims are frequently little more than paper constructions, abandoned as soon as the project is underway. Stimulating intellectual discussions are a scarce commodity in most academic contexts where the adversarial model reigns supreme.

The project described above could, therefore, be regarded as nothing more than 'business as usual' for academic research enterprises. That's not the way we saw it, of course. Since it was a women's studies project, most of us expected something far better than 'business as usual': stimulating discussions in a friendly mode; an egalitarian organisational structure; a shared theoretical and methodological perspective – in short, a project which would not only fulfil the requirements of the funding agency but contribute to the furtherance of feminist scholarship. As the project deteriorated, our reactions were different (panic, disapproval, anger), our analyses of the problem varied, and our coping strategies were diverse (coercion, denial or evasion). Our disappointment was the same, however. Our frustrations provided fuel for further conflict and estrangement until, finally, our project had become much worse than 'business as usual'.

One explanation for this debacle is that academic feminists have problems with power. In the hierarchical world of the academy, power is pretty much 'old hat'. Those who have it (in the Netherlands, the full professors) are expected to run departments, manage research projects and chair committee meetings.[3] We all hope that they will exercise their power wisely and judiciously and most of us would definitely prefer a democratic organisational structure to an autocratic rule-by-decree.

As women's studies gains a foothold in the academy, hierarchical relations between women are inevitable. Feminist academics occupy different positions in the institutional pecking-order. The full-time professor, the lecturer with tenure, the researcher on contract and the unemployed scholar no longer form an unproblematic 'we'; they have different interests, different goals, different allegiances. When the professor in women's studies does not take responsibility for a project or refuses to mediate a difficult conflict, the rank-and-file becomes angry. She is not doing her job, they think. (Secretly, of course, each of us wonders whether she might not do a better job herself.) The 'tyranny of structurelessness' – once the bane of grassroots feminism – joins the university pecking order with disastrous results. Feminist academics can no longer join forces, united against a common foe. Now it's every woman for herself. But who is running the store?

Of course, it's not easy for the newly-appointed women's studies professor. She has reached the top apparently, but she rarely has access to the same resources or opportunities as her male colleagues. Her discipline may be institutionalised, but it continues to be marginal and a source of constant concern. She often does not have the experience which would enable her to exercise power effectively and with authority. She cannot draw upon the habitus of masculinity as a resource whereby competition is kept in line by adherence to the rules of hard-ball committee politics tempered by a friendly beer in the local pub where all can be forgotten until the next morning. She lacks the backing of the venerable 'old boys' network' and, while feminists do have their own networks, they are a long way off from providing the support needed to move about easily in the world of the academy.

While the female professor who is not a feminist may be regarded as someone who just needs to 'learn the ropes', her feminist colleague will not have the same options. The traditional feminist ethic of solidarity and egalitarianism makes hierarchies between women problematic and, in the most extreme case, antithetical to feminism. When the feminist professor engages in displays of public bicep-flexing, retreats into the exclusive inner circle rather than engaging with her cohorts, or resorts to the 'bureaucratic fix', she will be viewed with suspicion. In short, the feminist professor is expected to exercise power, but to exercise it differently. It's a pretty tall order.

'Is That All There Is?' (Peggy Lee)

The institutionalisation of women's studies tends to be regarded as the pinnacle of success for academic feminism. It is something which we fought hard for. However, as I contemplate the war-zone which is women's studies in the Netherlands, feeling tired and not-a-little shell-shocked, I wonder whether the outcome has been worth the effort or whether I am, perhaps, just the wrong woman in the wrong place at the wrong time. My feminism feels more like a burden than an asset, a source of disappointment and confusion rather than inspiration and empowerment. Perhaps women's studies should be left to those academic women who are not encumbered by a feminist past, who can approach the field as an interesting novelty or a convenient stepping stone in their academic careers. Women's studies – at least, in the Netherlands – may just not be the place for a feminist to be.

As a long-time American ex-patriate, this state of not quite belonging is well familiar and, in the process of rethinking my allegiances and reconsidering my options, I begin to wonder whether the geographical solution might not be in order: perhaps the chilly climate described above is a typically Dutch phenomenon and I should think seriously about trying my hand at academic life in the US. At first glance, my occasional visits – professional and otherwise – to my former homeland suggest that academic feminism in the US lacks much of the atmospheric harshness which pervades Dutch women's studies. In my – admittedly limited – experiences as a guest scholar, conference participant or collaborator on publications with American colleagues, I have often had a sense of 'coming in out of the cold'. This might, of course, just be a matter of the grass being greener on the other side of the ocean. However, my impression that women's studies is a more pleasant place to be in the US is confirmed by many of my American colleagues as well. As one long-time sociologist friend told me, 'Women's studies is my home away from home.' In her view, the university is a hostile environment for feminist academics, while women's studies is a haven – a place to go for encouragement, discussions about issues she cares about, practical support or just to let off steam about university politics.

It is not my contention that women's studies in the US is a paradise. Feminist academics become entangled in interpersonal conflicts there just as they do in Europe and even the sturdiest 'old girls' network' does not guarantee unquestioning loyalty or automatic support. Nevertheless, women's studies in the US is a more hospitable place for feminist academics than in the Netherlands. One possible explanation for this difference in climate might be found in the different ways in which women's studies is organised within the university structure.

In the US, women's studies is far less institutionalised than in the Netherlands. Women's studies departments do not generally exist as separate entities. Instead, feminist academics work in disciplinary departments and participate in loosely organised, interdisciplinary teaching or research programmes in women's studies. These progammes are notoriously underfunded, understaffed, and dependent on the commitment of feminist academics for their survival. They are managed by an overburdened director who may or may not be a full professor and whose primary responsibility resides in managing tight resources, negotiating a position in the university, and generally keeping the programme going for 'just one more year'. Unlike the Netherlands, where feminist scholars can work together in their own departments, in the US academic women tend to be isolated, 'token feminists' in male-dominated departments. Unlike the Netherlands, where women's studies has received formal recognition, in the US it has a marginal position in the university structure.

Thus, differences in the status and organisation of women's studies – in particular, the degree of institutionalisation – have somewhat paradoxical consequences for the overall climate of women's studies and the degree to which women's studies is hospitable to its practitioners. While women's studies in the

Netherlands has the advantages of being institutionalised, it has the disadvantages of an internal culture based on animosity and competitiveness. In the US, on the other hand, women's studies programmes have to struggle with the problems associated with marginality, but many feminist academics have a vested interest in helping one another get tenured positions at the university as well as joining forces to ensure the continuity of women's studies as a programme. The alternatives of, on the one hand, the security of institutionalisation and, on the other hand, solidarity in marginality, present a hard choice indeed. As a feminist academic, I would really prefer – when all is said and done – not to have to choose, but to have it all instead. Why isn't it possible to have the best of both worlds?

The best of both worlds

Women's studies – whether in the Netherlands or the US or other parts of the world – is invariably caught between the necessity of achieving a foothold in the university structure and the necessity of maintaining a position of relative autonomy. The former is essential for safeguarding the continuity of feminist scholarship as well as the careers of individual feminist scholars; the latter for ensuring that academic feminism remains at a critical distance to 'normal science' and provides space for innovative feminist scholarship. This tension between the risk of marginalisation and the risk of co-optation is a characteristic feature of women's studies. It not only places individual feminist academics under pressures which are quite different from those encountered by academic men and non-feminist academic women, but it unmistakably shapes the cultural climate of women's studies in general.

When women's studies shows systematic signs of becoming unpleasant, conflictual, or destructive for its practitioners – as is the case in the Netherlands – the initial response is to point a finger at the individual (poor management skills) or to shrug the problem off as endemic to any academic setting (*jalousie de métier*). Both responses ignore the specific tensions under which academic feminism exists – tensions which are, indeed, in 'the nature of the beast'.

I do not believe in feminist utopias, particularly within the walls of the academy. However, women's studies is still in transition and, therefore, subject to change. While we can't get rid of the need for some institutionalisation, we also need to find ways to maintain supportive encouragement and affirmation which will enable individual feminist scholars not only to survive but also to thrive. To this end, I propose several avenues which might be helpful for making the current climate in academic feminism more hospitable to its practitioners. While I have generated these proposals from the vantage point of my experience within women's studies in the Netherlands, they can provide a framework for thinking about the quality and organisation of women's studies in other contexts as well.

First, women's studies should not be divorced from the context of women's participation in the academy. Women's studies as an autonomous discipline necessarily functions as an alibi when the overall position of women at the university is deteriorating. Thus, a reluctance to deal with emancipation issues – as is the case in the Netherlands – is misled. As long as talented women are unable to get tenured positions at the university, women's studies will remain limited to the privileged few. Academic feminism and the feminisation of the university are separate but, nevertheless, related issues.[4]

Second, academic feminists everywhere cannot afford to ignore the desires and disappointments of professional feminism. The fallacy that we have finally arrived together with our idealisation of academic life are 'patriarchal fantasies' (Sayers, 1994). Our deep-seated longing for support and recognition from other women and the often bitter reality of envy, anger and betrayal need to be brought out in the open and analysed. This would entail a self-critical and reflexive approach to professional feminism as ambivalent, contradictory, and, to some extent, impossible.

Third, as professional feminists in the academy, we cannot afford to be ambivalent about power. The notion that there is a space within the academy which is devoid of power is an illusion and a dangerous one at that. Ignoring power does not make it go away. It simply absolves us from the task of taking a critical look at our own relationships and organisational structures. We need to find ways to mediate our differences and exercise our newly-gained power constructively: democratically, but with authority.

Fourth, women's studies will never become a 'discipline like any other'. It remains – and indeed, should remain – at a critical distance from the centre. To have it otherwise would mean that we have lost our critical edge, have been assimilated or co-opted by what we set out to criticise. This is not a rendition of the old autonomy-integration discussion, nor is it an attempt to iron out the differences among women working inside and outside the academy. I agree with bell hooks (1990), who argues that marginality is not something which should be relegated to the past when we were the victims of exclusion. Marginality is not simply a symptom of oppression, but a site which can be chosen as a location for radical critique, creativity and openness. For academic feminism, it is a space from which to develop alliances without encroaching on one another's autonomy or imposing a shared feminist identity.

Acknowledgement

I would like to thank Mieneke Wolffensperger for our many conversations about the joys and pitfalls of feminist projects. These conversations inspired me to write this paper. I would also like to thank Willem de Haan, Helma Lutz and Liz Stanley for their encouragement and helpful comments.

Notes

1. In the US, 26% of academics are women and 14% of them have achieved the position of full-professor. In the UK, 20.5% of academics are women, but only 4.9% are full professors (Lie et al., 1994: 208), although these figures are by no means easily compared as 'professor' in the

UK is a very different rank and status than it is in the US, and is somewhat more akin to the Dutch notion of professor.

2 Dutch universities provide a limited number of grant-cum-teaching assistant positions for dissertation research. In addition to these positions, some dissertation research is financed by the Dutch Council for Academic Research. In order to have access to these positions, women's studies has to have a formal status within the university. At present, the tenured staff of women's studies can devote about one half of their time to research. This is in contrast with, for example, the UK where only the teaching programmes have a formal status and much of feminist research has to be brought in through external funding or carried out under the auspices of a 'regular' department (Brouns, 1988; Brouns and Harber, 1994: Chapter 3).

3. In the Netherlands, professorships are life-time appointments rather than promotions on the basis of merit and/or seniority. Full professors are not only responsible for the scientific output of their departments, but are expected to bear the brunt of the administration as well. This is different than, for example, in the US, where the tenure system ensures that once an academic has achieved tenure, s/he automatically becomes an associate professor (senior lecturer) and – barring some unforeseen disaster – will be promoted to full professor several years later. Moreover, in the US, the chairing of departments tends to be rotated among the senior staff and everyone is expected to take part in committee work. Thus, while there are power hierarchies between staff members, they are less formally structured than in the Netherlands.

4. The situation seems to be different in the US, where individual feminist academics are concerned about getting more women hired into their departments and where affirmative action is generally regarded as a feminist issue.

References

Benjamin, Jessica (1986) 'A desire of one's own: Psychoanalytic feminism and intersubjective space', in Teresa de Lauretis (ed.), *Feminist Studies/Critical Studies*. Bloomington: Indiana University Press. pp. 78–101.

Brouns, Margo (1988) *The Development of Women's Studies. A Report from the Netherlands*. The Hague: STEO.

Brouns, Margo and Harber, Hans (1994) *Kwaliteit in meervoud. Reflectie op kwaliteiten van vrouwenstudies in Nederland*. The Hague: VUGA.

Brückner, Margrit (1995) 'Professional feminist caught between solidarity and disappointment', *The European Journal of Women's Studies*, 2: 77–94.

Davis, Kathy and Grünell, Marianne (1994) 'The Dutch case: An interview with Margo Brouns,' *European Journal of Women's Studies*, 1: 100–6.

Flax, Jane (1978) 'The conflict between nurturance and autonomy in mother-daughter relationship and within feminism', *Feminist Studies*, 4 (2): 171–89.

hooks, bell (1990) *Yearning. Race, Gender, and Cultural Politics*. Boston: South End Press.

Lie, Suzanne, Malik, Lynda and Harris, D. (eds) (1994) *The Gender Gap in Higher Education*. London: World Yearbook of Education.

Meulenbelt, Anja (1992) 'Over liefde en afgunst tussen vrouwen: op naar een sterkere beweging' in A. Meulenbelt (ed.), *Visies op feministische therapie. Over liefde, geweld en racisme*. Amsterdam: De Maan. pp. 23–38.

Noordenbos, Greta (1994) 'Women academics in the Netherlands: between exclusion and positive action', in S.S. Lie, L. Malik and D. Harris (eds), *The Gender Gap in Higher Education: World Yearbook of Education*. London. pp. 106–16.

Orbach, Susie and Eichenbaum, Luise (1987) *Between Women. Love, Envy & Competition in Women's Friendships*. London: Arrow.

Sayers, Janet (1994) 'Psychoanalysing patriarchy's ills', *European Journal of Women's Studies*, 1: 227–39.

Sheppard, Deborah L. (1989) 'Organizations, power and sexuality: the image and self-image of women managers', in Jeff Hearn, Deborah L. Sheppard, Peta Tancred-Sheriff and Gibson Burrell (eds), *The Sexuality of Organization*. London: Sage. pp. 139–57.

17

Knowing Feminisms and Passing Women: a Conclusion

Liz Stanley

Is the now visible if still not readily welcomed presence of feminisms within the academy, in the university, a success story, a version of 'rags to riches'? Are those of us who are feminists present therein the harbingers and agents of change, and sources of empowerment? Are we radical bastions against the incursions of conservatism and control? Or is this a fairy story for our times, a feminist myth, a romanticism that comforts and shields from our sight what is actually going on?

But perhaps it might be more complex than this, more awkward to describe and explain than either of these two positions suggests. Perhaps there is truth on both sides here, but not the whole truth, nor nothing but the truth, in either of them, and the truth might differ in different contexts. It is this ground – the in-between which separates the happy-as-a-clam romanticism of 'we're here, it's all changing' from the gloomy insistence that this is mere myth-making and that 'it's awful' – that the chapters in this book interrogate and explore. What has been said, and how does it fit together? Does any pattern emerge?

The backcloth has been one of concerted and often savage incursions into the organisation, management, finances, teaching and research of 'the university', which in the UK has taken the form of an unmistakable attack on its central values of independence and thoughtfulness as much as on its finances or the working practices and conditions of its academics. Elsewhere, these state incursions have focused more on finance than intellectual practices, or have been experienced as assimilation within pre-existing structures which have bent what was once Other into conforming shape, or have appeared as troops viciously attacking those who dare to protest, or have been terrorist snipers leaving the dissident dead in their own blood (and remember Canadian Marc Lépine murdering women students, as well as troops storming their way into Nigerian and Argentinian university campuses). But still, such state incursions, such bendings and shapings if not forcings and murderings, have occurred and are occurring in university systems in most parts of the world.

These incursions have been marked by the insistence that thinking is a wasteful luxury and one that cannot be afforded: to think is to waste; to think is too radical; to think is to be like the lilies of the field which neither toil nor spin nor do anything very useful at all. This is the Gradgrind notion of what it's all about – what we should be doing is producing 'units' who possess certain 'skills', defined as those directly usable within the market-places of capitalism, conforming to its certain needs, and being of known shape and capacity and activity. For such a mind-set, the university is pre-capitalistic, hedonistic, anarchic: thinking independently for its own sake, what greater danger could be posed than this, an activity without apparent profit?

If a danger to the very idea of 'the university' is being experienced from the managerialist impulse within, as well as from without, then can the university be both defended and attacked at the same time? Can it be radically changed in one set of ways (those that constrain and confine minds but also bodies), but still remain fundamentally intact in others (those which liberate by encouraging intellectual and all other independence)? These are central questions for feminists, for they raise associated issues concerning whether feminism can be done within such an institutional setting or whether it is always a matter of being at a skew to it, an irritant rather than the body politic itself. But then again, we also need to ask just why it is that we, and many like us, continue to call 'the university' those managerial position-holders, those 'I'm just doing my job' sources of paper edicts that tell us what to do and when to do it as defined by our political task-masters. We too are the university, those of us who teach and those of us who learn. We feminists also need to recognise that ours is not the sole nor necessarily the most important presence within this, and that there is no need for us to assume, nor accept when others attempt to thrust upon us, responsibility for the survival of those attributes of the university which we wish to preserve, indeed to enhance: its transformative capacities. If 'they' tell us that our protestations are too loud, too wild, and damage the university, then, instead of becoming quiet, let us rather inquire in whose interest it is to shut us up, make us quiescent.

In piecing together the threads of what is happening, the considerable organisational complexities of 'academia' have to be recognised, composed as it is by overlapping sets of activities: in the 'intellectual' aspects of research and publication; in the 'teaching' aspects of engagements with students, classrooms and graduate supervisions; in the 'administrative' aspects of carrying out the now required administrative tasks of the organisation. And also, of course, here the activities of 'those who teach and those who learn' are surrounded not only by an army of university administrators and support staff and by departmental and faculty structures, but by state-imposed systems of regulation, and also by the less forceful but no less important presence of 'the disciplines', with their own boundaries and borders, apparatus for self-constitution, systems of communication, regulatory mechanisms and gate-keeping activities. There can be, there typically are, rather different conditions and relations pertaining in different conjunctions of the complex institutional structure of higher education. It is not therefore surprising that it is correspondingly difficult to analyse 'what's going on'. It's getting much worse, is one message; but it's also getting much better too, for some.

The academic disciplines have attracted and repelled many feminist academics in just about equal measure; indeed it has often been the same thing that has attracted and repelled at one and the same time. An important example here has been the promise of the disciplines, indeed of the university more generally, that they can and do provide the means of 'seeing "reality" as it truly and objectively is'. This is the promise of power as the product of specialist secret knowledge, the promise of knowing what others do not, the arcane, the mysterious. But feminist academics are and remain women, those who have been Other and object to this process and its resulting set of organisational practices: subservient presences within, 'samples' who have been the focus of the investigatory gaze without. If universities are mechanisms for the construction and the getting of that which comes to be defined as knowledge, then to come inside, to be the constructors and enforcers of, and not merely the subjugated others to, this process and its product is more than double-edged. For one thing, feminist as well as other critiques of the foundationalist pretensions of all versions of 'science' have insisted that the emperor actually has few clothes, that 'knowledge' in these terms is a chimera. For another, this is the direct opposite of 'going native', for it is to leave the native colonised peoples, to join the ranks of the colonisers. And for another, 'they' always know that we are Other to 'them', for we bear the indelible signs with us when we enter. So why do feminists want to enter, then, if this is all there is? Certainly some want these 'Othering' aspects of the academy, with gender as the means of gaining ingress as the source of specialist knowledge claims, promising really true knowledge about women. 'Feminism is not unitary', write 500 times.

One of the many separations within feminist thinking, as well as between 'it' and other systems of thought, has cohered around the centrality of binary thinking to the academy and the related assumption of universalism. Cartesian thinking insists that there can be, indeed within the university there must be, a divorce between thinking and being, between mind and body, between thinking and feeling, between feeling and knowing, because one end of these binaries gives rise to universal statements of 'the facts' which imply no politics of location: the knower is transcendent, and so the knowledge is general, universal. Feminism entered the academy on a wave rolling across the intellectual mindscape of the West, a wave composed by movements, social as well as political and intellectual, which insisted upon first revaluing these binaries and then rejecting the view that they are actually binaries: as Adrienne Rich insisted, 'objectivity is what men call their subjectivity'. The insistence on the need for embodied theory, situated knowledges and the politics of location have all energised and propelled feminism. More recently these seem to have been lost sight of in the drive to come inside, away from the margins and into the centre, into the university as one site of knowledge and so power, to take up the tools of the master's house and to produce Theory as abstract and disembodied as was ever produced herein. However, the more subversive ways of thinking and conceptualising have remained, although they have been often denied or trivialised, and there are signs they are once more being revalued, a new generation thinking differently from the margins in shrill voices, being and being seen as uppity, difficult women. But now more inside than before, and more troublesome.

So are there better, more enhancing, things that 'inside' of academia confers? The expectation many people have when they enter higher education is that this experience will be about developing new ways of thinking, new ways of being, new knowledges. But often what they find instead is boring, badly or carelessly done, or is openly repressive, or indirectly so in the sense that whatever women (working class, black, 'mature', disabled) are is 'wrong' in some indefinable way. They find themselves not simply at odds with the dominant values and practices of the place (for they often embrace these, wanting knowledge/power themselves), but in some more fundamental sense they are the wrong kind of person, even when they do exactly the right things in terms of custom and practice. They enter bearing the signs of their Otherness. What dispowers women and other Others within the academy can be the alien way in which ideas are formulated and expressed, can be the kind of space that it is, can be the way that roles and expectations are distributed within it. But it can also be the contention that we are inside when really we oughtn't to be, when we just do not belong, when it is our being that is difficult, wrong. Other. 'We' make 'them' uncomfortable.

But of course 'we' do not exist. 'We' are many and varied, and our names are legion. What is it that shapes 'identity' and the ways we come to understand what it is to be us, our kind of person? There are the easy answers, that this is the product of biology or of upbringing, that we are creatures of gender and 'race' and ethnicity and class and age-cohort, or that there are other broader processes at work, discovered in the mind as much as the body, deep structures albeit shifted and changed by surface and outer ones. Then there are the things that can no longer be said without someone assuming that any mention of individuality is a retreat into the taboo individualism: that, for example, we can be female and black and lesbian but unique, like no other of our kind. What, thankfully, remains is the sheer bloody-mindedness of people, who behave and understand themselves this way and that, outside the law of what knowledge tells us. How else can we explain the ingress of women into the academy in spite of the bars to doing so within the supposedly egalitarian but actually highly élitist and competitive teaching and examination system? If knowledge actually knew what it claims to know, this would not, could not, be happening. No wonder the lineages of ideas and theories are not often traced, for 'knowledge' is not cumulative but is rather that which brown-noses the prevailing orthodoxies of its day.

There are, of course, mechanisms for the exclusion of difference and the control of 'different' people once they manage ingress, the management of those who are perceived as 'Other'. These mechanisms are not additional to, but are rather constitutive of, 'the organisation', and they operate in every aspect of academic life, at formal as well as informal levels, including through the evaluation of applications for funding and for jobs, through short-listing, interviewing, appointment, and through evaluation and promotions reviews.

At every point where people are judged, they can be found wanting because of who they are as well as what they do and how they do it. 'Standards' and 'ability', like 'skills', are socially and politically constructed, part and parcel of the procedures by which entry into the organisation and mobility within it are managed and controlled, and the constitution of disciplines can reinforce as much as undercut these organisational processes. 'The institution' of higher education is more than the form of organisation that is termed the university. Disciplines are no refuge from the organisation of the university or the institution of higher education; the disciplines are central: the patterns of inclusion and exclusion could not be as they are without them. They are deeply implicated; but even so they are among the few interstices left, another in-between where the in-betweenies can go, meet, think, plan, organise.

Women in general, feminist women and black women perhaps especially, are Other to this last most zealously guarded boys' club that is the university. All women therein have to pass, have to become passing women. At its most basic this means becoming invisible. Women are the means that make it work, its chief labour power, the source of its divisions of labour, so that men at all levels can have their organisational noses and bums wiped and nicely flattering and size-enhancing mirrors held up before them. Power dressing, power behaving, competitiveness, are all aspects of women's passing: they are ways of seeming to be just as the men herein are. There are other more subtle forms of passing too: we do not scream, rage, run amok; we nod and smile and agree. To be fully out would mean being in a constant state of revolt, of opposition. To pass is the price of admission and the cost of remaining. We pay or we go – we cannot have clean hands, wash the contamination away through protestations of revolutionary sentiment or intent. There are things feminisms and feminists want, indeed desire, here. This is why so many attempt to enter, this is why so many struggle and compete to remain. As for what these things are, let us be clear that these are the other side of the very things that we despise or criticise, the sickle side of the moon; they are knowledge, independence of mind, intellectual space, transformative thought.

Passing does things to how we are and what we do and what we can become. There are ontological significances here as well as epistemological consequences, and there are also ethical as well as political ramifications. Passing as an ontological state contains notions of liminality and transformation: you can only be in the closet if you are concomitantly, at one and the same time, somewhere else as well and always on the move from one to the other. One place, another place, and moving in-between. No wonder that in becoming politicised passing peoples claim an identity they were taught to despise, for to be, to become, *someone* is an ontological revolution for those who have had no one state of body and mind to be.

Do knowing feminisms, then, confront the passing women of the academy, as a new kind of Other within? And is passing here to be seen as a kind of epistemological as well as ontological betrayal? But another way to see this relationship is that passing is, by definition, a condition and a product of knowledge, of knowing from the underside and then knowing the dissimulations that result as those under and other *pass*. Being within but passing is the first stage in coming out, along with knowing other passing people and together creating that liminal space where masks are dropped, or rather other masks are donned. Coming out as a passing black person, as a passing lesbian woman or gay man, are well documented processes as well as well trodden paths in the lives of many people who have lived passing, liminality, politicisation; but what would coming out look like in terms of the feminist academic? Can we already see this within the pedagogical practices associated within feminism in the academy, or is this something different?

Of course attempts to challenge and change the stultification of convention have occurred through the introduction of feminist practices within the academy, and within feminist pedagogy in particular. Here for many there has been a proclamation of the transformative relationship between teaching/learning/being/becoming – teaching as a means of taking a stand against the institution and thereby empowering students, a collective moral statement. But this is a praxis which takes place in a context where failure is in-built – 'power' and 'hierarchy' permeate everything in the interface between teacher and taught, those that mark and those that are marked, those that evaluate and judge and those who are evaluated and judged. To deny this is romanticism indeed, and it also de-skills and dis-empowers those of us within the university as its teachers and researchers, within because we do know that which neophytes do not. The conjunctions of knowledge and power are by no means simple or one-dimensional: neither innately good nor bad, it all depends on who, what, how and with what effects; but, whichever or both, within an institutional context it retains a hierarchical form.

Paradoxically, it is sometimes the conditions of the harshest exclusion, the most repressive mechanisms of internal control, that enable the creation of enclaves, free(er) zones within, on the borders, around the peripheries. To be inside the academy is to collude, there should be no doubt about that. The currency of money and publishing creates the only value valued – these things buy organisational acceptability, indeed kudos, even for the morally vile. The question is, can collusion coexist with the continued impulse to challenge and to change? How many of the feminist professoriat, the full professors and heads of departments, can be counted on here? Or indeed how many of the rest of us? But academic mainstreams are not absolute; they change over time, and, amongst things, academic reproduction involves the processes of incorporation of that which was formerly Other. It may be that incorporation and assimilation are the surest forms of change, neither complete nor total but at least something. To be 'Other' is no simple point of stasis.

Colonial otherness – isn't colonialism always a matter of predicating one form of being upon another which is privileged over and above it? First Peoples should perhaps resist plurality and interculturalism, for these are terms and processes which stand for their dissolution into that which is privileged. This is not 'intercultural' but subservience and subjugation of one culture within, rather than, as before, without a dominant one; and nor is it plural, for it is 'the one' which is dominant and superordinate and not 'the

Other'. Perhaps academic feminism should think about itself and its relationship with 'women' in these terms, with the attractions yet the dangers of gender implicated here. The comfort of the similarities with other women is that the academic and the feminist have a value-added effect rather than producing a difference in kind, but privileging gender may make class, sexuality, 'race' and ethnicity and other structured inequalities and identities vanish. And the theorisation of this privileged view can become a new field of expertise, the creation of new academic élites and their incorporation: 'we = feminist experts who theorise gender; you = women who merely experience it'.

There are no easy or permanent answers to such complexities, for as conditions change so too may the configuration of these issues and of suitable feminist responses to them. There is no 'home' anymore, if there ever was. 'Inside' isn't home to the other Others; it provides only the grounds for a transit camp, a shanty town along the walls of the great city of Academia. And once inside, it is no longer possible to claim to be 'an activist' in any former sense, for one result of being inside is that entrants take on a different point of view, a habit of critical thinking about everything; everything, including what you are and have been, so that 'being Other' is the ontological state of Academia, surrounded by performances of belonging. Outside, this is to have become different, but sometimes not different enough, as when the promised goods – knowledge, power, change – are not forthcoming. This happens when the very kind of academic that someone is requires continued dealings with some organisational aspect of 'outside', differently premised and constituted around different ontological as well as epistemological states. The peculiar conditions of the applied disciplines and multidisciplines can condition what their inhabitants see as intellectually 'proper', for the professions outside can respond to 'their' academics as by definition deficient: knowledge lies in practice, not in theory; those who can do, those who can't teach.

But of course 'they' do not exist in any unitary sense either. We are all 'outside' as well as 'inside' at one and the same time, and there is a multiplicity of borders and border-crossings within. Within is not, has never been, a unitary place and space, and such complexity is not a deviance introduced by the contaminating presence of women/feminisms. The regulations and customs and the language and uniforms of the university exist, but so too do seething intellectual discontents and jealousies of those who are superior and shouldn't be, and angers at those who are inferior but don't know their place. Putsches and palace revolutions take place within disciplines as well as in departments and faculties, as erstwhile mainstreams are displaced, ruling groups are toppled, canonical ideas are challenged and abandoned. The times are always turbulent, change is always occurring, things are never quite as they are represented. Women's studies is no home either, for this too is not one but many, inhabited by proponents of women's studies or gender studies or feminist research or of none of these or of all, and it has its own regulations and observances, its own ruling groups and rebellions, its own emergent and displaced canonical ideas.

A more interesting point to contemplate is why should anyone want 'home', should want this particular version of home. Why should an academic want a sense of intellectual belonging? Isn't thinking best done from the margins? Shouldn't it be a case of reading Virginia Woolf each morning and bell hooks each evening? But there are other things to be found 'inside' of the university than those already catalogued, and perhaps these are the things that are truly desired, that continue, rightly, to inspire. Let us not forget, let us also remember each morning and each evening, that, with all its problems and faults, nonetheless the existence of the university is a mechanism permitting critical, independent and creative thought. In this respect, the university enables the presence and persistence of intellectual complexity and dissent, and it is founded on principled ways of doing things and principled beliefs in knowledge and the freedom of mind. These things are worth having and worth defending. These are the things that continue to attract, to seduce, for such attributes are those which underpin individual and collective struggles to understand the world and then, in some small measure, also to change it.

References

Cliff, Michelle (1980) *Claiming An Identity They Taught Me To Despise*. Watertown, MA: Persephone Press.

hooks, bell (1984) *Feminist Theory, From Margin to Center*. Boston: South End Press.

hooks, bell (1989) *Talking Back: Feminist Thinking – Thinking Black*. London: Sheba Feminist Publishers.

Hunt, Marsha (1996) *Repossessing Ernestine: The Search for a Lost Soul*. London: Harper Collins.

Lorde, Audre (1984) *Sister/Outsider*. New York: Crossing Press.

Luke, Carmen and Gore, Jennifer (eds) (1992) *Feminisms and Critical Pedagogy*. London: Routledge.

Morley, Louise and Walsh, Val (eds) (1995) *Feminist Academics, Creative Agents for Change*. London: Taylor & Francis.

Rich, Adrienne (1979) *On Lies, Secrets and Silence*. London: Virago Press.

Woolf, Virginia (1929) *A Room of One's Own*. London: The Hogarth Press.

Woolf, Virginia (1938) *Three Guineas*. London: The Hogarth Press.

Biographies

Johanna Alberti has taught all her adult life and now teaches mainly history, mainly for the Open University, and also for the Universities of Newcastle and Northumbria, and the Worker's Educational Association. She has written *Beyond Suffrage: Feminists in War and Peace. 1914–28* (1989), *Eleanor Rathbone: Woman of Ideas* (1996), and a number of articles.

Carol Brown is an independent choreographer, a dance lecturer and performer. She teaches choreography and dance and gender studies at the University of Surrey. Her dance theatre company, Subrosa, has performed in Europe and Australasia. Her major work, *Eve's Tattoo*, was premiered in England in Spring 1996.

Chris Corrin teaches politics and women's studies in Glasgow. Her current work is concerned with feminist analyses of and resistance to violence against women; comparative research on women's changing realities in East–Central and Eastern Europe; and aspects of lesbian politics. The central focus of her life is spending time with women in many different situations, enjoying learning and laughing together.

Kathy Davis was born in the US and has taught (medical) sociology, psychology and women's studies at various European universities. She is currently a senior lecturer in the Women's Studies Department at Utrecht University in the Netherlands. She is the author of *Power Under the Microscope* (1988), *Reshaping the Female Body* (1995) and co-editor of several books on gender, power and discourse.

Mary Evans was educated at the London School of Economics and the University of Sussex. She has taught sociology and women's studies at the University of Kent since 1971. Her main academic interests are in nineteenth- and twentieth-century Western feminist literature. This is fortunate, because it precisely coincides with her taste in reading. Published works include *Jane Austen and the State* (1987), *The Woman Question* (1993), *A Good School* (1994) and *Simone de Beauvoir* (1996).

Elaine Graham is a lecturer in social and pastoral theology and has been Director of the Centre for Feminist Studies in Theology, Department of Religions and Theology, University of Manchester since 1988. After a first degree in social history and sociology (Bristol), she worked in adult education and higher education chaplaincy. Her research interests are theories of gender, feminist theological praxis. Her publications include *Life-Cycles: Women and Pastoral Care* (1993) (co-edited with M. Halsey) and *Making the Difference: Gender, Personhood and Theology* (1995).

Uma Kothari is currently a lecturer in development studies at the Institute for Development Policy and Management at the University of Manchester. Her teaching and research interests include gender and development theory and practice, agricultural and rural development, and colonial discourse and post-colonial theory in development studies. More recently her work has concentrated on migration, culture and identity: the experiences of contemporary migrants to Britain, and labour migration to Mauritius.

Gina Mercer is currently lecturing in women's studies, creative writing and literature at James Cook University in Townsville, Australia. Her most recent publication is a controversial book-length study entitled *Janet Frame: Subversive Fictions* (1994). She has published both creative and academic work in Australian and international journals. At the moment she is Director of the Centre for Women's Studies, as well as juggling her other academic commitments, writing a novel and mothering a powerful five-year-old daughter – she sometimes enjoys a challenge!

Angela Montgomery has worked in a range of higher education institutions, primarily teaching law, criminal justice and equality, and has worked on both gender issues in education and race issues in criminal justice within the public sector. Additionally, she has acted as consultant on a range of equality issues.

Jean Orr was born in Belfast and trained as a nurse in the Royal Victoria Hospital before becoming a health visitor. She studied for a BA in social administration at the then Ulster Polytechnic. Following this, she became a manager of community nursing services, but decided that academia was where she wanted to be. In 1977/8 she undertook a MSc in nursing at the University of Manchester where her research was on 'Women's Views of the Health Visiting Service'. From 1978–81 she taught at the Ulster Polytechnic and returned to Manchester University in 1981. Among her other activities, she became a member of the statutory body regulating nursing, midwifery and health visiting. In 1991 she returned to Belfast to take up the foundation Chair of Nursing at Queen's University. She has written on women's health, health visiting, community health and nurse education. Her overseas work has focused on women's health in developing countries and has acted as a consultant to the World Health Organisation and World Bank. She enjoys travelling, good wine, good food and good company.

Anne Seller has taught philosophy at the University of Kent since 1965 and has leavened this with several visits to the University of Colorado at Boulder, where she taught her first course in women and philosophy in 1978. At Kent she participated in setting up the first MA in women's studies in Britain, and regularly contributes an option on philosophy and feminism to it. She was a founder member of the Society for Women in Philosophy and has twice taught at a women's university in south India. She has published articles in various anthologies of feminist philosophy, and is currently writing a book for Sage on Hannah Arendt.

Ailbhe Smyth is a feminist activist, researcher and writer. She is Director of the Women's Education, Research and Resource Centre at University College Dublin, Ireland, and a co-editor of *Women's Studies International Forum*. Books she has edited include *The Abortion Papers: Ireland* (1992), *The Irish Women's Studies Reader* (1993), and *Wildish Things: An Anthology of New Irish Women's Writing* (1989). Recently she co-edited the fiftieth birthday issue of *Feminist Review* on the theme 'The Irish Issue: The British Question' (1995). She is currently working on a collection of essays: *Outings, Guilt Trips and Other Kinds of Excursions*.

Liz Stanley is a connoisseur of brief biographies, food, books, music, 'lurve', wine, writing and cats, in changing permutations of this order, and editor of the *Women of Ideas* series published by Sage. Recent books include *The Auto/Biographical I: The Theory and Practice of Feminist Auto/Biography* (1992), *Debates in Sociology* (1992, with David Morgan), *Breaking Out Again* (1993, with Sue Wise) and *Sex Surveyed, 1949–1994* (1995).

Sue Wilkinson is based in the Department of Social Sciences at Loughborough University, where she teaches social psychology and women's studies. She is the founding – and current – editor of *Feminism & Psychology: An International Journal* and also edits a book series called *Gender and Psychology: Feminist and Critical Perspectives* (both Sage). Her books include *Feminist Social Psychology*, *Feminist Social Psychologies: International Perspectives*, and (with Celia Kitzinger) *Heterosexuality, Women and Health, Feminism and Discourse* and *Representing the Other*. She is a founder member of Women in Psychology; the Psychology of Women Section of the British Psychological Society (BPS); the Alliance of Women in Psychology; and the Lesbians in Psychology Sisterhood, which is currently working to set up a BPS Lesbian and Gay Psychology Section. Her current research interests are in women and health (especially breast cancer), and the social construction of sexual identities (especially heterosexual feminist identities).

Sue Wise is a senior lecturer in applied social science at Lancaster University. She has previously been a professional social worker and has published widely on feminist theory, child abuse and feminist social work.

Name Index

Subject Index

DATE DUE

7/14/2000		
APR 1 2001		

GAYLORD   PRINTED IN U.S.A.